TOO MUCH
OF A GOOD THING

TOO MUCH
OF A GOOD THING

Mae West as Cultural Icon

Ramona Curry

University of Minnesota Press
Minneapolis
London

Published by the University of Minnesota Press
111 Third Avenue South, Suite 290, Minneapolis, MN 55401-2520
Printed in the United States of America on acid-free paper

Library of Congress Cataloging-in-Publication Data

Curry, Ramona, 1951-
     Too much of a good thing : Mae West as cultural icon / Ramona
     Curry.
       p.   cm.
     Includes bibliographical references and index.
     ISBN 0-8166-2790-8 (alk. paper). — ISBN 0-8166-2791-6 (pbk. :
     alk. paper)
       1. West, Mae—Criticism and interpretation.   I. Title.
     PN2287.W4566C87   1996
     791.43'028'092—dc20
     [B]   95-25838

The University of Minnesota is an equal-opportunity educator and employer.

To the memory of Ann T. Brumbach (1956-1992)

Contents

Acknowledgments

Like any publication, this book has come to print through the work of many people besides the named author. Librarians and editors, friends and family fostered the project through generous acts that ranged from sharing ideas and offering research suggestions to furnishing ready meals and good humor when I needed such support at stages of the research and writing. I acknowledge all contributions with appreciation.

Among the individuals and institutions that provided access to diverse historical data, staff members at the Margaret Herrick Library of the Academy of Motion Picture Arts and Sciences, including Sam Gill, Kristine Krueger, and Howard Prouty, have earned my fervent gratitude. Others who thoughtfully drew my attention to valuable cultural documents include Patricia Erens, Robin Fitzpatrick, Ed Husayko, Helen Murray, Mary Ann Oshana, Gordon Quinn, Milos Stehlik, and Virginia Wright Wexman, all of Chicago, and Nancy Abelmann, Dan Majdiak, and Kathy Parham of Champaign-Urbana, Illinois. My longtime friends Doreen Bartoni, Gretchen Elsner-Sommer, Kapra Fleming, Kate Kane and Fran Parr, Scott Levine, Christine List, and Fred Strodtbeck supplied Westian tidbits, steady encouragement, and nourishing conviviality from the project's outset. Kara Lindstrom was a generous Los Angeles host, as was Alison Pinsler, who, as a staff member at the Margaret Herrick Library, also professionally aided the research.

Besides volunteering numerous research tips, Chuck Kleinhans, Craig Kois, and Kate Kane devoted many hours to critiquing early drafts of the manuscript; Christine List, Deborah Tudor, and Virginia Keller also gave unstintingly of their time and intellectual acumen. Other friends and media scholars who made insightful responses to portions of the work in progress include Michelle Citron, Corey Creekmur, Alex Doty, Richard Dyer, Lucy Fischer, Henry Jenkins, Kristine Karnick, Richard Maltby, Dana Polan, Barbara Scharres, Ted Shen, Chris Straayer, and Mimi White.

My wonderfully good-natured, astute, and nurturant husband, Gene

Bild, has promoted my work in all of the ways mentioned, and more. Besides to him, I have incurred the largest debt in bringing this book to press to several University of Illinois colleagues. My friend Richard Mohr thoroughly copyedited an advanced draft of the book and otherwise repeatedly brought fresh insights to the material and offered spritely advice about shaping it into a lively publication. As senior film scholar in the Department of English, Robert Carringer patiently read and responded to several drafts and rendered other measures of collegial encouragement.

Robert D. Parker, Brigit Pegeen Kelly, Michael Bérubé, John Frayne, Bruce Michelson, and James Hurt commented judiciously on extensive sections of the manuscript. David Desser, Zohreh Sullivan, Michael Shapiro, and Cary Nelson also contributed their time and professional expertise. The thriving University of Illinois feminist community nourished this project and my other work by reliably fusing intellectual challenge with social embrace, mentoring with recognition. Among its many members, I wish to thank especially Cheris Kramarae, Leigh Star, Kal Alston, Melanie Loots, H. Jeanie Taylor, and Sonya Michel.

A Wallace Annenberg Foundation fellowship, awarded through the organization Women in Film, supported an early phase of the research and writing; a released time grant from the University of Illinois Humanities Research Board enabled concentrated work on revisions. Richard Wheeler, as head of the Department of English, maintained an invigorating interest in the project and consistently tendered professional guidance and support. Rebecca Morrow executed numerous research and editorial tasks with cheerfulness and creativity. Durrell Dew, Carine Melkom-Mardorossian, and Craig Fischer ably assisted with proofreading and manuscript preparation, and Elin Slavick helped with the photographs. Marlyn Ehlers, Rene Wahlfeldt, Sharon Decker, and Joan Maiden repeatedly facilitated the project and the quality of my working life through their reliability and friendliness in helping with administrative matters.

Thanks are due a number of other people who made important contributions as the book neared completion, particularly my editor, Janaki Bakhle, and her assistant, Jeff Moen, as well as Mary Byers and other members of the University of Minnesota Press staff. Judy Selhorst copyedited the manuscript with a fine sense of nuance and a keen eye for detail. I wish also to thank the anonymous press readers. Charles Pierce, West Graphics of South San Francisco, Dennis Livingston, Rosetta Reitz, Terry O'Neill and Hamiltons Gallery in London, Gene Trindl, Diana Spence, and Jennifer McNeil graciously helped me secure reprint permissions.

Finally, I wish to acknowledge publicly an outstanding debt to Ann Brumbach, who died, much, much too young, of ovarian cancer while I was writing this book. Ann left her signature on my scholarship, and my life, as a respectful and loyal friend, a feminist fan of popular culture, playful admirer of camp, inveterate reader, and all-around smart and creative woman. I would have loved to place the published work into my friend's receptive hands, and it is to her memory that I dedicate this book.

Introduction:
Posthumous Citings from Pistol to Puddle

"Mae West Remains Hot Number," declared a newspaper headline on 15 August 1993, above an article that detailed events around the United States observing the centenary of that entertainer's birth. A Los Angeles museum, for example, would celebrate the 17 August birth date with film screenings, costume and photo exhibits, and a female impersonator's performance.[1] A piece in the Sunday New York Times, also on 15 August, announced the first release of West's 1930s films on videotape, which MCA/ Universal had timed for the occasion.[2] Not long before, following the fall 1992 release of Madonna's controversial book Sex, a Los Angeles Times movie column had compared the living megastar to Mae West.[3]

Even though most contemporary media consumers have seen, at best, only brief clips from West's twelve films (ten of which appeared between 1932 and 1943), these recent articles in newspaper entertainment sections all presumed that readers recognize West as a movie icon and enjoy references to her, more than fifteen years after her death. Indeed, the column comparing Madonna to Mae West appealed to readers' appreciation of the older star as grounds for accepting her controversial successor. Advertisers, publishers of "memorable quotations" books and calendars, cartoonists, and television writers appear to share the newspapers' assumptions. Those purveyors of American culture all believe that "West still sells": verbal phrases associated with the star currently market restaurants and bars, bras, movies, even key chains.[4]

"Come up and see me sometime," a variant of a line West directs at Cary Grant's character in her first star vehicle, She Done Him Wrong (1933), crops up repeatedly more than sixty years after it first laced popular oral culture across the United States.[5] Another Westian phrase, "Is that a gun in your pocket, or are you just glad to see me?" also pops up in joke books and advertisements. (Sometimes in verbal accounts the word "banana," "pistol," or even, diminutively, "pickle" appears in place of gun.)[6] The quip is generally thought to derive from one of West's early films. In fact, West never utters this line in any of her 1930s movies, nor does it show up in any correspondence concerning their censorship. According to one story, West once made the remark to an enthusiastic reporter awaiting her arrival at the Pasadena train station. When West does deliver the line (to George Hamilton, playing a gangster) in a film she made two years before her death, *Sextette* (1978), it occurs as an intertextual citation, meaningful precisely because of its established attribution to the star.

The presumption that Mae West can still sell media extends beyond newspapers and videotapes. Since West's death at age eighty-seven in 1980, four substantial biographies have appeared in bookstores and two biographical films have run on U.S. television, one a feature film first broadcast on network TV in 1982 and that occasionally runs on cable stations; the other, a recent documentary.[7] And at least two murder mysteries featuring the movie star as a central character have come out.[8] Specialty book or music stores sometimes carry audiocassettes of West's radio and television appearances and song recordings, and movie memorabilia shops almost always offer posters and cards depicting West. Their frequent display alongside images of Marlene Dietrich, Greta Garbo, and Madonna, and near glossy black-and-white blowups of muscular male pinup models, bespeaks West's continuing appeal as a gay cult figure. Gay-sponsored costume balls usually have one or more Mae Wests in attendance, and several movies with settings in gay nightclubs include West impersonations; so do female impersonation shows in clubs that also cater to straight audiences.[9]

The book before you shares the popular media's assumptions that the reader (of gay or straight or other sexual self-definition) has at least a sketchy recognition of West as a long-standing cultural icon *and* is interested in learning more about that icon—but from a perspective somewhat different from that offered by previous works about the star. In offering "more" and "different"—not to say "too much"—I am not promising to bring to light any closeted skeletons or stories that might contradict previous biographies. Although I shall perhaps supply fresh information and propose interpretations new even to readers with extensive previous knowledge of the star, I give no definitive account of West's experiences or personality, for my purpose is not biography. Instead, I take biographies as an instance of "Mae West"—a popular media phenomenon that has generated a range of functions and meanings in U.S. cultural history. Although Mae West certainly had agency as a historical subject, as her biographies (and 1959 autobiography) argue in detail, my concern is the social significance of West's widespread *reputation* for possessing creative and economic powers rare among female entertainers. In short, this book examines not Mae West, the person and performer, but rather the sustained interest in "Mae West" as a popular American icon.

The cover art suggests the book's perspective, for it records an internationally recognized artist's engagement with West as a popular figure. Salvador Dalí created the color drawing (gouache on newspaper) in 1934-35, dubbing it *The Face of Mae West, Usable as a Surrealist Apartment*. The image depicts the star's face as a stage. West's eyes emerge out of paintings hanging on the stage backdrop, her hair drapes as stage curtains. Her nose doubles as a standard theatrical prop in drawing room comedies and dramas: a decorative fireplace. The rounded stage edge forms her chin and neck; a plushly upholstered couch marks her mouth. Two years later, Dalí commissioned a three-dimensional full-size version of the lips sofa covered in shocking pink velvet; it is now on display in the National Film Museum in London. Another functional version in red leather has smiled since 1974 in the Dalí Museum room that realizes the collage title's suggestion: eye-pictures hang on a red wall, a flesh-colored fireplace breathes fire from one nostril and stores firewood in the other, oversized locks of golden hair drape the room's entrance.[10]

Although the Art Institute of Chicago deems the paper original in its collection too fragile for exhibition, the image circulates on museum shop postcards, in art history texts, and in occasional newspaper articles.[11] In simultaneously constructing and deconstructing West's face as a theatrical artifice, Dalí's work provides visual evidence that since the beginning of her movie fame, some cultural observers have construed West's appearance and performance as an elaborate masquerade. This book explores the sociopolitical and cultural implications of the public's grasping West's image as a masquerade of gender, race, and class.

I address "Mae West" from three intertwined perspectives: first, as a singular case history revealing how star images emerge and circulate as cultural signs; second, as a social phenomenon that played a central role in the emergence of Hollywood's internal film censorship and in U.S. cultural politics in the 1930s; and third, as a site at which we can interrogate and develop critical media theories about sexual representation, notably about the spectacle, excess, and parody that constitute masquerade. My work draws on previous research about film stardom but extends beyond accounting for a particular star. It develops an approach to media phenomena that synthesizes cultural studies, close textual analysis, and feminist-inflected psychoanalytic theories with detailed research in film and social history.

In this volume, I argue for a historical understanding of popular cultural signs as dynamic constructions in relation to specific audiences and issues in the public sphere.[12] The project illustrates how stars and celebrities signify in cultural context by documenting and interpreting in nuanced detail what and for whom a particular star image has signified. Among the public discourses that have centrally engaged "Mae West" are the institutional responses to the economic depression of the 1930s, the gay and women's rights movements of the 1970s, and the identity politics of the 1980s and 1990s. Like Madonna's image, and that of TV star Roseanne, both of which extend some of West's cultural functions, "Mae West" has encompassed multiple and often contradictory meanings, even within a discrete discourse such as feminist critical reception. Indeed, the cultural renewability of West's image, like that of other enduring popular icons, derives, I argue, from its complex structuring and adaptability.

One frequently mentioned characteristic of West's image is its "sexiness." Even many current consumers of popular culture who cannot fathom the performer Mae West ever having been sexually appealing recognize the icon as somehow symbolizing "sex." But it is not self-evident what kind of sex "Mae West" signifies, nor with whom, or on whose terms. Two recent jokes about Mae West, one that has appeared in print and one that to my knowledge has heretofore existed only in oral form, illustrate this point.

A greeting card available in the late 1980s in card and novelty shops features a man (female impersonator Charles Pierce) made up, costumed, and posed as Mae West. The figure, wearing a glittery black dress, holds a white rose hip high; a champagne bottle ranges up alongside, its shiny gold foil neck emerging from a collar of fur (see Figure 1). A phrase across the top of the picture proposes, "I hear you practice safe sex." Inside, the punch line concludes: "Call me when you're through practicing." The joke, which, like many of West's own quips, turns on a pun, conflates two desires in the playful refusal to "practice" safe sex: a demand for an experienced lover and an impulse toward wild, unbounded sex without thought of consequences.

For the gay men targeted as buyers, the card articulates a bold, transgressive fantasy: unprotected sex in the midst of the AIDS epidemic, despite public pleas for health-conscious sexual behaviors and presumably also the shop browser/reader's own sense of care and responsibility. The humor arises from the sheer audacity of the declaration, underscored visually by the lasciviously erect champagne bottle and the heavily bejeweled and blond bewigged but nonetheless clearly male poseur. Recognition of West's persona in the figure anchors the joke, for the (wo)man presumably speaking was herself a female impersonator (or, rumor had it, maybe really a man!) who was long recognized as a comedic "camp"—a figure who through excessive artifice and outrageous, ironic performance violates prescribed gender behaviors. The card employs "Mae West" as a sign that in the late 1980s embodied the delights and potential dangers of gay sexuality.

A joke in even more recent circulation relates West to homoeroticism from another angle:

> Mae West sees a woman looking at her. West goes up to her and asks, "Is that a puddle you're standing in or are you just glad to see me?"

This joke, which passed at least among media scholars in the early 1990s, simultaneously cites and rewrites the standard "gun in the pocket" quip. The variant shifts attention from the male physiology of sexual desire to that of the female, and focuses on a woman's presumed desire for West as a woman. Unlike her contemporaries Marlene Dietrich and Greta Garbo, West has usually not been considered lesbian or bisexual, nor her performances generally to signal lesbian sexuality. But this joke postulates West's current appeal to lesbians—possibly as an object of desire, more clearly as a parodic, campy figure overdetermined as a site of gender transgression. Although not itself evidence of any strong lesbian following for West, the joke underscores and expands the star's association with transgressive sexualities in addition to the heterosexual promiscuity that West herself supposedly practiced.

The displacement from hard pistol to viscous puddle traces the parameters of West's shifting reception and sociohistorical functions: a phallic sign transfigured as a mark of female desire. The tumescent (and presumably heterosexual) male reporter at the Pasadena station extends to encompass the gay male audiences who enjoy the line in *Sextette*, who transmute into the 1990s woman who cannot contain her pleasure over West's persona. The differently engendered audiences augment rather than supplant their predecessors. As Charles Pierce's bottle prop attests, the sign "Mae West" remains largely phallic; it also remains largely consonant with the dominant, heterosexist popular culture that initially shaped and profited from West's performances and image.

Sixty years ago, as today, the star represented both an excessively yet earnestly feminine woman and an implicitly gay male female impersonator. If, in current reception, the latter persona has largely displaced the former,

the two readings together mark a site of contention among those who (re)
produce and circulate "Mae West" as a sign, to diverse and sometimes
competing ends. I discuss in detail the historical moment of West's reception by some early 1970s feminist critics who argued that West's image perpetuates masculinist subjugation of women through their bodies and criticized West's status among gay men as a well-aged campy movie queen.
From my own feminist position, I argue for a reading of the excessively
feminine woman reflected in the glistening puddle as female drag and as
woman-positive camp.

The shifting figuration of West's image charts transformations in central
tropes of twentieth-century popular culture that have enacted and negotiated sexual difference, gender distinctions, and delineations in social
power. I argue that even as a variable signifier in a range of contexts, "Mae
West" has consistently signified transgressive sexuality, in combination
with other recurrent attributes: power, ambiguous gender positioning, and
comedy, the mode in which she couched her sexual performance. The pis-
tol-to-puddle sex change underscores a persistent source of West's
appeal—and of her capacity to offend: her image encodes *multiple* sociosexual transgressions. "Mae West" compounds implications of sexual and
gender deviance with class and racial markings. As a glamorized bleached
blonde, West herself is visually encoded, like so many other American female stars, as a fetishized white woman. But her image, particularly from
the 1920s through the 1950s, also hints at the violation of sociosexual
boundaries between races and social classes. Indeed, as I will argue, representational techniques contributing to West's star image draw on long-
standing conventions of pornography that suggestively violate social taboos to enhance erotic pleasure. The taboo that West most consistently
and obviously broke—that against heterosexual female promiscuity—
shades into the violation of more rigid, less publicly acknowledged sociosexual taboos.

My position that the icon "Mae West" has diverse though structured
meanings that have emerged through its historical circulation entails an
understanding that popular cultural consumers are themselves producers.
These "coproducing" consumers jointly and variably ascribe meanings to a
cultural sign nominally fashioned by *material* producers of American mass
culture, who in the 1990s, as in the 1930s, operate largely out of New York
City and Hollywood. I recognize that both sets of producers have some
agency in their involvement with mass cultural forms, and also that institutional and social factors, including gender, class position, and racial

identity, may variously structure their pleasures and goals in mass cultural production and consumption. Thus, although I carefully examine West's institutional production as an icon, my account of that icon's workings does not posit a hypothetical, exclusively male cinema spectator perceiving woman as phallic signifier, or otherwise privilege presumably heterosexual men's readings of West. I attempt instead to explicate the icon's meanings for contemporary women and gay men, audiences that I construe as socially and politically, rather than primarily psychologically, constituted. I also aim to identify commonalities in the possible pleasures and challenges that West may offer female and gay audiences.

Clearly, my own interests and biases as a generally straight, middle-class, fortyish Anglo-American woman critically engaged in academia inform not only my consumption, but also my authorial contribution to the ongoing production of an icon. My analysis of West's image unavoidably argues for a particular reading. The project of situating a transmutable star sign within the network of historical relations that have yielded its meanings also cannot escape other hermeneutic limitations—or, if one will, consequences of the project's own historical position. Even the extensive research I have conducted (into official correspondence and censorship records, publicity and promotion materials, newspaper and trade journal accounts of audience responses, and published and oral reviews of West's films and other appearances) cannot enable a full reconstruction of the meanings that West's image signified at earlier periods or a surety about how viewers interpreted her films on their initial release, except through reports by contemporary commentators.

This limitation arises in part because some materials that might have given a somewhat different picture may have never been recorded or archived or are otherwise unavailable.[13] More crucially, all of the correspondence, reviews, and other materials that I cite are themselves texts requiring interpretation. While I have striven to offer a historically informed analysis, my reading remains a perspective from the present. The current content of "Mae West" necessarily informs any understanding of, even any interest in, the sign's historical functions. A present-day reader will unavoidably approach a report of West's reception in 1933 with some knowledge of "what happened to Mae West" subsequently, if only that she continued to make films and lived to an advanced age. Whatever view a contemporary consumer may have of West, it is necessarily a cumulative, retrospective image.

West's current star image has arisen from numerous written, visual, and aural representations. In addition to film roles and recorded performances on stage, radio, television, and even record albums, a plethora of promotional and critical texts about those performances and about West's own actions and words (including clearly fictional accounts, like the murder mysteries) contribute to the composite image of the star now available. The debates in film theory of the past two decades that have targeted West's image have also propagated "Mae West" as a sign, even while evaluating and revising what it signifies.

My study offers close textual analysis of West's visual and aural manifestations but grounds these as much as possible in the historical record of their cultural impact. Besides approaching "Mae West" overall as a case history revealing the complex workings of popular cultural signs, I present detailed case studies of selected performances by West (in films, radio, and television) during four historical periods: 1926-33, when West's status as a national icon was forged; 1933-37, when West played an emblematic role in American moral and political discourse; 1937-64, during which time West's public reception shifted as she moved from film to radio to stage to television; and 1964 to the present, as West's dominant reception has come to be determined by self-declared gay men and feminists, sometimes in contest, sometimes jointly.

The organization of the book adheres to those stages of West's career, with each chapter focusing on one or two dominant elements in her star image. Chapter 1 departs from an article that appeared under West's byline in 1929 in *Parade*, a New York theater publication, to explore West's iconographic construction in the decade prior to her 1932 Hollywood debut, tracing the genesis of her image's later manifestations. The chapter investigates how movie costumes, sets, and performance style widely imbued "Mae West" with emphatic sexual associations, as did publicity about the star's personal tastes in clothes and home decor and about her preferred activities and companions—among them, African American men. This overview of West's star image provides a basis for analyzing how "Mae West" has served at once to confirm and to contravene standard representations of gender, race, and class in popular American culture. It also reveals how both West's performance style and her credits as author of her own screenplays, supplemented by studio publicity, invited her reception as an exceptional woman who controlled her career, her finances, and her personal autonomy. In conclusion, the chapter addresses a paradox: West's much-touted role in exacerbating the U.S. film industry's internal censorship identifies the star's greatest historical impact in her capacity to disrupt the very system—Hollywood—that empowered her.

Recurrent elements in West's image receive closer examination in the next five chapters. Chapters 2 and 3 reveal the key emblematic—rather than causal—role that West's image played in 1930s discourses about movie reform, which I argue correlated with national and film industrial economic and political crises. Chapter 2 presents a case history of *She Done Him Wrong* (1933) to examine how West's characterization as a successful prostitute in this and her subsequent three starring vehicles (*I'm No Angel*, 1933; *Belle of the Nineties*, 1934; *Goin' to Town*, 1935) functioned in the context of the Depression as a challenge to hegemonic middle-class values.

Chapter 3 continues the analysis of the icon's functions within the political and economic circumstances of the Depression, highlighting the internal censorship the Production Code Administration required after 1934. The production and reception of the 1936 West vehicle *Klondike Annie* reveal how the movie reform discourse, which centered from 1933 to 1937 on West's persona, successfully deployed her image as a foil in its political and economic conflicts with Hollywood.

Chapter 4 returns to close analysis of the performative strategies contributing to West's image, to examine the workings and implications of the comedienne's bawdy humor. A discussion of Sigmund Freud's analysis of joke telling brings insights about the social impact of West's sexually aggressive comedic performance. But West's enunciatory position in cinematic narratives and her powerful star image as a comedienne fundamentally contradict Freud's—and other psychoanalysts'—presumptions about gender difference in relation to humor. I argue that dominant feminist psychoanalytic media theories cannot adequately account for viewers' grasp of the star's spectacular excesses in dress, setting, and verbal performance in the context of West's identity as a star comedienne.

The chapter departs from a discussion of West's 1937 scandal-provoking radio parody of the biblical Eve and concludes with an analysis of West's 1964 guest appearance as herself on the television situation comedy *Mister Ed*. I argue that although the dominant perception of West's comedic mode has shifted over the decades from satire to parody to self-parody, the shift has resulted more from the altered media and social climates within which she performed than from any changes in her performative style. Strong social taboos against the visibly aging sexual female body have also contributed to widespread perceptions of West as self-parody. Yet to the extent the performer is perceived as a "camp," I argue, West's comedic self-parody can effect further parodies as well as renew the social satire many critics discover in her early films.

In chapter 5, I consider the reception of West's image from the mid-1960s, when West began to be discussed in print as a high camp figure, through the early 1980s. I examine particularly how West's performances in *Myra Breckinridge* (1970) and *Sextette* (1978) built on her prior image as a "(female) female impersonator" and influenced her popularity among gay men and often controversial reception from feminist media critics of the period. I also demonstrate how *Mae West* (1982), a made-for-TV posthumous film biography, marked a largely ineffective mainstream attempt to refigure the star's image in terms of current middle-class, heterosexual feminist concerns. That biographical film presented West as a woman whose professional interests interfered with her personal satisfaction in love.

Rather than following the biographical film's cue in redefining West's image, feminist media critics began in the 1980s to approach West from perspectives that could account for women's pleasures in fantasy figures like West. In chapter 6, which a set of Westian jokes structures as a summary, I propose a fresh analysis of West's psychoanalytic, as well as cultural, impact that reveals how the star may appeal to contemporary feminists as well as to gay men as a parodic feminine masquerade and also as "phallic mother." Analysis of how "Mae West" works as camp points to the shared interests that women—lesbian and straight or bisexual—and gay men may have in "Mae West" as a sign of gender *and* sexual transgression.

Mae West, who was born in New York probably in 1893 and died in Hollywood in 1980, was an entertainer who worked at various periods of her life as a stage and film actor, a playwright and screenwriter, a singer, an author, and a real estate investor. The result of this work was "Mae West," the quotation marks distinguishing the name as a sign representing not a person but an icon in American popular culture.[14] This book's subject is the workings of that icon within the specific historical and political economic contexts that created it: how "Mae West" has functioned for much of the twentieth century as a sign, what the sign has signified in the past, and how and what it represents currently.

1

The Sex "Queen"

Almost seven decades prior to the release of Madonna's *Sex*, Mae West shocked New York by using that laden word as the title of the first play she wrote and coproduced on Broadway. West's *Sex* featured the actress in the lead role of Margie LaMonte, a gold-hearted prostitute who plied the wharves. The play ran for 375 performances in 1926-27 before a court decision that it violated public decency led to its closing and West's brief jailing. Even after the verdict curtailed the thriving ticket sales that publicity about the pending case had fostered, media reports and photographs of West in the hands of the law augmented the national reputation she had been garnering for more than a decade as an overtly sexual performer.[1] (See Figure 2.)

West's performances had incorporated sexual suggestiveness as early as 1908-12, when, still in her teens, she began touring on vaudeville circuits and appearing in minor roles on Broadway's musical stage.[2] West's style was reportedly influenced by that of vaudeville star Eva Tanguay and speakeasy owner and burlesque performer Texas Guinan, both known for shocking audiences with the brash sexual license in their songs and catchphrases.[3] West not only knew Guinan and her act, but even posed with her for a publicity photograph around 1928 (Figure 3). Five years later, West concluded her opening musical number in her attendance-record-breaking film *I'm No Angel* with an utterance ("Suckers!") that echoed Guinan's own well-known tag line, "So long, suckers!"

West's appearance in Hollywood movies after 1932 further enhanced her celebrity and gave her persona a lively visual and aural embodiment for movie audiences across the United States and internationally. In managing to extend a performance style resembling popular musical theater and burlesque into sound film, West asserted for that medium the degree of public sexual display and verbal play allowed on the New York stage. Issues of cinematic sexual license soon became anchored to West's persona. Within months of the release in March 1933 of her first starring vehicle,

She Done Him Wrong, West's name had come to signify in public discourse the qualities and behaviors constituting "the transgressive woman." Central among the qualities that "Mae West" represented in 1933 were an active, even predatory, sexuality and a bold, mocking manner, particularly toward men, whom she appeared to desire sexually but otherwise not to need. Much of West's appeal—and her capacity to shock—derived from the way her image systematically contradicted the period's middle-class social ideals of female chastity and feminine modesty.

West's sexualized image had distinct class and racial overtones. According to West's autobiography, *Goodness Had Nothing to Do with It*, and several biographies that accept its claims, West originated the stage performance of the "shimmy dance" around 1911 after observing it in Chicago's South Side nightclubs.[4] The attribution both enhances West's reputation as an artistic innovator and identifies a specific gesture—hip swiveling—in her sexually suggestive performance that links the German-Irish American star to urban African American culture. West's later performance of jazz and blues songs on stage and screen further associated the white star with the unrestrained sexual behavior that racist U.S. society attributes to lower-class African Americans. For many consumers, such cross-racial associations inflected West's image with the allure of the exotic or forbidden.

Assertions that Mae West introduced the shimmy to the stage indicate another facet of the star's image that has endured for decades: that of the author and creative force. West is said to have written or otherwise determined most of her own material, including the screenplays of her films. Her capacity to "author" her own persona distinguishes her as an accomplished woman who managed through talent and nerve to achieve a degree of power within the U.S. entertainment industry that remains rare for female entertainers. The star's reputation for professional iconoclasm (she repeatedly provoked censorship) and personal autonomy (she was never a conventional wife or mother) augments the aura of power emanating from West's performance and her central, heroic position in her films' narratives. West's evident power in her professional and personal life is key to the star's recent feminist reception and also to her long-standing status as gay icon.

The intersection of power and sexuality represented in "Mae West" fosters her continuing appeal as a cultural sign. The conjunction of remarkable professional success and sexual appeal still stands in contrast to conventional female representations. West's historical impact in entertainment and

American culture arguably arose from her comedic depiction of a taboo sexuality marked by race and class as well as gender deviance. West's contributions to twentieth-century American popular culture emerged from her iconographically representing multiple social transgressions.

Parade-ing Sex on Stage

An article that appeared in the New York theater publication *Parade* in September 1929 vividly documents the sexually transgressive encoding of West's image prior to her 1932 move to Hollywood. Titled "Sex in the Theatre" and attributed to West herself, the article discusses West's reputation for depicting improper or censorable sexual practices on stage:

> For years I have been devoting my career in the theater to the education of the masses to certain sex truths. My last four plays, "Sex," "Pleasure Man," "Drag" and "Diamond Lil" have all dealt with major, vital sex problems. (12)

The author goes on to argue that each of her plays teaches morality by portraying deviation from sexual mores:

> In my play "Sex," I presented the picture of a girl whose great beauty and economic poverty forced her into bad ways. . . . "Sex" has its educational value because it shows the life and psychology of a prostitute and also has its moral. Many people who saw it learned a lesson.
>
> In my play, "Pleasure Man," I showed the true picture of a man who was weak and who forgot the wise law of moderation—who was oversexed. The man came to no good in the end and many young men learned a lesson from the play. A great majority of our young men are oversexed or repressed, which is the same thing because it is unnatural. . . .
>
> I admit that in my play "Drag" I was a little bit premature. The public is still too childlike to face like grown-ups the problem of homo-sexuality. How few are the people who even know what the word means? Because of this universal ignorance I wrote "Drag" with the intention of taking it to all the theaters in the country to teach the people. . . .
>
> In "Diamond Lil," the play in which I am acting now, [I play] a scarlet woman in the nineties on the Bowery. She is a woman who lives with different men. People have said that I must be bad myself because I play bad parts myself so well. They fail to credit me with intelligence and a love for my art. . . . [T]he story of "Diamond Lil" makes one think of a modern idea of the Single Standard. I believe in the Single Standard for men and women. I will tour in "Diamond Lil" for another season and I expect that at least three million people will be given something to think about that they never thought of before its run is ended. And then I shall make a talkie out of it and enable thousands more to learn its lesson. (12-13)

The author's rhetorical strategy of presenting theater as a forum of sex education and her insistent moral posturing presumes that a reader in 1929 would associate the name "Mae West" with the depiction of excessive, taboo, or illicit sex. A brief boxed biography on the first page of the article, a photograph, and an ink sketch all contribute to the article's representation of West as sexually sophisticated and active, in her private life as well as in performance. The sidebar biography describes West as follows:

> Mae West was born in Brooklyn. Made her debut at eight, imitating Eddie Foy and Bert Williams at an amateur show. She is a golden blonde, 5 feet 5 inches tall and weighs 130 lbs. In "Diamond Lil" she makes up to look 5 feet 9 inches and 160 lbs. Does this by wearing a specially boned corset which brings the hips out, the waist in and the breasts up for sensual effect. Likes expensive, highly scented soaps, fresh fruits with heavy creams, long clinging gowns and rich shades of color. Has her suites hung with heavy draperies and demands liveried chauffeurs from her hotel. Hates night-clubs. Reads little. Dislikes wise-crackers. Likes soft-spoken people and studies all she meets for character. Is said to have invented the shimmy before Gilda Gray. Sophisticated mannerisms and languid speech. Eugene O'Neill her favorite author. Got tired of trouping and wrote "Sex." Made her overnight. Hates being looked at offstage. Interested only in men and sex plays. "I've had some big moments in my life" . . . with a smile. (12)

This verbal sketch presents West's body as glamorous and valuable: she is a "golden" blonde; indulges and adorns herself with expensive soaps, foods, and clothes; and requires luxurious housing and transportation. The description portrays West's figure in "Diamond Lil" as that of a sexually mature female: "the hips out, the waist in and the breasts up for sensual effect." A small stylized engraving next to the opening paragraph, showing a woman wearing a long, full-skirted dress and carrying a parasol, reiterates this exaggerated and, by 1929, outmoded representation of the female form. The next page features a closely cropped photograph of West's face surrounded by fluffy white fur and waves of light hair, her eyes looking away from the camera below dark eyebrows plucked to thin arches. The portrait represents West in conventional terms as feminine (averted eyes, face framed in soft materials) and sexual (use of make-up and fur's associations with sensuality and with animals).

The article and illustrations highlight certain elements of West's public image of the period while repressing or altering others. West's touting her professional goals as an educational and moral mission, however ironically, justifies the article's voyeuristic focus on taboo sex. While the biographical sketch hints at West's own social deviance in having as an eight-year-old impersonated male performers such as African American vaudevillian Bert Williams, it emphasizes that West is conventionally feminine in describing her beauty care regime and obliquely affirming her heterosexuality (she is "interested only in men"). The description counters the socially disruptive implications of the star's expressed desire to promote knowledge of taboo sexualities, which she names in succession as prostitution, excessive male desire, male homosexuality, and female promiscuity. Notably, the latter two practices violate not only middle-class social mores but also the conventional delineation of behaviors and traits into those belonging properly—and distinctively—to men and women. Indeed, the compulsive male heterosexual conquest upon which *Pleasure Man* ostensibly focused supplies a foil for male homosexuality. The play, which opened 1 October 1928 on Broadway but closed by court order after only two performances, incorporated many lines and characters, including evidently gay female impersonators, from the previously forbidden *The Drag*.[5] And, as I will demonstrate in chapters 2 and 3, West's self-characterization equated female prostitution to a woman's pursuit of pleasurable sex with a succession of partners. The two most gender-transgressive practices that West describes—male homosexuality and female sexual promiscuity—are precisely those that most permeate her persona.

The 1929 *Parade* article is emblematic of innumerable subsequent accounts of West's persona. These and other sources of West's image, including her recorded performances, yield the impression that the star repeatedly transgressed social boundaries, including the received binary demarcation of gender. Five particular facets of West's image already evident in the *Parade* article served jointly throughout her career to create its aura of social and sexual transgression: (1) her spectacular costumes and sets, (2) her relations to African Americans and other racial and ethnic groups that dominant Anglo-American society marks as "different" or "other," (3) her associations with men encoded as gay, (4) her central narrative position and distinctive performance style, and (5) her powers of authorship, with its attendant economic and social privileges. The balance of this chapter addresses these aspects of West's star image in sequence.

Sex and Class in the Celluloid Scene

The flashy costumes Mae West wore and the baroquely luxurious settings she appeared in contribute significantly to the star's aura of transgressive sexuality. West's appearances in films built on her spectacular presentation

on stage, which itself drew heavily on nineteenth-century theatrical practices.[6] In films and in myriad publicity stills, West wears formfitting long
gowns of satin, velvet, and net, decorated with fur, feathers, lace, sequins,
and jewels (see Figures 4-14). Following long-standing conventions in European painting and theater that visually correlate material riches and sensuality, the luxurious materials arrayed on West's photographed body signal
wealth as well as sexual allure.[7] Carefully lit and posed, the rich textures
evoke a highly tactile sensuality and so metonymically encode West's image as sexual. West's highly decorative and evidently impractical costumes
also mark her as a creature of leisure, fitted for display rather than physical
labor. In this, West's appearance adheres to a Hollywood practice established by the 1920s—most notably by Cecil DeMille's domestic dramas
featuring Gloria Swanson—which dictated that only glamorous, visibly
well-off women appeared as sexually attractive.[8]

West's textured and bejeweled costumes thus suggest a gendered sexuality inflected with upper-class privilege. Many of her films and photographs
exude the romanticized aura of a time past. The elaborate designs and ornate decorations arrayed around West's image evoke the dress and home of
an upper-class woman of fashion in the late nineteenth century. The settings in which she frequently appears in photographs, including the Hollywood apartment where she lived for many years, also bespeak wealth and
even royalty: magazine profiles of her life at home reported the star's pref-
erence for Louis XV furnishings.[9] (See Figures 15 and 16.)

Yet other aspects of the star's appearance and performance mark her as
distinctly lower-class, particularly in her roles in *Night after Night* and her
first three star vehicles, as well as in her earliest publicity photos (see Figures 4-6). Although West's Hollywood costumes and decor generally connote "bygone luxury" and "Victorian upper middle class," the star's prevailing image recalls a specific period, place, and style of life: the "Gay
Nineties." Against this reading of West's appearance, French author
Colette remarked in a 1938 review that the costumes that Mae West
favored—giant hats, clinging dresses, straight corsets "that enclosed the
female body from under the arm to the knee"—derived from fashions
popular in 1907-8.[10] Yet West's widespread reception remains inflected as
Gay Nineties (1890s!), a period in American culture that has come to imply raucous scenes and comparative sexual license in the burgeoning
American urban scene, most notably in saloons.

Although only four of West's twelve films are set in the 1890s, her characterizations in these have propagated her dominant image as the "Belle of

the Nineties." West's roles in *She Done Him Wrong* (1933), *Belle of the Nineties* (1934), and *Klondike Annie* (1936) built on her role in the 1928-30 stage success *Diamond Lil*; in these films she plays the featured entertainer in a saloon or nightclub who is also implicitly a mistress, in both sexual and proprietary senses. Other West star vehicles also draw on her established image as a turn-of-the-century "showgirl." In *I'm No Angel* (1933), which costumes and props vaguely set in the 1930s, West plays a small-time circus entertainer who succeeds with her lion-tamer act in the "Big Time." *Goin' to Town* (1935) is also nominally set in the 1930s but opens in a suggestively nineteenth-century "Wild West"-style dance hall, in which West provides entertainment. West is also an entertainer in a Wild West saloon in *My Little Chickadee* (1940), which costumes, sets, and narrative put around 1870.

The unrestrained public behavior presumably allowed in Gay Nineties and Wild West saloons marks these settings as lower-class.[11] West's recurrent characterization as a Gay Nineties entertainer thus degrades her costumes and jewels from marks of a leisured lady's wealth and sexual allure to evidence of success as an entertainer: a woman of lower-class origins who has managed through "show business" to become rich. Like the 1929 *Parade* article, which, before describing West's expensive tastes and "sophisticated mannerisms," points out that she was "born in Brooklyn," West's early Hollywood publicity often emphasized the lower-class overtones of the star's origins and her personal preferences: her father was a boxer, she herself had a predilection for boxers and other muscle-bound men, she spent leisure time at prize fights.[12] West biographies often underscore the star's working-class origins, even though West had at times denied such a past.[13]

The plots of West's vehicles at Paramount from 1933 to 1935 (for which the star always received writer's credit) recapitulate the "poor young (wo)man makes good" narrative formula: each centers on the rapid rise in her character's fortunes and social standing. Building on West's "Diamond Lil" image, the films relate the success of West's characters (and of her star persona generally) to the judicious marketing of her sexuality through her performance as entertainer and also as mistress or prostitute. Her characters' status as sexual commodities both on and off the stages within the films draws on social tradition in nineteenth-century Britain, France, and the United States, which equated female stage performers with prostitutes. West's concurrent encoding as being of lower-class origins but gaining wealth through the suggestive use of sex in performance thus invited a reading of her luxurious costumes and settings as indications of lower-class, rather than upper-class, standing.

Without knowing West's films or much about her life, contemporary viewers may read the star's appearance as "lower-class" because her dress and surroundings seem excessive rather than elegantly upper-class. In most widely available film clips and stills, West wears not sequined *or* lacy gowns, furs *or* feathers, but often all of these materials draped about her body at once. The elaborate upswept hairdo crowned by a broad-brimmed hat and large, ornately set diamonds dangling from her ears and embellishing her deep neckline, wrists, and fingers emphatically supplement her richly textured clothing. The ornate, sensual furnishings surrounding her, including animal skins and paintings and marble statues of nude women, are extensions of her costumes.

Such ornamentation is generally read in the twentieth century as gaudy display rather than glamour or elegance. Especially the many diamonds and feathers adorning West's body and bleached blonde hair (or, later, wigs) combine to mark the bearer as a lower-class woman "on the make." That such garishness was taken also in the 1930s as a mark of lower-class taste is indicated by a scene in the 1937 version of *Stella Dallas* (directed by King Vidor and produced by Samuel Goldwyn), in which Stella (Barbara Stanwyck) tries to appear glamorous and upper-class to her daughter's friends by excessively ornamenting herself with jewelry and elaborately trimmed hat and dress. It is the failure of her attempt that gives the scene its meaning: her style of adornment marks Stella as inescapably lower-class. Yet Stella's ornamentation does not exceed what West characteristically displayed with impunity.

West's costuming worked with her bawdy dialogue and body language and her stage and film roles to encode her image as a lower-class, sexually available woman: obliquely, as a prostitute. This character typing has led some critics to conclude that West represents a powerless woman. Yet West represented a lower-class woman with a difference. Her excessively spectacular presentation, combined with her presence as star performer, exudes an aura of power.

In *I'm No Angel* (1933), six trumpeters herald the arrival of West's character "Tira" as she rides atop an elephant into a grand arena, wearing a bejeweled white pantsuit and plumed hat and waving a whip, before dismounting in the center ring to "tame" three lions (see Figure 37). In the opening scene of *Belle of the Nineties* (1934), West appears on stage wearing a formfitting glittering dress in a sequence of vignettes, first as a butterfly, then a bat, a rose, a spider, and finally, draped in slinky bunting, crowned and holding high a burning torch as the Statue of Liberty (see Figures 9-11). A tenor framed in separate shots intercut with West's display croons a rendition of "My American Beauty" to accompany the sequence. Further shots of a rapt, largely male diegetic audience (within the film) focus film viewers' attention on West as a performer offering an irresistible spectacle. West's number follows a chorus-line act of hefty women in white tights, which establishes the setting and tone of nineteenth-century burlesque and sets up a visual contrast for West's comparatively more impressive solo figure.[14]

West had previously masqueraded as a "spider woman" in *I'm No Angel*: she dons one of her most distinctive costumes in a scene where she aims to seduce the film's male lead, played by Cary Grant (Figure 8). In *Goin' to Town* (1935), West's operatic performance as Delilah provides a spectacular highlight primarily through her costume, a formfitting dark dress with glittering cones as breastplates and a cluster of golden braids accenting her hips and pubic area; her arms trail veils as she gestures broadly and sings the French lyrics in wavering soprano (Figure 13). West's "over the top" costume and gestures ensure her capacity to command viewers' attention; in film and stage presentation, that capacity represents a source of power.

Although West wears elaborate costumes in the stage acts she performs in all her films, the star's appearance in "offstage" settings in modern dress films such as *I'm No Angel*, *Goin' to Town*, and *Go West, Young Man* remain generally within the bounds of acceptable marks of glamour in the 1930s. Some publicity stills promoting West's forthcoming film productions showed her in relatively understated contemporary fashions (see, for example, Figures 24, 28, and 29). A portion of West's early film audiences did consider the star glamorous and beautiful, notwithstanding the deviation of her predominant style from the streamlined women's fashions that dominated much of the 1920s and 1930s. Articles in movie magazines and daily newspapers in 1933 attributed to West a distinct influence on high fashion (particularly owing to Edith Head's elaborate costumes for *She Done Him Wrong*) and also on prevailing ideals of women's body types, as a healthy corrective to a fixation on slimness.[15]

Reviews of West's first three vehicles frequently express admiration for the star's presentation. In August 1934, Los Angeles columnist Elizabeth Yeaman acclaimed the star's glamorous appearance and voluptuous costumes in the newly released *Belle of the Nineties* and praised West's songs. Yeaman also declared West "an ethereal young woman who is the essence of dainty refinement" in her private life and called her "well-bred."[16]

But beginning around 1935, newspaper reports increasingly criticized excess in West's costume, body style, and behavior. *New York Times* critic Andre Sennwald began his review of West's 1935 film *Goin' to Town* with floridly couched criticism of West's aging and her weight:

> Being one of Miss West's most abject idolators, your film reporter has the unhappy task this morning of hinting that the great lady is revealing intimations of mortality in her new picture. . . . Miss West continues to be, as she herself points out, a good woman for a bad man. But there are distressing signs that she is beginning to crack up. Perhaps you will agree that it is a legitimate form of criticism, rather than an ungracious personal comment on the distinguished star, to report that she seems to have gained weight in not altogether discreet localities since the bellowing days of "She Done Him Wrong" and "I'm No Angel." Nor has the change to modern dress improved her lure for those of us who loved her as the brewery beauty of her earlier masterpieces.[17]

Just two years after praising the star's appearance in *Belle of the Nineties*, Elizabeth Yeaman obliquely criticized West's taste in clothes and jewels following a personal interview with her during location shooting for *Go West, Young Man*:

> For her modern wardrobe, Mae has taken off 12 pounds and her corsets. . . . she lounged comfortably in a pair of grey crepe pajamas, a white broadtail swagger coat, white satin pumps and a heavy burden of jewelry. The jewelry was awe inspiring. On her left hand was a giant cabochon star sapphire of 75 carats, widely circled with diamonds. The ring was the size of a half dollar. On her left arm were three dazzling bracelets. The one next the wrist, about two inches wide, was of diamonds, surmounted by another star sapphire of 125 carats! Yea, verily! The other two were wide bands of diamonds. On her right hand was a diamond, held to the ring by invisible prongs. It looked as if it ought to be weighed in pound measure rather than in carats. The jewelry is not paste reproduction. It is genuine and is Mae's personal property. At her own insistence, she is wearing it in the picture. . . . And there should be a word about the modern wardrobe for her new picture. The gowns are all long and trailing. There are no sports clothes. No tailored garments. Mae doesn't have any of those in her private wardrobe. She'll wear evening dresses, negligees and plenty of monkey fur in "Go West Young Man."[18]

Other writers of the period condemned West's appearance more openly, addressing their barbs primarily at West's figure. One instance is an article in the November 1936 *Photoplay* by fashion consultant "Madame Sylvia," which asks "Is Mae West Skidding on the Curves?" In a 1938 article, French author Colette defended West against unnamed critics who had vividly reproached the star for her "corpulence," called her "an adipose beauty," and referred to her "fat haunches"; Colette herself criticized West for appearing thinner.[19]

Even presuming that West had grown heavier (a point difficult to verify from her films), her size alone could not have warranted her notably altered reception beginning in 1935. The rising criticism of West's excess around this period correlates with two factors: first, the star's growing importance as a powerful emblem of movie immorality, and as such a key target of moral reformers; second, the revelation in April 1935 that West had been married in 1911 at age eighteen, and the concomitant revelation of her age as forty-two, ten years older than previously assumed. Frequent condemnations after the mid-1930s of West's appearance for being "in poor taste" indicate a shift in her dominant reception as a sexually and professionally bold and original female type to her being considered a vain, aging, nouveau riche "hussy" who inappropriately displayed her body and wealth.

Such are the implications of an ironic *Life* magazine feature in 1940 about the star's Hollywood apartment, which reads in part: "Dominating the rooms, which resemble sets from her movies, are a nude statue of Miss West, two nude paintings and 26 mirrors. Most imposing is the gigantic clover-shaped one encircling her bed."[20] A caption under one of five photographs illustrating the article points out: "Her living room has a bear rug on the floor and a three-panelled mirror covering most of the south wall. All the tables are covered with porcelain and glass knick-knacks. The flowers are mostly artificial." In the photograph, West stands near the bear-skin rug facing the mirror, clad in a white satin gown, one bejeweled hand on her hip.

The *Los Angeles Times* had previously, on 22 December 1935, circulated accounts of West in her home surroundings (see Figure 15). These and other articles invariably depicted West's upholstered satin-draped bed, justifying the inclusion by asserting that the star and author wrote scripts in bed and drawing attention to the strategically placed ceiling mirror that allegedly enabled her to "see how I'm doin'!"[21] (See Figure 16.) Suggestions that West's bed served as work site and exhibitionistic performance stage underscored the star's sexual excess. West's decor offers evidence of sexual narcissism and vulgar display: the multiple nude representations, multiply mirrored; the sensuality of the bear fur; the orgy of polished glass and porcelain.

In 1965, the trade journal *Show* ran a feature on West with photographs and text by Diane Arbus; the article depicts West in word as sexually active and in image as excessive. One photo shows the septuagenarian West propped up in bed, embracing a monkey.[22] Four years later, *Life* ran on its cover a similar photo that shows West, now *sans* monkey, lounging in a mirrored bed amid satin, brocade, velvet, and lace. Inside, old publicity stills and contemporary photos of West at home in her Ravenswood apartment illustrate a long interview with the star.[23] (Figure 17 resembles the "at-home" images printed in *Life.*) Except for West's aging, little had changed in *Life*'s visual representation of the star between its 1940 and 1969 feature articles. But the evident public response to West had changed: *Life*'s 1969 cover elicited responses from readers such as "It's absolutely bizarre! Give me nudity any time," and "[It] has all the opulence of an expensive casket." Other letters to the editor described the magazine's presentation of West as "lavish" and "camp."[24]

These letters point to reception of West in 1969, at age seventy-five, as a sign of excess that is implicitly sexual ("give me nudity") but that is also related to gender violations (the mention of gay-associated "camp"). Public response to the *Life* illustrations and the interest expressed in the star by Arbus, known for her photographs of the grotesque, confirm how West signaled sexual and gender deviance in the 1960s. This was a period of popular revival for West, a revival that clearly drew on the star's established transgressive status. A source of the deviance in West's image, besides her appearance and behavior, was her frequent association with persons marked by dominant U.S. society—and by Hollywood—as racially and culturally "different" from the supposed norm.

Race Relations in West's Image and Performance

West's musical performances contributed to her image as an actively sexual, persistently "low-class" woman, for she frequently delivered songs in the "dirty blues" style. A musical tradition of stylized sexual display through innuendo-laden lyrics, the "dirty blues" is associated with African American performers such as Ma Rainey and Bessie Smith and accordingly bears specific racial and class connotations.[25] "Dirty blues" lyrics delivered by a female narrator/singer usually proclaim humorously that the singer is eager for sex, promiscuous, and often intent on garnering financial gain for her sexual performance.

West had adopted a dirty blues musical style in her years in vaudeville and popular theater and maintained it in her film roles, albeit in continually modified form. In *She Done Him Wrong*, West sings not only a version of the popular ballad "Frankie and Johnny," with which she had become closely identified during the run of *Diamond Lil*,[26] but also two numbers derived from the dirty blues tradition: a version of "Easy Rider," a Bessie Smith song, and "A Guy What Takes His Time." The lyrics of the latter include such phrases as "I'm a fast movin' gal that likes 'em slow" and "I'd be satisfied, electrified to know a guy what takes his time."*

West's opening number in *I'm No Angel* is a bluesy tune titled "They Call Me Sister Honky-Tonk" that identifies the star as a hardworking cooch dancer in a traveling carnival. The song includes such lyrics as "I'm a devil in disguise," "I'm fire and I'm flame," and "I'm not looking for a true man, all I want to do is have my way."* In *Belle of the Nineties*, West performs versions of "St. Louis Woman," "Memphis Blues," and "My Old Flame," accompanied in onscreen performance by Duke Ellington and His Orchestra. "St. Louis Woman" is a 1914 William Handy song that West renders in a style reminiscent of Ma Rainey. It includes lyrics such as "I lived six flights up but he sure did like to climb" and "Oh, bring on those fancy loving papas!"

West's cinematic presentation as she sings "St. Louis Woman" complements the racial implications in the song's lyrics and style. West sings on the stage of the "Sensation House," a private New Orleans gambling club at which liveried African American doormen grant the evidently rich male patrons entrance. The camera frames most of West's performance in medium and medium long shots that emphasize her waving a feathered fan to punctuate the lyrics and swiveling her hips, tightly clad in a sequined white dress with a darker glittering zigzag down the midsection. (See Figures 12 and 18.) Cutaway shots show Duke Ellington on piano and other

---

* "A Guy What Takes His Time," written by Ralph Rainger, copyright 1932, 1933, renewed 1961, 1962 Famous Music Corporation, reprinted by permission, all rights reserved. "They Call Me Sister Honky-Tonk," words by Gladys Dubois and Ben Ellison, music by Harvey Brooks, copyright 1933 Shapiro, Bernstein and Co., Inc., New York, copyright renewed, international copyright secured, all rights reserved, lyrics reprinted with permission.

individual musicians, all African American, vivaciously playing their in-
struments. The *mise-en-scène* that establishes the milieu and the editing of
the scene augments the festive and forbidden aura of West's sexually suggestive performance.

In another remarkable scene in this film, which was directed by Leo Mc-
Carey, West sings a pensive, hymnlike number titled "Troubled Waters,"
which bewails the calumny directed at her "good name."[27] West's character sings the number after strolling out onto a balcony to contemplate the
African American Christian revival meeting along the river nearby. The
editing connects the star to the revivalists through a series of stunning audio and visual dissolves between West and the spiritual meeting. The series
culminates in a sustained superimposition of West's face in close-up over
an extreme long shot, from her point of view, showing the group singing
and dancing in religious frenzy around a bonfire. The circle of brightly lit
writhing bodies sparkles like diamonds strewn over West's platinum hair
and low neckline while the audio track mixes the two hymns. (See Figure
19.) A montage of the singers' faces in close-up, overlaying the previous
composition, concludes the sequence. The repeated quick motion of the
camera dollying in to frame individual faces accentuates the rising mo-
mentum of dancing and singing. West's bright white visage remains static
as a backdrop; the black faces supplant her image as her performance incorporates theirs.

Although more African American performers appear in *Belle of the
Nineties* than in any other West film, this film typifies West's and other
Hollywood films of the period in its casting of African Americans as entertainers and servants. African American women play the star's personal
maids in West's first three star vehicles: Louise Beavers as Pearl in *She
Done Him Wrong*; Gertrude Howard as Beulah; and Libby Taylor, Hattie
McDaniel, and an uncredited fourth woman in *I'm No Angel* (Figure 20);
and again Libby Taylor, who was also West's personal employee, as Jasmine
in *Belle of the Nineties* (see Figure 21). Most of the maids have comparatively extended speaking roles in exchanges with the star.

In both *I'm No Angel* and *Goin' to Town*, African American men appear
in uncredited bit parts as attendants heralding West's stage performances.[28] The actor Nicodemus appears in a demeaning stereotypical role
of the lazy, dumb sidekick (what African American film historian Donald
Bogle classifies as a "coon") in *Go West, Young Man* (1936), and Louis
Armstrong has a cameo role as a street sweeper and band leader in *Every
Day's a Holiday* (1938). However, West does not appear onscreen with ei-

ther of those two characters. West's characters had no interactions with
African Americans in films following *Goin' to Town* until the star's appearance in 1970 in *Myra Breckinridge*, in which Calvin Lockhart plays a gay
student at an acting school and other African American men dance in
Latin-influenced musical numbers.[29]

Although the presence of African Americans in West's films diminished
following *Belle of the Nineties*, other actors of color and also locales that
many U.S. viewers might consider exotic appeared in increasing numbers.[30] In *Goin' to Town*, two characters are cast as Native Americans (Tito
Coral as Taho; Joe Frye as Laughing Eagle, a jockey); the film is set in part
in Argentina. In *Klondike Annie* (1936), a number of Chinese American
men appear in the initial setting in San Francisco's Chinatown, and West's
character has a Chinese maid (Soo Young as Fah Wong), with whom she
speaks in Chinese. (Maids in West's subsequent starring vehicles are all
"French," i.e., exotic but white.) In *My Little Chickadee* (1940), set in "the
West," a stereotypical Native American character is the object of many
jokes told by West's costar, W. C. Fields. Several of West's jokes in that
film also take Indians as "butts," as she coolly shoots down the line of
mounted warriors attacking her train. *The Heat's On* (1943) (initially
titled *Tropicana*) features jazz performed by Trinidad-born pianist Hazel
Scott and Latin American rhythms by Xavier Cugat's Orchestra.[31]

West's recurrent juxtaposition with characters cast as racially distinct
emphasizes the star's own identity, enhanced through her blondness, as a
privileged white woman. The actors cast as servants also narratively accentuate the lead character's acquisition of wealth and social status, as her
maids increase in number with her success (see Figure 20). The interracial
exchanges in which the star engages onscreen also charge her image with
an undercurrent of exoticism and sexual taboo. Of all West's films, *Klondike Annie* most overtly violates the taboo in U.S. society against interracial sexual relations, for as the film opens, West's character is mistress to
Chan Lo, owner of a Chinatown nightclub (Figure 22). In keeping with
industry casting practices, the Chinese man is played by a Caucasian actor,
Harold Huber.[32] West's entrance in that film, following on a typical verbal
buildup by other characters, occurs on an ornately decorated stage in Chan
Lo's club, as veil-like curtains lift to reveal her strumming a mandolin
and singing "I'm an Occidental Woman in an Oriental Mood for Love."
An audience of Chinese men watches (see Figure 23). Through a process
of displacement, the represented racial difference enhances West's desirability as a precious commodity: while the blonde star herself remains dis-

tinctly white, her persona encompasses the allure of the forbidden through her character's play with cross-racial relations.

The representational strategy fetishizing white female sexuality by suggesting the potential violation of interracial sexual taboos is of course not unique to West's films. Indeed, the comedy of West's films somewhat effaces the technique's effects, compared with its more obvious use in other films of the same period that juxtapose American blondes with (supposed) "racial others" in exotic locales, such as *The Bitter Tea of General Yen* (1933) with Barbara Stanwyck and *King Kong* (1933) with Fay Wray.[33] However, publicity about West's offscreen associations and interests in racial difference contributed to the star's representing outlawed sex in a way that other 1930s blonde stars did not. An article that appeared in the *Los Angeles Times* around the release of *Belle of the Nineties* suggests that West sexually desired Native American men:

> In my next film I'm going to have an Indian in one of the principal roles, and I want a real Indian. . . . He's got to be just right, and one that the ladies will love. Of course, you understand, I sort of like him myself, and when I meet him I look him over carefully.[34]

The star's reported interest in "a real Indian" complemented previous accounts of her personal and professional interest in men of racial and cultural backgrounds distinct from her own, particularly African American men. West's novel *Babe Gordon*, published in 1930 and reprinted in 1931 under the title *The Constant Sinner*, has as its protagonist a character embodying the West persona who takes as one of her lovers "Money Jackson," in West's words, "the Negro king of the Harlem numbers racket."[35] West reports that the novel, which formed the basis for her last Broadway production before her move to Hollywood, went through five editions.[36] Studio publicity from 1934-36 about West's personal life included photographs of West's African American maids and her chauffeur in 1935-36, boxer Chalky Wright (see Figures 21, 24, 25, and 26). Newspaper publicity about the chauffeur who succeeded Wright, a "Filipino pugilist" called Speedy Dado, extended West's interracial associations.[37]

Twenty years later, in an article headed "Mae West's Open-Door Policy," the magazine *Confidential* linked West's image with Wright again by suggesting that the two had maintained "more than an employer-employee relationship," in West's own words.[38] West eventually pressed charges of libel and won. But the lawsuit managed to move the "exposé" about the star's willful violation of taboos against interracial sex (and adultery, for both Wright and West were married at the time) from the pages of a tabloid into the daily press and also into West's autobiography, even as she denied the story.

Recent West biographies that embellish the details of West and Wright's relationship uphold the racially encoded sexual transgression in West's image.[39] Long before megastar Madonna replicated the practice by hiring Asian and African American backup singers and dancers, West's image embodied cross-racial associations that at once augmented and displaced other facets of her image, including the transgression of middle-class norms of monogamous heterosexuality.

Gender Impersonation in West's Performance and Image

West's contemporary audiences often focus on the star's presumed violations of socially prescribed gender roles, and particularly on her complex relation to gay male subculture. Associations with male homosexuality that had arisen during West's days on the stage carried over into her movie career, obliquely fostered by theater critics, Paramount studio publicity, and the star's films. In winter 1927, West's play *The Drag* had opened for tryouts in Bridgeport, Connecticut, and then Paterson, New Jersey, in anticipation of a Broadway run. Extensive publicity about its focus on obviously gay characters, including female impersonators, and its exceptional box-office success out of town made the play a target in New York political struggles that had crystallized around theater censorship. West's *Sex* and two other long-running plays that had themes of "sexual deviance" were also targeted, although the police raid on *Sex* was no doubt aimed primarily at precluding *The Drag* from opening on Broadway. But extensive publicity about *The Drag* and, eighteen months later, *Pleasure Man* securely anchored West's image to associations with homosexuality and transvestism.[40]

Although cross-dressing is not necessarily correlated with sexual orientation, its representation in American popular culture conventionally signals homosexuality or at least a socially disruptive gender ambiguity. West's "deviant" image also arises from her own exaggerated performance of gender characteristics, both male and female. West herself has long been recognized as a gender impersonator. Hollywood publicity and popular biographies have occasionally recalled the childhood act in which West imitated male vaudevillians, as did the *Parade* feature and an article about West in *Movie Classic* in January 1934.[41] But West's image has been more broadly and frequently associated with *female* than with male impersonation, implying, paradoxically, that West herself was performing (or even really was!) a man impersonating a woman—by popular reasoning, a gay male. West's association with transvestism differs from that of Marlene Dietrich and Greta Garbo, who are recognized as having expressed a strong female—and often implicitly lesbian—identity through their male masquerades.[42]

In the May 1934 *Vanity Fair*, critic George Davis proclaimed West "the greatest female impersonator of all time" and celebrated the male homoerotic implications in West's image in ironic tones:

> Miss West, long have I loved you. Ay, long before *I'm No Angel*. Long before *Diamond Lil*. Long, even before your first great play, *Sex*. . . . Though my love for you has never been the fleshly one proclaimed by so many of your admirers, it has withstood true-blue the test of time. I can pay you no greater tribute, dear lady, than to say that it has healed the wound in my heart caused by the death of the one and only Bert Savoy.[43]

Most contemporary biographies trace West's performance style to female impersonators in vaudeville, including Savoy and Julian Eltinge.[44] Although West mentions neither of these performers in her 1959 autobiography, she does recount at length how theater director Edward Elsner helped her with *Sex*. She first implies that he was gay, then quotes him praising her performance style for having "a definite *sexual* quality, gay and unrepressed. It even mocks you personally." A few pages later, in the chapter titled "SEX, More Sex and the Cooler," West writes first about a bisexual man who pursued her, then recounts her impulse to write *The Drag* ("Some force that was perverse, some strange thing, was compelling me to write it"), and thereupon launches into a moralistic discussion of homosexuality "as a danger to the entire system of western civilization," which her play sets out to defuse by bringing "its secret antisocial aspects . . . into the sun."[45] Despite West's homophobic phrasing, the overall effect of the chapter, like that of the *Parade* article published thirty years earlier, is to underscore West's own unconventional engenderment and obliquely to celebrate the gay male sensibility she attributes to theater director Elsner, her bisexual lover, and the actors she cast in *The Drag*.

Paramount's publicity department built on the appeal of West's presumed deviance, notwithstanding the extensive application after mid-1934 of the 1930 Motion Picture Production Code to studio publicity as well as to film scripts (a development I discuss in chapters 2 and 3). The studio

promoted *Belle of the Nineties* (originally titled *It Ain't No Sin*) with a photograph of West and director Leo McCarey that was issued in June 1934
with the following suggested caption:

> TALKING IT OVER WITH THE QUEEN—Around Hollywood the boys and girls of
> filmdom call Mae West "the Queen." . . . Although screen folk call Mae
> "the Queen" just for fun, she is injecting a royal sequence into her new
> Paramount picture to emerge as a queen in a burlesque skit.

The caption echoes *Vanity Fair*'s acclamation of West's gender ambiguity
in its sly reference to the coterie of "boys and girls" playfully naming West
"the Queen." By 1934 that term was well-established slang for a man enacting an exaggerated femininity.[46] The caption's timing within a month
of Davis's essay at once prized and contributed to expanded public recognition of West as a female impersonator.

Just over a year later, in October 1935, Paramount released a publicity
photo series featuring a Los Angeles Police Department officer who had
masqueraded as West in an effort to capture an extortionist. One photo
that shows Chalky Wright and a plain-clothed officer flanking the West
impersonator integrates the cross-racial and gay implications in the star's
image (see Figure 26). The *Los Angeles Examiner* illustrated its coverage of
the extortion threats against West with a photo of Harry Dean in his "Mae
West" disguise standing next to the star. The eye-catching front-page image appeared below the headline "Mae West Guarded after Threat" and
the subhead "Doubled in Furs—They Stole Act"; the photo caption read
"Harry Dean and Mae West (right) as the detective donned feminine attire in attempt to trap extortion suspects."[47]

Production Code administrators, the Hollywood-based employees of the
Motion Picture Producers and Distributors Association (MPPDA, also
known as the Hays Office, after its longtime director Will Hays), who were
charged with upholding Code guidelines, made no recorded objection to
such hints of "perversion." These men either did not recognize or consider
harmful or for other reasons did not object to elements in West's films that
similarly drew on and augmented the star's associations with cross-dressing
and other conventional representations of homosexuality. This was the
case notwithstanding the Code's official prohibition of the representation
of homosexuality under the rubric "sex perversion."

Production Code Administration (PCA) director Joseph Breen did caution Paramount in correspondence about the script for *Goin' to Town* that
an interior decorator was not to be a "nance"; the character was subse-

quently deleted.[48] PCA correspondence on West's 1938 film *Every Day's a Holiday*, which was independently produced by former Paramount production chief Emanuel Cohen, warned that the film should not imply that West's character lived with two men.[49] But the characterization of one of the men, a butler called "Graves," was neither noted in correspondence nor censored upon final PCA review of the film; that character is played by Charles Butterworth as a "queen." In one scene, West's character, "Peaches O'Day," tricks the stereotypically effeminate Graves into climbing into a showcase window to steal an elegant costume for her. Following her instructions, Graves tries on various women's capes and feathered hats and at one point hides from a passing policeman by posing behind a headless dress form, in effect appearing in drag. Paramount, which distributed the film, made stills from the scene for its advertising campaign (see Figure 27).

West's last films, *Myra Breckinridge* (1970) and *Sextette* (1978), are most obviously constructed—and have been almost exclusively received—as "gay camp," as I discuss in chapter 5. But West's camp reception emerged long before the rise of the gay rights movement, prior to the star's aging to a point that made her excessive feminine mask obvious to all (as the letters to *Life* in 1969 suggested), prior also to the easing of Production Code enforcement. West's image signaled complex homosexual and other "gender-deviant" associations from her earliest stardom. Her contemporary reception as camp has as its historical foundation the oblique representations of male homosexuality in her 1930s films, fostered by long-standing critical discussion of West as female impersonator and Hollywood's own promotion of West as a "queen."

The Power of Character and Authorship

Mae West's designation as "queen" points to a compounded social deviance in her image. Besides its gender-transgressive slang connotation, the term does, after all, refer to the traditionally most powerful and presumably richest female member of a royal family. But even while West, surrounded by Louis XV furniture, presents a regal queenly figure, she emanates the style of a lower-class woman. Yet the lower-class woman usually suffers socioeconomic subordination, whereas the cultural sign "Mae West" manifests power relations that seem to challenge long-entrenched patterns of male and upper-class dominance. West's moniker "Queen" thus doubly registers how the star inverts historical patterns of power distribution correlated to gender and class: a lower-class woman enacts through her costuming, physical mannerisms, and narrative positioning in films a power-ful masculine figure who exhibits a luxurious and excessive feminine mas-querade.

West's masquerade as a flamboyantly royal female impersonator exuded an aura of power grounded in material wealth that far surpassed any power ceded lower-class women in economic and political practice. But the mas-querade also enabled West, the actress from Brooklyn, actually to amass such wealth and power. West's image encapsulated the potential for a woman of lower-class background to ascend to a throne, at least in Holly-wood, U.S.A.

West's characterization as a woman with royal power derived in part from her systematically playing famous female personages such as Cleo-patra, Delilah, and Catherine the Great.[50] In Goin' to Town, West's per-formance incorporates the power and sexuality attributed in popular his-tories to the first two figures: as "Cleo" Borden, West sings the female lead in the opera Samson and Delilah, justifying her plan to do so by declaring to her butler, "I gotta lotta respect for that dame. Now there's a lady barber that made good!" Prior publicity had suggested that West would play an-other assertively sexual and powerful female biblical figure, the Queen of Sheba.[51] In September 1934, Edwin Schallert declared in his Los Angeles Times column that recently adopted "rules and regulations" made the pro-duction of the proposed Queen of Sheba impossible "for the time being," but remarked that West might play "Catherine the Great during the ro-mantically tempestuous part of her career."

Of all these royal female figures, West's image is most closely aligned with Catherine the Great, who, popular legend holds, was insatiable in her quest for sexual and political power.[52] West's autobiography recounts her attempts in 1938-39 to make a film featuring herself as the Russian em-press in her own script Catherine Was Great and her success in 1944-45 with the work as a Broadway play.[53] Newspaper and magazine reviews panned the production, but noted that it was a tremendous popular suc-cess.[54] Even after the play's closing, press reports of a legal suit charging West with plagiarism of the material kept active the star's associations with Czarina Catherine. West biographies similarly propagate the associa-tion, as does a line of dialogue in West's highly self-referential film Sextette, which asserts that West's character, Marlo Manners, herself a movie queen, will soon star in the Technicolor picture Catherine Was Great.

West described her play's version of the czarina as "a pre-incarnation of myself. A Slavic-Germanic Diamond Lil, just as low in vivid sexuality, but on a higher plane of authority."[55] Although West's image, like the legend of Catherine, combines sexuality and power, the sexual component is more central to West's persona than to Catherine's. The czarina may have wielded her political power to exercise wanton sexuality (including sex with horses); twentieth-century observers attribute West's power precisely to her exercise of wanton sexuality in both her films and her life.

Besides West's "royal" roles and her power as spectacle, the star's performance style and narrative position in films after *Night after Night* (1932) contributed to her reception as a sign of a powerful woman. Many critics have noted that West's characters, especially in her first two or three star vehicles, avoid the punishment or restraint at tale's end that typically befalls many Hollywood female characters.[56] French author Colette expressed in 1938 what many subsequent critics have found remarkable about West:

> She alone, out of an enormous and dull catalogue of heroines, does not get married at the end of the film, does not die, does not take the road to exile, does not gaze sadly at her declining youth in a silver-framed mirror in the worst possible taste; and she alone does not experience the bitterness of the abandoned "older woman." She alone has no parents, no children, no husband. This impudent woman is, in her style, as solitary as Chaplin used to be.[57]

Beyond its catchy turn of phrase even in translation, this formulation evokes interest for its association with Colette, whose persona incorporates a life narratively similar to that of the movie star and characters she describes. This association paradoxically undercuts Colette's assertion that West is unique: "She alone . . . ."

Numerous critics writing in the past two decades have discussed West's display of "freedom," "self-sufficiency," "independence," "strength," and other characteristics that in twentieth-century American parlance denote power.[58] These authors read the star's behavior in films as embodying her personal autonomy and control. For example, feminist critic Marjorie Rosen, writing in 1973, discusses West in the following terms:

> [A]s the powerhouse, the aggressor, she controlled plots and manipulated males with the deftness of a puppeteer, as dispassionate and calculating as any woman might dream of becoming. Mae herself admitted that she existed as "the woman's ego." It is this aspect of her screen image more than her sardonic sexual cynicism which so aggravated her detractors.
>
> Never before, and never since, has a woman in films been so thoroughly in control of her destiny. First of all, she was usually self-employed and

self-supporting. Mae's character adored herself with a passion that didn't leave room for men. They were interchangeable; she could afford the luxury of showering kindness on them but always remained diffident, distant, even if—as in the end of *She Done Him Wrong*—she bows to Cary Grant's charms and they go off together.[59]

In Rosen's and other critics' interpretations, the narcissism, promiscuity, and indifference to romantic attachment that West enacts are evidence of the star's own power to achieve her desires, however transgressive, both on and off the screen. Critical accounts also discover West's *extra*cinematic power in her ability to resist or even control powerful men such as Adolph Zukor, head of Paramount, in her professional and private life. These discussions often conflate West's film characters and West as actor and persona.

While this is a common phenomenon of star images that movie scripts and publicity materials have long cultivated, West's image evinces a particularly emphatic equivalence between actor and character.[60] The trial scene in *I'm No Angel* (1933) recalls West's widely reported court appearances on charges of indecency in 1927 and again in 1930, for corrupting minors with her play *Pleasure Man*. A caricature of West in the Walt Disney cartoon "Who Killed Cock Robin?" (1935) in turn parodies the courtroom scene in *I'm No Angel*.[61] In *Night after Night*, West plays a sympathetic former girlfriend of star George Raft's character. West's casting coalesces with later biographers' assertions that she and Raft had been lovers in the late 1920s and that their continued friendship led Raft to request West for a supporting role, more or less as herself, in his first starring vehicle. Several of West's own starring vehicles (*I'm No Angel*, *Goin' to Town*) integrate her birth date, August 17, into the dialogue or settings, notably through calendars on display in the background.

West's autobiography *Goodness Had Nothing to Do with It* further perpetuates the illusion of continuity between her screen and personal identities. The book's title is a much-quoted line of West's dialogue in her first film, *Night after Night*, her retort to a hatcheck girl who exclaims, "Goodness, what beautiful jewels!" The autobiography points out that a scene in *Belle of the Nineties* in which West's character, Ruby Carter, is robbed of jewels duplicates the actress's personal experience of being robbed in the fall of 1932, an incident widely reported when it happened and again in 1933–34 when suspects were prosecuted.[62] Paramount took advantage of publicity about the crime to stage a photo series of West with a representative from the Los Angeles District Attorney's office, showing the star "trying out" a

selection of firearms, from pistols to machine guns. The studio's photo captions emphasize West's implicitly masculine power and expertise with large
guns and, drawing on West's own style of sexual innuendo, assert that she
chose the larger of two pistols offered her for target practice (see Figure 28).

Film reviews in the 1930s noted the consistency of West's performances
from film to film and the unity between her characters and her star persona, arguing, sometimes critically, that West always played herself. These
and more recent discussions frequently attribute such unity to West's authorship of her own material.[63] Recognition that West managed largely to
determine and sustain her career in the face of very limited opportunities
for women enhances her aura of power. Such power adheres to West's image notwithstanding disputes over the legitimacy of some of her claims of
authorship. Newspaper accounts of the many litigations to which West was
party focus on her powerful star status even when they sometimes doubt
her rights in the cases at hand.[64] Even biographies that question the credits' validity note that West managed to lay convincing claim to all her material, whether she wrote it or not. Skeptics attribute West's extensive authorship credits to an overweening ego that awed her coworkers.[65]

In the early 1930s, Paramount considered the image of an all-powerful
female star a marketable asset. Studio publicity for West's first three starring vehicles propagated her image as a powerful, multitalented woman engaged in every aspect of her movies' production. Promotion for *Belle of the
Nineties* included photographs of West ostensibly consulting with Adolph
Zukor and director Leo McCarey, as well as with her cameraman, the script
girl, costumers and propmen, a dramatic adviser, and even with the studio's
"censorship expert," John Hammell (see Figures 29-32). A publicity photo
of West wearing modern clothes and sitting with McCarey at a table bears
the following suggested caption:

> ONE WOMAN PRODUCTION STAFF—Mae West does everything but
> build the sets for her Paramount productions. She writes her stories, offers
> directorial suggestions, has her hand in costume designing and knows her
> music. Here she is on the set of her next sinema, *It Ain't No Sin*, with her
> director Leo McCarey, going over her new script. Although she will
> blossom out again in the amazing gowns of the Naughty Nineties, she
> chooses as "working clothes" a sweater ensemble and a topcoat. [Figure 29]

The remarkable economic success and business acumen frequently attributed to the star complement the aura of power in her image. Accounts
of her financial success circulated widely in the early 1930s and recur in

later discussions of West. Many reports assert not only that her first two starring vehicles broke box-office records but also that the profits saved Paramount from bankruptcy. A number of biographers note her status, by 1936, as the highest-paid star in Hollywood, commanding $300,000 per picture and an additional $100,000 for screenplay or scenario. In this period the average annual U.S. income was about $1,600. A frequently cited figure for West's 1936 income is $480,833.[66]

Some biographers point to West's wisdom in investments. During the Depression, she savvily bought real estate in the San Fernando Valley near Los Angeles, which she parlayed into an estate worth millions.[67] Such information contributes to West's power, as it is well understood in American terms: her capacity to earn and control material wealth. Remarkably, even accounts of West's eventual failure in Hollywood augment her status as a sign of power, for these trace her eventual decline to her having disrupted society sufficiently to provoke film censorship.

Mae West as "Great (Wo)Man" in Hollywood History

Hollywood lore holds that Mae West individually occasioned rigorous enforcement of the Motion Picture Production Code, which delimited the content and, to an extent, the ideology of Hollywood movies from the 1930s through the mid-1960s. Standard U.S. film histories frequently draw direct causal links among West's 1933 productions, the formation in 1934 of the Catholic Legion of Decency, which threatened to boycott theaters that showed offensive movies, and the subsequent enforcement of the Production Code by the Hays Office. Although recent detailed historical studies invalidate this reductionistic account of events, the popular claim that "Mae West caused Hollywood censorship" continues to circulate and to support the star's characterization as a powerful woman.

In his book *Hollywood Babylon*, underground filmmaker Kenneth Anger recounts the formation of the Legion of Decency in a vivid passage in keeping with the work's style as a behind-the-scenes exposé of film history:

> Stronger disapprobation of Mae's fun-loving views on sex came spewing forth from Cardinal Mundelein of Chicago. The cardinal ordered one of his professional prigs, the Jesuit Rev. Daniel A. Lord, to pen a pamphlet, "The Motion Pictures Betray America," in which Catholic youth was urged to boycott the "obnoxious pictures" of Mae West. All of them would henceforth be blacklisted in Father Lord's magazine, *The Queen's Work*.
>   The Catholic sodality were so gratified by the response that they decided to put their anti-sex boycott on a national level. Bernard J. Sheil, auxiliary

bishop of Chicago, set about organizing a pressure group: the National
Legion of Decency, was formed in October 1933, six months after the
release of *She Done Him Wrong*. The Legion heavies cited the menace Mae
West represented as one of the major reasons for the "necessity" of their
organization.[68]

A more recent popular history of Hollywood film censorship affirms
West's responsibility for the foundation of the Legion of Decency even
while ostensibly dismissing such claims:

> Hollywood historians have propounded the theory that the Legion of
> Decency was established primarily to remove Mae West from the screen. It
> was scarcely six months after the release of her salacious *She Done Him
> Wrong* that the most virulent form of censorship took hold in the movie
> colony. Undoubtedly, the clerical reformers had more to be disturbed about
> than the buxom Miss West, but the theory of cause and effect has much to
> commend it.[69]

These and similar histories assert that the Hays Office responded to the
Legion's powerful threat by immediately trying to eliminate West's indecency from the screen. Marjorie Rosen sketches an even more direct
course between West's actions and those of the film trade association, cu-
riously attributing the Legion organization to the Hays Office itself.[70] Although technically incorrect, Rosen's implicit identification of the PCA *as*
the Legion of Decency displaces equivalents in her history. The accounts
all narrate how West managed for several years to evade the Hays Office's
attempts to censor her. Some introduce Joseph Ignatius Breen, MPPDA
director Hays's appointee in 1934 to head the newly formed Production
Code Administration, as a principal character and often an embodiment of
that agency, much as Hays functions metonymically for the movie picture
trade organization.[71] Breen's Catholicism often serves as an oblique explanation for his stance vis-à-vis West. Popular historical narratives thus set
up a series of continuities among the Catholic Church, the Legion of Decency, the MPPDA under Hays, and the PCA under Breen, all marshaled
against West.

The narrative histories usually contend that Breen eventually managed
to muzzle West only with the help of media magnate William Randolph
Hearst, who had taken personal offense at the star. Even then, Breen succeeded only after West had shrunk in popularity to become a box-office
liability for Paramount.[72] In these accounts, West's Hollywood career
moves in an arc from immediate financial and professional triumph in
1932-33 to ultimate inevitable defeat over the next three to five years un-

der the weight of the cumulative opposition of powerful leaders (or, alternately, minions) of the Catholic Church and the movie industry: variously Hays, Breen, Hearst, and Paramount studio executives.

Such explanations of West's role in Production Code enforcement adhere to a common American model of social causation that portrays complex social, political, and technological changes as the consequences of particular individuals' actions or the results of pitched conflicts, often with a personal basis, between a few powerful figures: a history of "great men."[73] Accounts of West's provoking and resisting censorship cast the star distinctly as a "great man" in Hollywood, placing her in the company of others who have had a wide-reaching impact in American film history, such as D. W. Griffith, Charlie Chaplin, Louis B. Mayer, and Irving Thalberg. In keeping with the resemblance of this model of history to classical tragedy, West as hero suffers setbacks and loses battles to worthy opponents, and the West versus PCA battle ends in the star's preliminary personal defeat. But only three powerful men backed by wealthy traditional cultural institutions can defeat her, and then only temporarily. And even as West bows to her opponents' superior power, she remains heroic in acceding with grace, as she leaves Hollywood to revive her stage career.

This popular view of the major personal role West played in Hollywood history derives from reports about the events as they occurred. A lengthy article about the MPPDA that *Fortune* magazine published in 1938 uses "Mae West" as a metonym in explaining the advent of internal film industry censorship:

> Frightened by the falling-off in film attendance, some producers tried to reverse the trend with liberal applications of sex, this technique reaching its flower in the Mae West pictures that appeared in 1932 and 1933.[74]

Such historical attribution, whether contemporaneous or retrospective, casts West as the embodiment of the American myth of success and its costs. As Richard Dyer has argued, movie stars often exemplify this myth.[75] Yet West's career narrative emphasizes her greater impact compared with most other stars, for it relates not one actor's personal successes and failures, but rather broad developments in the U.S. movie industry and in American social history. In the next two chapters, I offer an alternative history to the oversimplified claim that West caused censorship, by documenting how her image as a powerful, transgressive, comedic female actor functioned as a controversial cultural emblem amid the economic and social crises in the United States during the 1930s.

2

The Prostitute, the Production Code, and the Depression

Contrary to popular claims, the actress and screenplay author Mae West did not occasion American film censorship, nor did she provoke the film industry to adopt its self-regulatory Motion Picture Production Code. Yet the *icon* "Mae West" did play a central *emblematic* role in American public discourse about movie reform during the 1930s. The distinction is important for a grasp of the complexities of film history and the workings of cultural icons. Historical analysis of West's early star vehicles reveals how the star's image as a brashly sexual and persistently autonomous woman came, in the context of the Depression, to represent a challenge to the dominant but besieged values of the American middle class.

West's characterization as a successful and happy prostitute in her first five star vehicles (*She Done Him Wrong*, 1933; *I'm No Angel*, 1933; *Belle of the Nineties*, 1934; *Goin' to Town*, 1935; and *Klondike Annie*, 1936) was arguably the basis of West's perceived threat, but also of her popular appeal to the films' original audiences, including many middle-class cinema patrons. Particularly in the first four, West's characters exploit their sexual allure as a means to wealth, power, enhanced class status, and personal pleasure. Unlike most other Hollywood movies of the 1930s, West's films do not suggest that morality or questions of taste dictate female sexual behavior. Instead, West's films and star image present female sexual allure as a commodity that women themselves can control and benefit from. In so doing, West's films deviated somewhat from narrative and representational conventions in American movies. More significantly, West's movie image exposed contradictions in the well-established American capitalist practice of simultaneously exploiting and repressing female sexuality as a commodity under men's control.

The production and consumption of "Mae West" as a movie star and popular cultural sign made visible such discrepancies in Hollywood's symbolic deployment of female sexuality. Documented negotiations among Paramount studio producers, MPPDA representatives, and state censorship boards preceding the January 1933 release of West's first star vehicle *She Done Him Wrong* reveal the star's initially mild effect on Motion Picture Production Code enforcement. The film's critical and popular reception yielded West's immediate positive impact on the economic state and morale of the film industry. But historical records also reveal incipient rumblings around "Mae West" as a locus in a long-standing U.S. controversy over "movie morality," which had newly burgeoned in the early 1930s in response to widespread middle-class concern about the beleaguered economy and social system.

The Case of She Done Him Wrong

The film industry expressed interest as early as 1930 in featuring West in screen adaptations of her most successful Broadway plays. Recruiting West fit within the industry drive after 1928 to offer "the biggest stars while they're still playing on Broadway."[1] In 1929-30, West toured major U.S. cities in *Diamond Lil*, following the play's successful Broadway run in 1928. In January 1930, Universal studio founder and head Carl Laemmle requested that Jason Joy, then head of the MPPDA's Studio Relations Committee (SRC), attend the production of *Diamond Lil* then running at the Los Angeles Biltmore Theater to evaluate its suitability for adaptation, with a view to its passing the state movie censor boards. Laemmle's gesture was in keeping with MPPDA policy since 1924 that member studios seek guidance in purchasing plays and novels for adaptation to the screen.[2]

The internal memo that opens the MPPDA case file for *She Done Him Wrong* reports:

> I have advised Mr. Laemmle that because of the vulgar dramatic situations and the highly censorable dialogue, in my opinion, an acceptable picture could not be made of the material suggested in the play. The possibility of employing Mae West as a member of Universal's writing staff was brought to my attention. Of course, I discouraged the idea.[3]

Undissuaded, in April, Universal submitted to the MPPDA's head office in New York its proposal to purchase not only *Diamond Lil*, but also West's plays *Sex* and *Pleasure Man*. The MPPDA board of directors (comprising executive directors of member film corporations) rejected all these properties as unsuitable.[4]

Two years later, another studio, Paramount, advanced further with its plans to adapt *Diamond Lil*, but only with Will Hays's oblique personal cooperation. In June 1932, Paramount signed West for a supporting role in

George Raft's first starring vehicle, *Night after Night*, which opened in mid-October 1932 to moderate business. Critics attributed much of the film's appeal to West's performance.[5] Emphasis on West in studio publicity and exhibitor press kits for *Night after Night*, notwithstanding her fourth-ranked billing, suggests that this film served to test and build the stage actress's crossover appeal to movie audiences.[6] Paramount clearly deemed West's screen debut a success and moved immediately toward producing a film starring West and based on her stage work.

Word reached Hays in early October that Paramount planned a production of *Diamond Lil* and hoped, by changing its title, to circumvent official MPPDA rejection of the play as screen material.[7] In a telegram to Hays on 19 October 1932, Harry Warner requested immediate clarification of Hollywood rumors that Paramount was proceeding with the production. Hays assured Warner in a return telegram that Paramount would not violate the industry agreement against producing *Diamond Lil*.

But the ensuing correspondence between the New York and Hollywood offices of MPPDA, including several telegrams in code, reveals Paramount's persistence in the matter. Studio production chief Emanuel Cohen, in California, had evidently enlisted the crucial support of taxicab magnate John Hertz, a Paramount board member and chair of its finance committee, who skillfully negotiated with Will Hays in New York.[8] At a special board meeting on 28 November 1932, the MPPDA board agreed to the adaptation of *Diamond Lil* if Paramount gave the film a different title and otherwise somewhat obscured the origin of the material.[9] The task of advising on revisions of the material to avoid objections by state and local censor boards in the United States and Canada and in other key foreign markets fell to the MPPDA Studio Relations Committee in Hollywood.

In the face of growing public objection to movies and rising calls for federal film censorship, as of October 1931 the MPPDA required member studios to submit scripts of prospective productions. Although this formal requirement aimed to enhance the credibility of MPPDA claims about industry self-regulation, the policy also represented an SRC service to save member studios the expense of reediting and reshooting to meet state censors' objections or even to prevent substantial losses should a film be banned. Seven U.S. states had established movie censorship boards by 1930: New York, Massachusetts, Maryland, Ohio, Pennsylvania, Virginia, and Kansas. Canadian provinces Alberta, British Columbia, Ontario, and

Quebec also had censor boards, as did a number of U.S. cities, including Chicago, Kansas City, and Milwaukee. In practice, decisions made by these censor boards determined the versions of film prints available in other states and provinces in the same distribution region.[10]

Paramount submitted the prospective *Diamond Lil* film production for SRC review several weeks before the MPPDA directors reluctantly lifted their ban on 28 November. The day after that meeting, Dr. James Wingate, who in September 1932 had succeeded Joy as director of the SRC, cautioned Paramount that the film could not be set "in a whore house" and that the characterization of "Pablo Juarez," a gigolo in *Diamond Lil*, would have to be changed to avoid offending South American markets.[11] Taking the mild, advisory tone then the norm in SRC correspondence with studios, Wingate suggested that the character might be played as "sexy" and "exotic," but without establishing his nationality. (This character became a Russian named Serge Stanieff.)

In his letter to Paramount on 29 November 1932, Wingate advised the following further changes in the script:

- elimination of "the slightest suspicion of white slavery"
- elimination of any suggestion that West's character, Lady Lou, is a "kept woman"
- use of a costume for Captain Cummings (a detective disguised as a rescue mission worker, played by Cary Grant) other than a regulation Salvation Army uniform
- elimination of a shot of the rear of a horse and a subsequent "gag" involving a street cleaner
- inclusion of a close-up cutaway shot of a photograph that Lady Lou shows to Serge while remarking that it is appropriate for the bedroom, with the picture showing her "clothed in good taste"
- elimination or change of the following words or phrases (words in italics are those Wingate indicated as offensive):
  "the last guy she *had*"
  "I've got to *have* you"
  "You got to give a man more than clothes"
  "Now—you can be *had*" and "I always knew you could be *had*"
  (Lady Lou's remarks to Captain Cummings, the latter the curtain line from *Diamond Lil*)

In his next weekly report to Hays in the New York office, dated 2 December 1932, Wingate expressed optimism about Paramount's cooperation:

With regard to *She Done Him Wrong* (the new title for the Mae West picture), upon receiving word from you of the clearance of this matter under the Formula, we had a conference with Mr. LeBaron, the producer, at which it became evident that not only was the studio willing to accept our suggestions concerning the script, but had even added a few of their own. Their major contribution consisted in changing the original element of the traffic in girls to counterfeiting, thereby removing every possible suggestion of white slavery. Our basic changes aimed at soft-pedalling the many references to the number of Lady Lou's previous affairs with men, and the suggestion, in view of the rather low tone of both the background and characters presented, that the whole picture be directed and played with sufficient emphasis on the comedy values, and exaggeration of the manners and customs of the period, as to remove it as far as possible from any feeling of sordid realism. With those suggestions the studio seemed to be in hearty accordance and so far they certainly seem to be doing their best to avoid the difficulties inherent in this subject.

Wingate's argument that the conventions of comedy and the "Gay Nineties" setting would counteract offensiveness in the story indicates the then current SRC interpretation of guidelines to motion picture morality.[12] This interpretation emphasized not the presence of potentially objectionable elements, but rather their mode of presentation. Still, Wingate's recommendations to the studio's liaison, Harold Hurley, made clear that one aspect of the original material had to be eliminated: any suggestion of prostitution. He argued specifically that Lady Lou not benefit economically from her relations to her suitors:

In order to counter the rather low general level of the background in this story, as well as of the type of woman portrayed by the principal character, it should be definitely established that neither Chick Clark, nor Flynn, nor any other man before Gus, has ever kept her. (Wingate to Hurley, 29 November 1932)

After previewing the movie on 9 January 1933, Wingate indicated to Hurley that he was not sure that suggestions of white slavery had been eradicated and warned him that the "general low tone of the action and backgrounds" did not make him optimistic about censorship (Wingate to Hurley, 11 January 1933). He nonetheless tentatively approved the film for release, contingent on a few changes in the ending.

Wingate's weekly report to Hays two days later alerted him to expect some difficulties with the film:

We did have one important preview this week—the Mae West picture, "She Done Him Wrong."

After reviewing the picture, our feeling is that it may cause a certain amount of trouble, and we so advised Mr. Hurley at Paramount. The script itself, as we reported, appeared satisfactory under the Code; but the basic elements of the original story and its Bowery backgrounds must of necessity bring it within the category of low-tone pictures. It is ribald comedy; but there are at least feeble elements of regeneration which can be argued in its defense, if anybody will stop to analyze and find them. Miss West gives a performance of strong realism. The film is very much toned down as compared to the play, which indicates that the company has made efforts to keep within such bounds of good taste as the Bowery background of the nineties would permit. The preview audience reaction (for whatever it is worth) was one of hearty, if somewhat rowdy amusement. We cannot help feeling, however, that a number of movie audiences, censor boards and other people in authority, will not be enthusiastic about it.

To gauge state censors' responses in order to avoid financial losses from having to alter released films, the Hays Office had begun submitting potentially controversial films first to the New York State Board of Censors. Negotiations between Hays and that board delayed the release of She Done Him Wrong until late January. West's performances of the two sexually suggestive songs "A Guy What Takes His Time" and "Easy Rider" were cut to retain only one opening and closing verse, and one chorus, respectively; cutaway shots of a woman pickpocket and a pianist ogling West as she sang were eliminated.

However, the primary point of contention with the board was the film's ending. At MPPDA insistence, West's final line, "I always knew you could be had," retained in the shooting script despite Wingate's suggestion, was cut. However, the MPPDA suggestion that a line of dialogue ("as soon as you are clear with the law") be added to avoid any objection that Lady Lou "commits homicide and connives to conceal the body, both serious crimes which go unpunished" (Hays to Wingate, 28 February 1933), was not heeded.

The MPPDA proposal that an added line of dialogue would rectify the violations of moral and legal order depicted in the film was consistent with the SRC policy at that time of evaluating the "effect of the whole," even though, in practice, few state censors accepted the argument that endings had a retroactive compensatory effect on the moral value of a film.[13] Nor, in terms of contemporary mores, was Lou's killing another woman the only ambiguous or potentially objectionable act in She Done Him Wrong. In the version eventually released, West's character lies to Chick, a former lover imprisoned for stealing diamonds, that she is "true" to him. The dialogue suggests that Lou has retained the stolen diamonds and does not contemplate returning them. Lou helps a bereft young woman, Sally, and asks her current lover Gus, a saloon keeper, to find Sally a job. The scene strongly implies that the young woman will be sent as a prostitute to San Francisco ("the Barbary Coast"). Lou's degree of participation in this scheme is unclear, for to Captain Cummings she displays convincing ignorance of her lover's traffic in women, but in later dialogue with Gus, she reveals her knowledge of the business.

Lou is a largely amoral character whose actions seem determined by narcissism and expediency. However, dialogue does emphasize the honesty of West's character in financial exchanges: Lady Lou: "Never heard of me cheating anyone, have you?" Mr. Jacobson (a realtor and diamond dealer, played as a Jewish ethnic stereotype): "Not about money!" The joke turns on the implication that Lou does cheat about other matters—that is, she "cheats" on men, flouting conventions of sexual fidelity.

The title of the film plays on the tag line ("he done her wrong") of the popular song "Frankie and Johnnie," which was featured in the stage performances of Diamond Lil. In both gender permutations, the phrase invites interpretation of the word wrong as referring exclusively to sexual behavior. She Done Him Wrong incorporates further associations with the song (and thereby with the play Diamond Lil) by using its musical motifs under the opening credits and by West's performing a shortened version of the song near the film's end.[14]

The lyrics of the traditional song make clear that he (Johnnie) is the perpetrator and she (Frankie) the victim of the initial wrong: Johnnie has betrayed Frankie by having sex with another woman. She Done Him Wrong inverts the gender relationship: West's character "does wrong," in conventional moral terms, by being sexually unfaithful not just to one but to several male characters. Besides lying to her imprisoned lover Chick, she clearly considers her current lover Gus no obstacle to either her eager flirtations with Serge and with Captain Cummings or her reluctant acquiescence to the amorous attentions of Flynn, Gus's political rival.

However, the film's narrative transforms the song's account of cause and consequences and thereby its moral pronouncements. In the song, Frankie exacts revenge for Johnnie's wrong by murdering him, a further wrong deed for which, in some versions of the song, she herself will be punished with imprisonment. In a different formulation of crime and punishment, West's character Lou displaces the murderous consequences of her betrayals onto the victims themselves by sending the unwelcome would-be lover

Flynn to her room, where a vengeful Chick waits in ambush. Cummings arrests Gus for his illegal operations (after Flynn gives him the tip-off) and then rescues Lou from strangulation at Chick's hands. Lou's only "punishment" is Cummings's love, a love the film has shown that she much desires, but one that need not cramp her promiscuous style, or so the final scene in the studio-released print implies. Lou/West thus enjoys a moral and economic victory that enables the character's rise in class status as the mate, at least temporarily (whether married or not is ambiguous), of a handsome young detective. Thus, whereas the lyrics of "Frankie and Johnnie" relate a minor romantic tragic tale, the story of She Done Him Wrong undercuts the basis of romantic tragedy by suggesting that motives of self-interest—predominantly a desire for money, sex, and/or power—create and maintain the heterosexual couple, rather than any deep emotional ties or spiritual commitments.

SRC files on She Done Him Wrong do not reveal censors' general reactions to the sympathetic portrayal of the amoral leading character. However, records of specific deletions required by seven U.S. state censor boards, three Canadian provinces, and four further export markets after the film's release yield a distinct pattern.[15] Except for foreign censors' cuts of suggested crime and violence (in Sweden, Quebec, and Britain, where censors cut a scene in which a prisoner threatens jailbreak), all the censored lines and images recorded in the SRC case file carry sexual innuendo, almost always the sexual behavior and attitudes of West's character.

Censor boards most frequently ordered deletions in the verbal exchanges between Lou and another character, as noted below (deleted lines appear in italics and the figure numbers in parentheses refer to still photographs drawn from the scene in which the uncut dialogue occurs):

Lou greets a female acquaintance on the street.
WOMAN: Ah, Lady Lou, you're a fine gal, a fine woman!
LOU: *One of the finest women who ever walked the streets!*

Rita, a counterfeiting partner of Lou's current lover, Gus, introduces her young companion to Lou (Figure 33).
RITA: Sergei is my new assistant.
LOU: *Day or night work, Rita?*

Lou counsels Sally, who just been prevented from committing suicide (Figure 34).
SALLY: How did you know there was a man?

LOU: There always is. You know, *it takes two to get one in trouble*. . . .
Forget about this guy. See that you get a good one the next time.
SALLY: Who'd want me after what I've done?
LOU: *Listen, when women go wrong, men go right after them!*

Dan Flynn, an aspiring Bowery boss who plots to replace Gus as
Lou's protector, tells Lou: "*You can't expect to go round getting men all
on fire and think they're going to forget all about it.*"
Captain Cummings has come to Lou's room to discuss Sally's fate;
the talk turns to Lou's moral character.
CUMMINGS: Well, I guess I'm taking your time.
LOU: *What do you suppose my time's for?* . . .
CUMMINGS: Haven't you ever met a man who could make you
happy?
LOU: *Sure, lots of times!*

Cummings, now revealed to be a detective intent on shutting down
Gus's counterfeiting and prostitution ring, attempts to handcuff Lou.
LOU: Are those absolutely necessary? You know, I wasn't born with
them.
CUMMINGS: A lot of men would have been safer if you had!
LOU: Oh, I don't know, *hands ain't everything!*

As Wingate warned, West's parting line "you can be had," in the scene
where she invites the apparently upstanding character played by Cary
Grant to "come up and see me," was considered censorable in several
states and Canadian provinces.[16] That knowing Westian declaration had
remained in her first scene with Grant, despite deletion before the film's
general release of her original closing line, as the two embrace, "I always
knew you could be had!" The released version ends in the following exchange:

CUMMINGS: You're my prisoner and I'm going to be your jailer for a
long, long time—and you can start doing that stretch right now! [He
slips a small diamond onto her ring finger.]
LOU: [smiling] Um, oh yeh? [She admires ring; cut to close-up of her
hand] Where'd you get that . . . dark and handsome?
CUMMINGS: [shaking head as he leans to kiss her] You bad girl!
LOU: Um, you'll find out! [They kiss. Screen fades to black.]

The Ohio censor board eliminated this scene altogether, leaving the prior scene, which implies Cummings is taking Lou to jail, as the film's ending. The censor board in Australia required that the film end after Cummings's declaration that he was "imprisoning" Lou; state of Virginia censors deleted West/Lou's last line, "You'll find out," and the embrace that followed.

A number of censor boards objected to two visual representations that West's verbal or physical performance drew attention to: a painting of a female nude (supposedly Lou/West) hung over the bar in the saloon, about which she remarks, "I wish Gus hadn't hung it above the 'free lunch'!"; and medium close-up shots of West making rocking and whipping gestures as if she were a jockey riding a horse, as she sings "Where has my Easy Rider gone?" West's censored quips all emphasize her character's—and her own—extensive experience and pleasure in sex, as do the lyrics of "Easy Rider" and "A Guy What Takes His Time," even after these were trimmed during production.[17] Such frequently deleted lines as "you can be had!" and "when women go wrong, men go right after them!" assert that transgressive female sexuality exerts great power over men. West/Lou's leering invitation, "Come up and see me, anytime," suggests the constant sexual availability of a prostitute—or a nymphomaniac. In the film's release version, Lou is clearly promiscuous; in spite of Wingate's cautions during the film's production, she is just as clearly a "kept woman," a status conventionally little distinguished from that of prostitute.[18] West/Lou's line early in the film proclaiming that she is "one of the finest women that ever walked the streets" even humorously boasts of her characterization as a prostitute.

In calling for particular deletions, U.S. state censors were exercising their authority as public representatives to designate and maintain guidelines for "movie morality," as each construed it. The U.S. state boards operating in 1933 differed in the number and extent of deletions they regularly demanded. In the case of She Done Him Wrong, the Pennsylvania board of censors called for twenty-one distinct cuts, including all those listed above, whereas the Kansas board required six deletions in dialogue— three at points frequently cut and three of lines uttered by male characters that other boards left untouched.[19] One can attribute these regular divergences to the influence of prevalent local social and political circumstances and to the history and individual composition of each censor board. However, there is every indication that board members shared class backgrounds and professional status: they were middle-class community leaders and educators appointed by state governors and mayors. Many were women.[20] The female censors' unusual status at the period as political appointees vested with power over the public sphere shrinks when one considers that their mission fit entirely within the traditional social function of middle- and upper-class women: to uphold cultural and moral standards.

Despite differences in the specific cuts made in She Done Him Wrong, the apparent agendas of the U.S. state censor boards seem strikingly consistent: to reduce or eliminate the film's visual and verbal depiction of active female sexuality as a source of economic gain, power, and pleasure. When the boards censored the cinematic suggestion of a close relationship between female sexuality and money and rise in class, they were censoring the representation of prostitution, in its broadest sense. But She Done Him Wrong does not depict prostitution as the unfortunate practice of a socially stigmatized group of lower-class or morally errant women. Rather, the film depicts prostitution as the basis of the heterosexual couple, as set terms of exchange that evade legal and moral regulation. Most important, it depicts prostitution as the successful management of a woman's own sexuality as a commodity under her own exclusive control.

Yet the censors' deletions hardly effaced the depiction of female sexuality in She Done Him Wrong as operating outside state and moral law: an occasional cut scarcely diminished the outlaw sexuality structured through the film's narrative and West's performance. Further, despite any censors' pruning, West's already widely publicized name and persona bore an aura of sexual transgression that would have permeated the movie for many moviegoers. Contemporary reviews of She Done Him Wrong in industry trade journals presume that movie exhibitors and other readers were well familiar with West's image. A critical notice in The Film Daily promotes the film with phrases associating West with working-class prostitution and also male homosexuality and transvestism:

BOX-OFFICE STUFF, WITH MAE WEST TREATING THE FANS TO A BIG LOAD OF HER GLAMOUR AND WISECRACKS.

As queen of the underworld, ensconced in a gay resort on the Bowery back in the 90s, Mae West puts on a show that's a robust treat for those who like lusty laughs. In a class by herself when it comes to this sort of stuff, Miss West lets the double entendre nifties fall from her lips in such a disarming manner that they never seem offensive. Her personal attractiveness, plus her kidding and burlesquing of sex, keep the interest keyed up right to the finish, where an inane happy ending does pretty much to spoil what might have been a rich travesty for travesty's sake. The story, which is less important than Miss West, is a trifling episode about a gorgeous creature who has her pick of men, does plenty of picking, loads herself with diamonds all along the route, and finally is marked for marriage by a handsome detective who breaks up her underworld circle.[21]

A writer for the *Motion Picture Herald* also evaluates the film's financial prospects in light of West's established image:

> Mae West, heretofore the stage's chief exponent of the dramatization of sex machinations, comes to the screen in her first starring vehicle, a picturization of none other than the "Diamond Lil" of recent stage memory. That Miss West is here highly effective cannot be doubted, but of the adaptability of her vehicle, her material for the common denominator of the motion picture public, there is considerable doubt.
> ... The film is lively, contrives to be amusing, has an element of melodrama, but is rather several degrees south of the lower limit of propriety. Miss West sings several numbers which cannot be conscientiously recommended to any common or garden variety of choral society. The individual exhibitor will have to decide for himself whether he can afford to run the film, realizing that it is hard-boiled, spares the feelings of no Ladies' Aid Society.
> Playing it, the exhibitor must necessarily indicate what it is, and he has the selling angles of Miss West in a well known role, and the personal attractiveness of Cary Grant. No children, of course.[22]

The back cover of that issue of the *Motion Picture Herald* sports a full-page advertisement for *She Done Him Wrong*. The headline "SHE DONE HIM WRONG ... IN THESE KEY SPOTS!" heralds a report of the film's box-office successes in large and mid-sized cities across the United States.[23] Alongside the words, a sultry-looking West in a glittery off-the-shoulder dress barely covering her breasts leans against a bar, a smoking revolver in her hand. (West's pose in Figure 5 served as the basis for her image in this advertisement.) A man in Gay Nineties costume lies, shot, at her feet, the label "Mr. Low Gross" emblazoned across his white shirtfront. The Paramount ad on the *Motion Picture Herald*'s back cover the following week further promotes West's appeal as a highly successful social and sexual outlaw: the illustration shows West, a Roman centurion, and a man in a loin cloth (Buster Crabbe, standing immediately behind West), all holding what look like oversized heat guns aimed at a large snowball. Four little cartoon devils, naked and bearing pitchforks, dance alongside. The copy reads "Just as Long as Paramount Gives You Pictures like 'The Sign of the Cross,' 'She Done Him Wrong,' and 'King of the Jungle'—Box-Office Depression Has No More Chance Than the Proverbial Snowball!"[24]

The 18 February *Motion Picture Herald* review predicts that the transgressive sexuality West embodied would appeal to audiences but might also

elicit their moral objections. Paramount advertisements in that publication promote West by compounding the outlaw associations of her image,
in the first ad presenting the star as a gunslinger, and in the second depicting her as a denizen of hell. Public reaction emphatically echoed the industry's dual construction of West as immoral yet attractive and endearing.
Despite the presidential-decreed bank holiday, which generally cut cinema
attendance in the month following the film's release, *She Done Him Wrong*
did astounding, record-breaking box-office business.[25] More significant,
from a historical perspective, was that the film catapulted West's image
into the ongoing public discourse about moral reform of the movies, which
began in the early 1900s and reached an apex in 1933-34.[26]

The U.S. movie reform movement, begun early in the century, had by
1930 provoked the film industry to concerted actions to counter recurrent
calls for federal censorship.[27] The Motion Picture Production Code of that
year formalized the reform movement's objections to movies as guidelines
for internal industry regulation. While the MPPDA did not invoke the
Code by name in its attempts to persuade Paramount to bring *She Done
Him Wrong* into a form that would pass state censors and avoid protests
from reform organizations, all the material the state censor boards deleted
in the film could be construed as violating the Motion Picture Production
Code.[28] That document literally codified the hegemonic ideology setting
the standards by which moral reformers and official censors judged "Mae
West" and *She Done Him Wrong*.

The Production Code as Middle-Class Manifesto

Recent scholarship on American film censorship in the early 1930s has
focused on negotiations between the Hays Office and other institutions in
the production, exhibition, and reception of single films released in 1932
and 1933, prior to or simultaneous with the release of West's *She Done Him
Wrong* (January 1933) and *I'm No Angel* (October 1933).[29] The composite
history that emerges from that research demonstrates that film industry
self-regulation came about gradually, through a complex web of issues and
individual actions. Only a grasp of the competing ideologies and practical
fiscal considerations surrounding eventual Production Code enforcement
enables a nuanced historical understanding of West's influence on Hollywood censorship.

The film industry is commonly said to have adopted the 1930 Production Code reluctantly to deflect the criticisms of moral reformers who had

organized sufficiently to make their calls for federal movie censorship an effective threat. MPPDA head Will Hays first recruited Martin Quigley, the Chicago-based publisher of the *Motion Picture Herald* and a prominent lay Catholic, to convince powerful Catholics who had fostered Chicago's local movie censorship to support a self-regulating film industry moral code. The MPPDA then engaged Father Daniel A. Lord, S.J., a dramatics professor at St. Louis University who had acted as adviser on religious epic films, to draft the document. Quigley and Lord's work with the MPPDA secured the Catholic Church's established policy of attempting to counter movies' potentially harmful effects by eliciting industry cooperation and self-regulation, rather than by pressuring legislative bodies to pass censorship laws, as Protestant church leaders, Progressives, and women's federations across the United States had repeatedly done from early in the century.[30]

The Code specifies at the outset three general principles for maintaining morality in motion pictures:

1. No picture shall be produced which will lower the moral standards of those who see it. Hence the sympathy of the audience shall never be thrown to the side of crime, wrong-doing, evil or sin.
2. Correct standards of life, subject only to the requirements of drama and entertainment, shall be presented.
3. Law, natural or human, shall not be ridiculed, nor shall sympathy be created for its violation.[31]

The body of the Code delineates the following twelve areas of concern that might violate these principles: crimes against the law, sex, vulgarity, obscenity, profanity, costume, dances, religion, locations, national feelings, titles, and repellent subjects. Specific potential violations are listed under each term, most elaborately under "Crime" and "Sex." Under the designation "Crimes against the Law," for example, the Code limits how murder, methods of crime, illegal drug traffic, and alcohol use may be presented, emphasizing the principle that the depiction of crimes should never "throw sympathy with the crime as against law and justice or . . . inspire others with a desire for imitation."

The principle expressed under the designation "Sex" asserts the value of chastity before and within marriage: "The sanctity of the institution of marriage and the home shall be upheld. Pictures shall not infer [sic] that low forms of sex relationship are the accepted or common thing." The Code prohibits or strictly delimits representation of adultery and "illicit"

sex, "lustful kissing and embracing" or suggestive postures and gestures, seduction, "sex perversion," "white slavery," "miscegenation," "sex hygiene," childbirth, and exposure of children's sex organs. "Miscegenation"
is expressly defined as "sex relationship between the white and black
races." "Sex perversion" and "sex hygiene" refer obliquely to homosexuality and abortion, as later emendations to the text's wording reveal. The
prohibition on "white slavery" was subsequently rewritten to include prostitution explicitly:

> The methods and techniques of prostitution and white slavery shall never
> be presented in detail, nor shall the subjects be presented unless shown in
> contrast to right standards of behavior. Brothels in any clear identification
> may not be shown.

Even the sections of the Code addressing categories beyond "Sex" reveal primary concern with sexual matters. For example, under the subject
heading "Obscenity," the Code notes, "Obscenity in word, gesture, reference, song, joke or by suggestion (even when likely to be understood only
by part of the audience) is forbidden." The section "Profanity" lists almost
forty "profane or vulgar expressions" that are not to be uttered, most of
which have sexual implications, especially with reference to women, for
example, "alley cat," "broad," and "hot" when "applied to a woman";
"Madam (relating to prostitution)"; "slut" and "whore."

Restrictions on costumes and dances also bespeak sexual matters, for
those sections forbid nudity, indecent exposure, unnecessary undressing
scenes, and "dancing costumes intended to permit undue exposure of
indecent movements in the dance." Any dancing suggesting sexual actions or "indecent passion" counts as obscene. "Titles" cautions against
"salacious, indecent or obscene titles." Female prostitution, phrased as
"the sale of women, or a woman selling her virtue," appears as one of
seven "Repellent Subjects" (others include executions, branding of people
or animals, and surgical operations), which "must be treated within
the careful limits of good taste." "Locations" refers exclusively to bed-
rooms, the treatment of which "must be governed by good taste and
delicacy."

In proscribing overt sexual representations and in calling for the exercise of "good taste," the Code emphasizes bodily restraint, modesty, and
circumspect behavior as "correct standards of life." These guidelines express distinctly middle-class values. The Code's principles upholding law,
"natural or human," and constraining sexuality within marriage as an in-

violable institution also articulate facets of American middle-class ideology. The repeated appeal to "good taste," without definition of its standards, presumes the cultural dominance of the moral and aesthetic values that shaped the Code.

In the 1930s, as now, the American middle-class population evinced a range of conscious beliefs and behaviors and held diverse, sometimes self-contradictory, positions on movie censorship and on Mae West. Many members of the upper and working classes would have concurred in the social cosmology that the Code embodies, including its gender presumptions and behavioral ideals. An ideology holds in practice neither all-inclusive nor exclusive sway over the socioeconomic class whose interests it represents. Nor are class-correlated social precepts static or internally consistent, particularly during periods of rapid social change, such as followed World War I, and of retrenchment, as in the 1930s. In democratic capitalist societies, however, middle-class concerns tend to dominate public discourses that affect all classes. Despite the Code's universalizing language, its central tenets (positing marriage as a moral and religious contract grounded in shared community values, sentimental love, and sexual fidelity; privileging restrained speech and comportment; and requiring that no crime escape detection and punishment) clearly derived from turn-of-the-century white middle-class traditions and concerns.[32]

Thus, it was not owing to coincidental semantics that many critics couched their negative assessments of West's films and image in terms of her violating "good taste."[33] Aesthetic choices that are deemed matters of "taste" relate integrally to social class structure, for the use of language and gesture as well as body styles, behavior, and patterns of consumption function as signs in symbolic struggles among social classes.[34] Condemnations of West for offending standards of taste and decency arose from a class-bound system of social expectations that adjudged the star's demeanor and dress as impermissibly low-class. As French sociologist Pierre Bourdieu argues, dominant classes strive to distinguish themselves from economically disadvantaged classes by means of cultural consumption:

> The denial of lower, coarse, vulgar, venal, servile—in a word,
> natural—enjoyment, which constitutes the sacred sphere of culture, implies
> an affirmation of the superiority of those who can be satisfied with the
> sublimated, refined, disinterested, gratuitous, distinguished pleasures forever
> closed to the profane. That is why art and cultural consumption are
> predisposed, consciously and deliberately or not, to fulfill a social function
> of legitimating social differences.[35]

Bourdieu's analysis of the stake that social groups have in making cultural distinctions provides a useful perspective on the Code's aims and operations in the 1930s. The film industry adopted the Code in response to an ongoing middle-class reform movement that sought to eliminate the capacity of the movies to provide vulgar enjoyment that might "lower the moral standards" of viewers. While the reformers who patronized movies did not regard themselves as vulnerable to such dangers, most worried about the deleterious effects of unregulated films on children and other viewers they considered particularly impressionable or morally unformed.[36] These concerns extended to their own children, for by the mid-1910s, movies drew large audiences from among the middle as well as the working classes.[37] Movies' broad-based appeal undermined traditionally class-correlated patterns of cultural consumption, and by the late 1920s had helped efface the self-evident prestige and social dominance of higher class cultural forms.[38]

Reformers such as Father Lord and Quigley recognized that the nature of the new entertainment limited attempts to regulate its consumption, for as a mass-produced and -marketed medium, movies transcended local networks of control. By sharply delineating at the site of *production* between acceptable and unacceptable representations, the Motion Picture Production Code attempted to create a mark of distinction within a mass cultural form consumed by all social classes. The Code thus figured as a symbolic instrument in a middle-class struggle to reassert dominance over American culture, even as that culture proliferated in new mass media forms. As I shall argue in the next chapter, the Code's enforcement through the 1930s heightened Hollywood's gradually established practice of addressing audiences *as if they were middle-class consumers*.[39] The Code thereby augmented efforts by reformers as well as, obliquely, by film producers and exhibitors, to inscribe all movie viewers into the dominant social order.

The Code propagated middle-class morality especially by correlating class status and respectability with sexual propriety. The Code did not categorically reject the depiction of sex, even extramarital sex, but rather permitted the covert exploitation of provocative elements if these were sufficiently controlled (embedded within the narrative as "necessary plot material"). But the Code did restrict the representation of possible benefits of wealth or rise in class standing that might accrue from such illicit practices. Thus, a film might portray (and so covertly exploit as spectacle) female sexual behavior that transgresses middle-class mores, but only if the narrative condemned such acts and punished the miscreants by film's end.

In its attention to such distinctions, the Code illustrates how the mechanisms of censorship regulate sexuality not by silencing, but by proliferating public discourses concerned with sex.[40]

Movie Reform as Social Imperative

The MPPDA categorized *She Done Him Wrong* and West's subsequent three movies as "sex pictures." This was a loose group of films usually featuring female characters who engaged in sexual relations with rich men as a means to attain higher class status. Such films were also sometimes called "kept woman" pictures.[41] MPPDA correspondence suggests that films of this type caused recurrent problems with the censor boards and movie reform forces in the early 1930s. The industry's difficulties led to gradual expansion in the Code's interpretation and application to films portraying women who gain wealth and class status through extramarital sexual relations.

She Done Him Wrong and West's next four films show similarities to but also important differences from other Hollywood movies produced in the early 1930s that depict female prostitution or gold digging as a means to achieve higher class status.[42] West's films offered a key reform target due to their status as "kept woman" films, for some reformers made causal connections between such movies and the concomitant socioeconomic crisis of the Depression.

The major studios began to produce a cycle of "kept woman" films in mid-1931 as a response to the Hays Office's order to stop producing gangster films, which in 1930-31 drew large audiences but also vociferous criticism from reform groups. Among the "kept woman" cycle were the Metro-Goldwyn-Mayer productions *Possessed* (1931, with Joan Crawford and Clark Gable) and *Red-Headed Woman* (1932) and the Warner Bros. film *Baby Face* (1933). *Red-Headed Woman*, a comedy written by Anita Loos and starring Jean Harlow as a woman who makes her fortune through a series of affairs with rich men, created a particular controversy on its release in June 1932. This film, which makes light of the Harlow character's actions and has a happy ending (with the comic heroine living in luxury in Paris), antagonized the reform lobby and upset the delicate balance of cooperation that Hays had been attempting to engineer between MPPDA member studios and the reform forces.[43] Historian Richard Maltby argues that Paramount's signing West in June 1932 was a response to MGM's production of *Red-Headed Woman*. Within four months of that film's release,

Paramount was planning the production of *Diamond Lil*, despite the MPPDA ban on the production. Warner Bros. reacted to that industry development by producing *Baby Face*, a melodrama starring Barbara Stanwyck as a poor young woman who grows wealthy during the Depression by seducing successively more powerful and rich employees of a bank.

Heads of movie studios in the early 1930s recognized not only the spectacle of beautiful female stars, but also the representation of active, even predatory, female sexuality as a commodity that enhanced their products' marketability in a severely depressed economy. By 1931, the film industry as a whole had begun to feel the effects of the Depression; during 1932, it fell into a major fiscal crisis. A sharp decline in box-office receipts led film companies to institute cost-cutting programs, including the sale or closing of a number of movie theaters. Despite these measures, by the end of 1932 many studios faced financial ruin as the New York and Chicago banking institutions to which they were deeply indebted began to demand payment.

As a sector of the economy seriously threatened in the widespread collapse of the capitalist system, the movie industry took the tack of exploiting every available business advantage. As the reform lobby had pressured the MPPDA into forbidding the lucrative gangster cycle, the profitable exploitation of assertive female sexuality lay next at hand.[44]

Subsequent developments proved that this strategy could work only for the short term, given the reform forces' consistent opposition to the representation of women exercising their sexuality beyond the bounds of marriage, especially to any financial advantage. The standard solution that the SRC under Joy and Wingate had worked out—to show at film's end that the transgressor had gained nothing but indeed had only lost by her actions—did not satisfy many censor boards or the broader reform lobby, even when these endings seemed convincing.[45] In his capacity as spokesman for the MPPDA (and thereby the film industry), Hays concurred in communiqués and public speeches with movie reformers in insisting on the principles set out in the Motion Picture Production Code of 1930. However, through March 1933, as we have seen in the case of *She Done Him Wrong*, the SRC interpreted adherence to the Code more liberally than did the forces for reform, including a number of state censor boards.

Maltby situates the U.S. "movie morality" campaign within a reform drive, beginning in the 1920s, that arose from perceptions among white Protestants that the apparent permissiveness of the period following World War I threatened traditional patriarchal values. When the stock market crash greatly exacerbated the anxieties of the middle class about its social and economic hegemony, Maltby argues, "Victorian patriarchy strove to reassert itself by identifying the alleged permissiveness of the Jazz Age as the scapegoat for the collapse of the economy."[46] The reformers' line of causal attribution held Hollywood responsible for promoting the widespread social instability that movies depicted. Paradoxically, the film industry simultaneously concurred in and itself violated middle-class values. In its struggle to survive as a capitalist institution, Hollywood employed a technique—the exploitation of an unrestrained female sexuality—that reform groups considered precisely the source of imminent danger to the traditional American economic and social system.

Several conjoined factors led the MPPDA to accede to the reformers' arguments for rigorous applications of the Code. In February 1932, a resolution was introduced in the U.S. Senate to investigate the motion picture industry; the resolution expressly criticized Hays as a "fixer" to protect the industry against public action.[47] In January 1933, Franklin D. Roosevelt assumed office and Hays lost the personal contacts he had maintained with Republican administrations; rumors circulated that he might be replaced by a Democrat.[48] On 5 March 1933, the eve of the bank holiday declared by President Roosevelt, Hays called an emergency meeting of the MPPDA board of directors to consider the consequences of bank closings for the industry. Hays used the opportunity to persuade the directors that rigorous Code enforcement was necessary to enable the industry to withstand public pressure for federal intervention, which might, under Roosevelt's administration, extend from concern about film content into the film industry's financial operations. The outcome of the session, which lasted all night, was the MPPDA board adoption of a "Reaffirmation of Objectives" that empowered Hays to reorganize the administration of the Code. He immediately instructed SRC head Wingate to tighten Code enforcement over ongoing as well as new productions and enlisted Joseph Breen, who was then administering the Advertising Code, to assist Wingate in the task.[49]

Beginning in September 1932, the release of the Payne Fund Studies, a series of sociological investigations on the influence of movies on audiences, fueled the rising protest against Hollywood. These reports led to public criticism of the film industry and increased support for government regulation of film content.[50] One book in the series, *Movies and Conduct*, written by University of Chicago sociologist Herbert Blumer, cited essays solicited from adolescents to argue that movies and particularly movie stars influenced the young viewers' fantasies about wealth and affected their sexual attitudes and practices. These events preceded by more than a year the April 1934 founding of the Catholic Legion of Decency and its threat to organize a boycott against movies it deemed immoral.

She Done Him Wrong was thus released at a time of national economic crisis, political change, and social upheaval and into a vigorous public discourse on the effect of movies on society. The tremendous box-office successes of that film and *I'm No Angel*, released nine months later, temporarily helped revive the film industry by generating morale-building publicity about movie attendance and providing an economic boost.[51] Contrary to claims sometimes made, West's films did not "save Paramount from bankruptcy," for the company had already gone into receivership in January 1933.[52] The unexpectedly high profits from West's first two star vehicles did, however, measurably enhance the company's assets and aid in its eventually successful attempts to reorganize and recover as an intact corporation.[53]

However, West's popularity did not represent a trouble-free asset to the film industry, for the reams of publicity given the star also made West an obvious target for the reform lobby. One writer, discussing the reception of *I'm No Angel*, concluded:

> Needless to say, this opus will scarcely get on the reformers' recommended lists. But with the tide running the opposite way perhaps the spleen of the moralists isn't a factor right now. And anyway, Mae West is today the biggest conversation-provoker, free space grabber and all-around boxoffice bet in the country. She's as hot an issue as Hitler.[54]

Notwithstanding the media attention surrounding—and constituting— West's emergence as a film star, the release of her first star vehicles did not initiate, but rather came in the midst of, a campaign against the representation of crime and particularly of sex in the movies. The advent of rigorous Code enforcement can thus by no means be directly ascribed to West's star image or films.

However, "Mae West" did play a unique iconographic role in the public discourse of the period about movie morality and censorship. By mid-1934, West's photograph alone sufficed to signal controversy over sexual depictions. This capacity emerges from the contents as well as the cover of the 7 July 1934 issue of *Newsweek*, a picture of West in bejeweled Gay Nineties evening costume (Figure 6). The portrait shows West to the waist, one hand cupping a breast, the other splayed across her midriff. A phrase on the cover, "The Churches Protest," directs readers to a featured report on the threatened movie boycott by the newly formed Catholic Legion of Decency and other reform groups. The article recounts West's role in the affair as follows:

> SIN: In the heat of argument, buxom Miss West . . . became the personification of Hollywood's sins. . . . Last week the New York State Board of Regents refused to license her new film "It Ain't No Sin."
> She shrugged her rounded shoulders (see cover). "If they think it's too warm, I'll cool it off," she said. Monday Paramount announced that the film would be recast and retitled.
> It was not the first time the censors have got after Miss West. . . . In 1927 she did a ten-day stretch on Blackwell's Island for playing on Broadway in "Sex," a banned production.[55]

The popularity of West's "sex pictures" and of her established image as a sexual transgressor made the star a highly suitable "personification of Hollywood's sins." Why West—rather than another Hollywood star such as Stanwyck, Dietrich, or Harlow—should have become a central emblem in the reform drive arises from the conjunction of elements in West's persona. The inextricable interdependence of female sexuality, power, wealth, a rise in class, and pleasure in West's performances and image caused reformers during the Depression to regard the star particularly as a challenge to the dominance of middle-class ideology.

Confounding Morality and Class

MPPDA records indicate that both industry and state censors understood—and objected to—West's recurrent enactment of an unmarried woman of lower-class origins who exploits her sexuality to attain wealth and class status as equivalent to her playing a "kept woman," even an overt prostitute.[56] Case studies of other censored films in the "kept woman" cycle document how the SRC and, after July 1934, the newly organized and renamed PCA worked to eliminate any suggestions that women might gain any lasting economic and social advantage by exploiting their sexuality.[57] The concern in industry self-regulation of these films focused on showing that characters who aspired to a higher station through sex with rich men were punished in the course of the narrative—at best by being returned to their working-class origins, often also by suffering through the loss of a child or other family connections. The aim of such narrative recuperation of erring women, especially as enforced by PCA head Breen, was to illustrate that illicit sexuality does not pay. As film scholar Lea Jacobs points out, contradictions emerged repeatedly in "fallen woman" films made between 1930 and 1940: the pleasurable spectacle of upper-class glamour, luxury, and power present a rise in social standing as a highly desirable goal, but the narrative condemns as illegitimate and ultimately unsuccessful the only means of attaining higher class status available to lower-class protagonists.[58] Charles Eckert's analysis of *Marked Woman* (1937) shows how even a social realist "fallen woman" film works to displace and then generally to reassert established class hierarchies.[59] This 1930s film cycle thus communicated the pleasures of higher class status and conspicuous consumption while warning at least female viewers against aspiring to those.

Analyses of the censorship of *Blonde Venus* (1932) and *Baby Face* (1933) reveal that the SRC tried to eliminate not only overt representations of the exchange of sex for money, but also any causal links between illicit sexuality and the conditions of the Depression.[60] The point is relevant to evaluating West's role in Hollywood censorship history, for these analyses cumulatively reveal that the movie industry—of which the MPPDA was an integral part—recognized a stake in limiting depictions of any connections between licentious sexuality and failures of capitalism.

Although *She Done Him Wrong* is set not in the Depression, but rather amid a burgeoning turn-of-the-century economy, the film does depict close relations between sex and money. As we have seen, Paramount producers and West did not cooperate with the SRC in effacing this relation. Nor did censors' subsequent cuts manage to eliminate the film's connecting active female sexuality to the increase of riches, status, and power, for these terms of exchange pervade the narrative. The film makes West/Lou's status as a woman "kept" by a succession of men appear a pragmatic and rather pleasant means of achieving luxury and ample male attention. The character certainly does not suffer as a social pariah, nor, when given the opportunity, does she seem eager to settle into marriage.

The prospective fate of Sally, the young woman whom Gus and Rita plan to send to the Barbary Coast, is cast less rosily in *She Done Him Wrong* than is Lou's own behavior; Lou's denial to Captain Cummings that she knows about Gus's "white slavery" operation nominally acknowledges social condemnation of prostitution—probably, correspondence suggests, at the behest of SRC censors. But West's character is exempt from condemnation or any suggestion that she is a victim for engaging in sexual relations in exchange for wealth. Rather, she appears empowered through the practice.

West's next three star vehicles replicated the narrative of her character's rise in class through judicious exploitation of her sexuality. In *I'm No Angel*, West rises from honky-tonk dancer in a carnival on the verge of folding to a luxurious life in a New York penthouse, with wealthy playboy Jack Clayton (Cary Grant) proposing marriage and begging to be her slave. West's character in *I'm No Angel*, Tira, is less obviously a "kept woman" than is Lou in *She Done Him Wrong*. However, there are numerous suggestions—in song lyrics, dialogue, and gesture—that her work as a "honky-tonk queen" is closely related to and supplemented by that of a prostitute. Although Tira goes on to big success as a lion tamer, the narrative and editing suggest, as I discuss in chapter 4, that her wealth derives directly from her relationships with wealthy men, rather than from her circus work.

West's characterization in *Belle of the Nineties*, released in September 1934 after being retitled and undergoing numerous censors' cuts, resembles the star's role in *She Done Him Wrong*. West plays Ruby Carter, a Gay Nineties entertainer who attracts the interest and riches of wealthy men. But the films differ in that Ruby relinquishes her wealthiest and most conventionally handsome suitor, a playboy named Brooks Claybourne (John Mack Brown), and ends by marrying an earlier lover, a boxer called Tiger Kid (Roger Pryor). These differences came about primarily as the result of censorship by the PCA, which, during extended negotiations before the 1934 film's release, required that West's relationship to Brooks be "cleaned up" and that a wedding scene be added.

The ability of West's characters to acquire wealth and class status through men is most striking in the star's 1935 vehicle *Goin' to Town*. West as Cleo Borden rises from being a modest dance hall entertainer in what initially appears to be the "Wild West" to marry a British lord whose attentions she has actively pursued. Cleo gains her initial fortune from a rancher who has amassed wealth through cattle rustling; she then seeks, successfully, to buy class standing through a marriage of convenience to a profligate "blue blood."

Significantly, although West's characters aspire to—and achieve—wealth and social standing, they do so without changing their behavior or values. Even in *Goin' to Town*, when Cleo takes lessons in diction and stages a ball featuring herself singing opera—and so would seem to aspire to upper-class manners and tastes as well as the wealth—her efforts are motivated entirely by desires for personal gratification and sustained only as long as necessary for her to achieve her aims. The persistent disjunction

between Cleo's behavior and the upper-class manners of those who surround her offers material for comedy. For example, in response to Winslow,
her English business accountant, who remarks on Cleo's plan to enter a
horse in a race, "I didn't know you were a judge of horse flesh," West/Cleo
replies, "I'm not, I never ate any!" In response to her accountant's commenting, "I didn't know you could speak Spanish," West/Cleo retorts,
"Don't think I worked in Tijuana for nothing, do you?" Cleo and other
Westian characters aspire to higher class status only to gain riches and social power; they decline to adopt any upper-class distinctions in morality
or taste as the price or consequence of their new status. Whereas dialogue
and song lyrics in *I'm No Angel* and *Goin' to Town* emphasize that the protagonist becomes a "lady," the narratives and West's performances suggest
that the term designates only a state of material wealth and social standing
(e.g., living in luxurious surroundings, having maids, being accepted by
"high society") and bears no reference to the character's sexual behavior.

That female sexuality is a resource to be exchanged for wealth and class
status served as the recurrent theme not only of West's narratives, but also,
of course, of many 1930s Hollywood productions, including the series of
Warner Bros. musicals explicitly addressing "gold digging." It also was (and
to an extent remains) a central premise of American middle-class ideology.
This system of beliefs and practices holds that female sexuality has
commodity value in economic exchange: the "good" (i.e., chaste, vir-
ginal, sexually "unused") woman has higher value than an "experienced"
woman in the marriage market, especially if she has nothing to offer *but*
her beauty and her "virtue." The value accrues to the man who possesses
her legally through the institution of marriage. Yet the female sexual
"good" must be appropriately exercised as a means to an end: the woman
must rely on luck, rather than initiative, in gaining opportunities to display her feminine charms profitably, yet playfully and always virtuously,
until she achieves her goal of "making a good marriage." Not these
women, but only those who exercise their sexuality excessively or explicitly as a commodity, as in prostitution, are social pariahs.

Whereas films such as *Gold Diggers of 1933* adhered to such nuances,
thoroughly specularizing the female body while narratively containing it,
West's characters and image perversely ignored distinctions between
"good" and "bad" women. The Production Code carefully articulated this
standard middle-class distinction, which disperses across female bodies the
contradictory prescription that female sexuality should simultaneously be
displayed and repressed. The censorship of the "kept woman" films at-

tempted to efface any representation of the contradiction; in most cases, that effort succeeded after the advent of rigorous Code enforcement in mid-1934. But despite efforts by industry and state censors, West's films continued to foreground the commodity value of female sexuality and its exercise across class lines.

As we have seen, West's first four star vehicles consistently suggest in dialogue, performance, and narrative that virtually all relations between women and men, within or outside marriage, operate in terms of the ex-change of sex for money.[61] And, like *Red-Headed Woman* and other early 1930s movies in the "kept woman" cycle, West's films do not suggest that sexual exchange between men and women is wrong or leads to unhappi-ness. Like those films, too, West's star vehicles infuriated reformers who found the "successful prostitute" a doubly immoral, if not impossible, fig-ure. Her films did not represent prostitution as a realistically desirable pro-fessional option, but they did offer a spectacular fantasy of glorified pros-titution as a means for a woman to attain social and financial autonomy, at least from any one man.

During the 1930s, when most women had little hope of economic or social independence, the representation of a woman who gains riches, comfort, prestige, and personal pleasure through the self-willed exercise of her sexuality may well have offered a fantasy figure to some female audi-ences.[62] The figure's temporal displacement in *She Done Him Wrong* into the diffusely nostalgic Gay Nineties and its presentation within the con-ventions of comedy obviated any narrative requirements for a realistic de-piction of prostitution that might have offended reform-minded audiences even more. Yet it was not West's depiction of prostitutes per se that con-stituted her primary threat to the goals of the reform movement, but rather her evident pleasure and success in openly exploiting her own sexuality as a commodity, both as character and as star.

West's confounding of moral and class distinctions marked her as a tar-get in the reform discourse. Yet the star's image paradoxically shored up a powerful system that served to maintain the contradictory circumscription of female sexuality: the Hollywood cinema of which "Mae West" was an integral part. Much of West's initial popular appeal as a movie star arose from her unabashedly and comedically representing the "bad woman" type. One New York critic wrote soon after the release of *She Done Him Wrong*, which he deemed "hard-boiled hilarity," that West "is entirely and gallantly unashamed. . . . [She] is frankly and heroically proud of her roughness."[63]

West's representation of a gender- and class-deviant type was popular not only with those who might have wished to violate traditional social distinctions, but also with many movie patrons who generally subscribed to them. West's characterization of a prostitute may well have provided even middle-class male viewers with a fantasy figure. That is the suggestion of an internal MPPDA memo from staff member Ray Norr to Will Hays in October 1933 around the release of *I'm No Angel*. Norr reports,

> The very man who will guffaw at Mae West's performance as a reminder of the ribald days of his past will resent her effect upon the young, when his daughter imitates the Mae West wiggle before her boyfriends and mouths "Come up and see me sometime."[64]

The putative man's enjoyment of West's performance bespeaks sexual fantasies evoked by West that are entirely in keeping with conventional social and representational practice: that of the excessively sexual woman available to any male. Only his censorious reaction to his *daughter's* emulation of West's sassiness and sexual display recalls the socially disruptive potential of the female who speaks her own sexual desire and employs it to her own ends.

Such diverse and ambivalent reactions illustrate how West's image operated at once within and in potential violation of the dual cultural mandate, simultaneously to display and to repress female sexuality. Paramount evidently recognized the former impulse as it built West up as a movie star. But pressure to realize the latter mandate—to contain female sexuality—increased rapidly in the three years following the release of *She Done Him Wrong*. By 1936, not only the reformers and the censor boards but also the film industry itself had begun actively to suppress West's sexual display. The gradual repression of West's image by the same institutions that had constructed and deployed it reveal how "sexual morality" served as both a disguise and an instrument of middle-class dominance.

3

The Star Commodity from Asset
to Liability

Besides making the unwarranted assertion that Mae West caused Hollywood censorship, standard film histories frequently claim that the Production Code's rigorous application after 1934 so eviscerated West's film narratives and performance style that within a couple of years the star lost
much of her audience appeal. As a consequence, so go the popular accounts, West's economic worth to Paramount soon declined, and her loss
of star status quickly followed.[1] But the apparent diminishment of West's
popularity in the mid-1930s, most often associated with her 1936 film
Klondike Annie, did not result primarily from changes in her films, or from
shifting audience tastes. Rather, altering economic and political circumstances around 1936 led Paramount and other movie corporations and per-
sonnel *themselves* to discount West as a star. In effect, as this chapter will
reveal, the film industry itself undercut West's popular appeal—and her
economic value—in the interest of longer-term business aims.

In the preceding chapter, I argued that the sign "Mae West" played an
iconographic role in two historical struggles over meaning and money:
first, as an attractive commodity within the economic discourse of a capitalist industry, and second, as a sign of transgression against cultural norms
in a discourse on movie morality. In this chapter, I will demonstrate that
these two apparently opposed discourses were in fact profoundly comple-
mentary. The movie reformers, who in the early 1930s focused on eliminating representations of transgressive female sexuality, cast themselves as
opponents to Hollywood practices. Yet we have seen that this moral debate symbolized conflicts between economically opportunistic and more
traditional factions of the beleaguered middle class, jointly struggling to
maintain social and economic advantage. Among the dominant American
social values at stake was the primacy of unfettered individual enterprise
within a capitalist economy. The movie reform discourse supported but
also sought to limit this tenet, not from general considerations of social
justice, but rather specifically to restrain women's sexual practices. Para-

doxically, the American film industry concurred in the reformist position, identifying the control of female sexuality as the key to economic and ideological hegemony. The film industry actively constructed "Mae West" as a sign of excessively deviant sexuality only, ultimately, to sacrifice her for the greater social good.

Certainly, Hollywood producers, distributors, and exhibitors exploited representations of female sexuality (like West's star image) and reluctantly curbed the practice only when other major institutions threatened to seek federal legislation or to exert economic pressures; such opposing viewpoints and persistent contradictions abounded within middle-class social and economic practices. But the eight major film corporations soon turned the reform discourse to business advantage. The formulation and enforcement of the Production Code strengthened the MPPDA as the industry's central trade organization and supported its primary members, the major film companies, in their drive to operate as a powerful cartel.[2] By the mid-1930s, the majors had effectively eliminated competition from independent producers and distributors through oligopolistic trade practices that the MPPDA and also the Depression-era National Recovery Act fostered. Public demand for control of "Mae West" helped justify the MPPDA's strong industrial position, even as its operations, on behalf of its member corporations, effected illegal prior restraint of trade. West's status as a sign of sexual transgression thus benefited Paramount and the other major film corporations *both* as a box office commodity and as a controversial cultural emblem.

A case study of *Klondike Annie*, the sixth and last film Paramount produced with West, shows how the ostensibly moral discourse about female sexual representation masked a political and economic discourse about institutionalized power, status, and wealth. The case provides crucial insights particularly into Paramount's contradictory business practices in the mid-1930s. The controversies surrounding *Klondike Annie* also reveal how industry censorship worked *not* to eradicate depictions of illicit sexuality, but rather to suppress the power and pleasure that West's characters derived from such sexuality. By 1935-36, during the film's sustained production and reception, West's aura of power, rather than her generally transgressive sexuality, had come to dominate her emblematic function within the film industry and increasingly that in movie reform discourse. The case study thus traces unexpected causal connections in the 1933-38 period among forces of Hollywood self-censorship, public responses to West's perfor-

mances, and the film industry's sometimes conflicting economic and political interests in Mae West as a star and cultural icon.

The Case of Klondike Annie

Paramount started production of *Klondike Annie* in June 1935, in the
middle of Ernst Lubitsch's one-year tenure as production chief at Paramount.[3] Associate producer William LeBaron directly supervised the
project; Raoul Walsh directed. Credits attribute the screenplay to West,
who plays Rose Carleton, a.k.a. "the San Francisco Doll." Like *She Done
Him Wrong* (1933) and *Belle of the Nineties* (1934), *Klondike Annie* is set in
the 1890s. The film opens in San Francisco's Chinatown, where a Chinese
nightclub owner, Chan Lo, holds West's character captive as his mistress.
Doll escapes, killing Chan Lo during the attempt, and embarks on a freight
ship to Nome.[4] En route, the captain of the ship, Bull Brackett (Victor
McLaglen), becomes enamored of her. Doll initially shows little interest in
Bull, but begins to accept his attentions after he discovers her identity, to
prevent his turning her over to authorities. Evading arrest by the police
searching for her in Nome, Doll assumes the guise of a pious settlement
worker, Annie Alden, who has just died on board the ship. In this masquerade, Doll packs the Nome settlement house and enlivens the services
with rousing song and good-natured admonitions to the miners to give up
drink and live right. The policeman assigned to watch for the wanted
woman sees through Doll's disguise, but, luckily for her, not before he falls
hopelessly in love with her. Meanwhile, Bull threatens to kill both the policeman and Doll if she will not depart with him on his ship. She eventually chooses to leave with Bull, but asks him to direct the ship back to San
Francisco so that she can seek legal exoneration by pleading self-defense
for killing Chan Lo.

The plot summary signals a number of similarities between *Klondike Annie* and West's earlier films. As in all of her star vehicles, West clearly plays
the protagonist whose actions and joking repartee dominate and propel
the narrative. Doll/Annie resembles West's other characters in manner
and performance: she is a talented musical and comedic entertainer and a
sexually alluring, clever woman who asserts control over her personal and
professional destiny. West again portrays "herself," the character that had
become closely associated with her established star image. Even the film's
title points to continuity of character type. In its use of a woman's name

coupled with a term implying wealth, "Klondike Annie" recalls the title of West's highly successful play *Diamond Lil*. Until shortly before its release, *Klondike Annie* bore the working title "Klondike Lou," her character's name echoing thereby "Lady Lou" in *She Done Him Wrong*. "Sapphire Sue" also surfaced as a name for West's character in the 1936 picture.[5] As these character names and her additional appellation "the San Fran-cisco Doll" suggest, West again plays the happily promiscuous, glamorous woman as a barely disguised prostitute.

But both West's role in *Klondike Annie* and its narrative also deviated from her earlier films. Despite the hint of gold in "Klondike" (the site of the turn-of-the-century Yukon gold rush), West's character is not an active "gold digger," in contrast to previous roles in which she pointedly exercises her sexuality for material gain. West's character in her first four star ve-hicles engages only in affairs she chooses and enjoys, and in the end she always "gets it all": wealth, status, and the devoted love of the film's most attractive man, along with exemption from punishment or even nominal repentance for any violations of moral strictures. Whatever punishment the last reel of these films metes out falls upon other characters, not on West's, however much the star may have participated in acts depicted in the film that qualify conventionally as criminal or immoral.

In *Belle of the Nineties*, for example, West's character, Ruby Carter, takes revenge simultaneously on a former lover and a current sleazy suitor by "fixing" a boxing match, pilfering a safe, pitting the two men against each other, conspiring to conceal the subsequent death of one, and "acciden-tally" setting a building on fire. *Belle of the Nineties* downplays Ruby Car-ter's violation of sexual norms, an aspect of the script that the newly formed Production Code Administration closely monitored, but elaborates her violation of criminal law and of conventional standards of honor in financial dealings. In so doing, the narrative maintains West's established star image as a transgressor of convention, an outlaw, by augmenting and in part displacing her character's violation of *sexual* mores onto the violation of moral and legal precepts concerning fair play (her drugging the boxer) and property (robbing the safe). At the same time, the narrative subtly shifts responsibility for these wrongdoings onto other characters, who at film's end "take the rap" while West's character escapes all reprobation. The film in its final form thus satisfied the Code's guidelines that there be concluding compensation for wrongdoing, without West's character re-gretting or suffering from her behavior or otherwise being narratively or visually reinscribed within the bourgeois ideology that the Production Code Administration sought to uphold.

In *Klondike Annie*, made less than two years later, West's character has a far more restricted range of choices. For the first time, West plays the unwilling mistress of first one, then another man. Although her character ends up coupled romantically with the best-known actor in the cast (Victor McLaglen), the narrative does not portray him as the most appealing man available to her.[6] West wears her usual ostentatious costumes, especially before she begins masquerading in Salvation Army garb (see Figures 22, 23, 35, and 36).[7] However, Doll/Annie does not prosper financially from either the star's standard use of body or her new use of "soul" in this film, but instead several times relinquishes material accumulations.

An exchange between Doll and an old girlfriend (and implicitly fellow entertainer or prostitute) called Tess (Lucille Webster Gleason) points up the limits set on West's character (Figure 36). Doll, whose past only Tess and Bull Brackett recognize, seeks her friend's advice in choosing between Brackett and the good-looking young policeman (Philip Reed) she clearly prefers. Tess's first response captures the spirit of earlier West vehicles: "Do you have to pick either one?" When Doll replies that she must choose in order to escape jail on the one hand and Brackett's vengeful jealousy on the other, Tess quips, "Maybe you'll get lucky and they'll kill each other!"

Given Doll's restricted choices, Tess's retort comes across as one of the film's boldest and funniest lines. The dialogue ends in one of West's much-quoted punch lines, which expresses her usual daring and imagination: "When I'm caught between two evils, I generally like to take the one I've never tried!" However, in later deciding to go away with Brackett, purportedly to avoid endangering the policeman's life or career, West's character chooses the "evil" (sex with Brackett) that the narrative implies she *has* tried before.

These variations in *Klondike Annie* from the established pattern of West's narratives did result from tightened Code enforcement. Correspondence reveals the Production Code Administration's range of concerns during the film's production from June to December 1935. The initial script of *Klondike Annie* elicited rigorous PCA monitoring for its implications of interracial sex, representations of torture, and unpunished murder, and for its casting of West as a prostitute.[8]

From the earliest correspondence, primary concern focused on the sexual behavior of West's character. A letter at production outset from

Paramount liaison John Hammel to Will Hays, then visiting in California, promised, "The ending of our story will be a romance between West and one of the characters in our picture, and it will indicate for the future a normal life and nothing that will bring condemnation from the most scrupulous" (Hammel to Hays, 29 June 1935).

This and subsequent letters imply that the initial script allowed West's character to accept the policeman's love. Hays's immediate response questioned the leading character's sexual morality:

> We assume that there will be no suspicion of loose or illicit sex relationships between Miss West and the Chinese gambler or any of the other characters in your story; rather, as you suggested in the discussion here, it will be definitely indicated that the woman whom Miss West represents is basically good. (Hays to Hammel, 2 July 1935)

The letter concluded in a disarming paragraph intimating that the MPPDA anticipated unprecedented cooperation on the project not only from Paramount, but also from West herself:

> I am constrained to take this opportunity to compliment Miss West, the studio and all of you who have part in the development of this purpose. I think it is splendid from every standpoint and if it is carried out with the high integrity and completeness as planned it will involve elements of real industry service as well as the creation of new and, I think, lasting substantial values for you all.

Later correspondence indicates that the PCA "stick" immediately supplemented the "carrot" of Hays's politic phrasing. In memos written in September and October 1935, Joseph Breen required a number of changes in the script and in song lyrics; he also repeatedly cautioned the studio to maintain decency in costuming and camera framing and especially in West's style of verbal delivery.[9] Except for the violence in scenes showing Doll's escape, all material designated for change or deletion bore implications that West's character possessed sexual knowledge and experience. For example, the PCA prohibited West from saying, "I'm sorry I can't see you in private," while looking the young detective up and down; other West lines that Breen marked for deletion included "Men are at their best when women are at their worst" and "It's a mighty cold sheet that just one sleeps under." Song lyrics, the primary site of PCA censorship in West's previous star vehicle *Goin' to Town*, also received careful attention in the production of *Klondike Annie*.[10] Breen red-penciled such lyrics as "My brand new daddy does me so much good" and "It's never too late to say no," and the studio dropped the numbers containing those lines.

West's proposed missionary disguise caused Breen the greatest consternation. He argued repeatedly that any suggestion that West could successfully masquerade as a church leader would offend organized religion. He demanded deletion of references to West as "Soul-Savin' Annie" or "sort of a preacher woman" and required that dialogue and costume characterize her as a social worker, carrying not a Bible but a black-bound anthology of settlement maxims. To exclude any "religious flavor," Breen forbade hymns and called for the elimination of lines like "Bless you, Bro—come up often and leave your sins" and "You can't save a man's soul if you don't get close to him," which, in West's delivery, might take on provocative double meanings.[11]

Breen's anxiety that viewers might take the portrayal of any association between West and religion at best as satire, at worst as blasphemy anticipated responses upon the film's release like the following review in the *New York Sun*:

> Mae West as a comedienne burlesquing sexy dramas is not nearly as
> offensive as Mae West in a settlement worker's bonnet talking of religion.
> *Klondike Annie*, the dullest film she has made, is both the cleanest and the
> most offensive.[12]

A letter that Claude Shull, head of the San Francisco Motion Picture Council, sent to Paramount, with copies to Breen, Hays, Mae West herself, and Mrs. Thomas G. Winter (an MPPDA consultant and former president of the General Federation of Women's Clubs), also realized Breen's fearful expectations:

> Any picture that presents its heroine as a mistress to an Oriental, then as a
> murderess, then as a cheap imitator of a missionary—jazzing up religion—is
> not in harmony with the other educational forces of our social set-up. And
> these elements are particularly objectionable when they are interspersed
> with smutty wise-cracks. (Shull to Paramount, 1 May 1936)

The rewrites and retakes that Breen required, along with studio difficulties in creating the Yukon set, caused production delays and cost overruns. On viewing the film in late December 1935, Breen called for several cuts in scenes that implied sexual desire or activity between Brackett and Doll, but granted a PCA certificate of approval. Breen's brief evaluation in his weekly written report to his boss echoed the optimism Hays had expressed at the project's outset: "The Mae West picture presents a new type of characterization for the star, depending for entertainment less on her wise-cracks and more on a legitimate story and sincere characterizations" (Breen to Hays, 31 December 1935)

Up to this point, PCA records on *Klondike Annie* compare in number and format to those for the previous two West productions, which con-clude by documenting state censor boards' cuts in the release version. The *Klondike Annie* file reports action by nine government censor boards, in-cluding the film's outright rejection in Alberta as "an offensive mixture of religion and immorality." Only the Ontario board made extensive dele-tions, including West's quip about the choice between two evils and her also much-quoted line, "What's the good of resisting temptation, there'll always be more!"[13] But the *Klondike Annie* file differs from others in ex-tensively documenting responses to the film after state censorship. Besides recording a controversial response (which, after all, her earlier vehicles had also met), the expanded documentation reveals the PCA's increased interest in West's press and public reception, beyond overseeing her indi-vidual films through their release.

Postproduction controversies began during Hollywood previews of *Klondike Annie* in early February, when someone tipped Breen off that Paramount was exhibiting a print of the film containing material deleted from the PCA-approved version.[14] Breen immediately rescinded the Code seal and reopened negotiations with the studio that resulted in the elimi-nation of "love talk" and other hints at an "illicit sex affair," before he agreed on 10 February 1936 to the film's release. *Klondike Annie* opened five days later at a special public preview in Miami and was released na-tionwide the following week.

Concurrent with the film's official release on 21 February, newspaper magnate William Randolph Hearst issued a memo to the thirty papers in his media empire declaring that the editors should roundly condemn the film, Paramount studios, and everyone connected with the picture, espe-cially the star, as immoral. The editors should also criticize the Hays Office as ineffective and then never again mention West's films. The PCA file contains a typewritten, unsigned copy of the memo, which an editor or other person with access to it may have relayed by telephone to the PCA, with or without Hearst's knowledge and permission. The memo's colorful wording and its central role in resultant controversies around West war-rants its citation here:

To Koblentz, copy to all managing editors:

The Mae West picture, KLONDIKE ANNIE, is a filthy picture.

I think we should have editorials roasting the picture and Mae West, and the Paramount Company for producing such a picture—the producer—director and everyone concerned.

We should say it is an affront to the decency of the public and to the interest of the motion picture profession.

Will Hays must be asleep to allow such a thing to come out but it is to be hoped that the churches of the community are awake to the necessity of boycotting such a picture and demanding its (word indistinct but probably withdrawal) [sic].

After you have had a couple of good editorials regarding the indecency of this picture, then DO NOT MENTION MAE WEST IN OUR PAPERS AGAIN WHILE SHE IS ON THE SCREEN AND DO NOT ACCEPT ANY ADVERTISING OF THIS PICTURE.

It is astounding that the Paramount people should have had the stupidity to produce such a picture when it has been demonstrated to what a degree the screen has been benefited by the clean pictures that have been made since the public uproar against screen filth.

It goes to show that screen producers are not influenced by any moral consideration but only by fear of public indignation.

And the only way of influencing such producers is by the people saying that a pandering to the lewd element of the community is not profitable.[15]

The *Klondike Annie* file contains several clipped editorials that appeared in Hearst papers beginning 20 February, which rephrase or slightly condense the memo, along with reviews of *Klondike Annie* and several reader letters printed in non-Hearst papers, most of which defend the film and criticize Hearst as a hypocrite.[16] Some Hollywood press notices speculate about Hearst's personal motivations for the campaign.[17]

A unique item tops the PCA file: an unsigned and undated personal testimonial in a one-page typed memo, purportedly, so states an introductory paragraph, from "a liberal minded and intelligent social worker about thirty years of age. She is not connected with the motion picture industry." The explanatory note asserts that the essay was collected in conjunction with a survey of audience reaction to *Klondike Annie* at a first-run Indianapolis theater, but does not specify exactly who solicited the reaction or when, why, or how it came to be in the file. The writer echoes views put forward in many reviews of *Klondike Annie*, that West's box-office draw and value as a star had substantially declined compared with her earlier appeal. More noteworthy than the testimonial's contents is its exceptional presence in the file, apparently as a sampling or documentation of "direct" popular sentiment. But despite the opinions expressed in letters and reviews about West's diminished box office appeal, *Klondike Annie* did above-average business. The Hearst campaign probably augmented the film's commercial success.[18]

In reporting on 10 February his reinstatement of the certificate of approval, Breen defended *Klondike Annie* to Hays, arguing that although it was somewhat salacious, it was not a travesty of religion. But in an internal PCA memo ten days later, on the same day that Hearst released his memo nationwide, Breen passed a summary judgment on West's productions:

> The important thing in this entire report is this: Just so long as we have Mae West on our hands with the particular kind of story which she goes in for, we are going to have trouble.
>
> Difficulty is inherent with a Mae West picture. Lines and pieces of business, which in the script seem to be thoroughly innocuous, turn out when shown on the screen to be questionable at best, when they are not definitely offensive. A special memorandum should be prepared on this matter for presentation to Mr. Hays. (Breen PCA office memo, 20 February 1936)

Although he had approved the film, Breen continued through the end of February to demand that Paramount make further cuts (for example, of West's line "Give a man a free hand and he'll put it all over you"). The studio replied that prints had already been sent out from the exchanges.[19]

Meanwhile, prior to the film's release, West herself had left town amid rumors about a feud with Ernst Lubitsch, just deposed as production chief at Paramount, and about her own intentions to leave the studio to work with former Paramount production head Emanuel Cohen, under whom West's first star vehicles had appeared. On 22 February 1936 an article appeared in the *Los Angeles Examiner*, remarkably enough a Hearst-owned newspaper, under the byline of Louella O. Parsons, film critic and Hollywood gossip columnist, asserting that West, "registering violent displeasure" toward Paramount, had refused to extend her contract with Paramount and that she had already signed to make two pictures with Cohen, with whom she was traveling East in search of new material.[20] Despite its echo in later publications, this account cannot fully explain the break between West and Paramount, for the corporation's New York office had deposed Lubitsch as production chief prior to West's departure.[21]

The identity of Lubitsch's replacement makes the parting of ways between star and studio all the more remarkable, for longtime Paramount associate William LeBaron, who had produced all of West's films, including *Klondike Annie*, assumed the position. Whatever the reasons for her leaving Paramount (an issue I take up again below), West did sign with Cohen, who produced two films with her, *Go West, Young Man* (1936) and *Every Day's a Holiday* (1938), through his newly formed independent unit, Major Pictures. Although Paramount Pictures distributed both films, after *Klondike Annie*, West no longer qualified as a Paramount "property." Even though West's popular appeal continued strong, her worth to Paramount had plummeted from its ranking three years earlier as a prime source of the company's fortunes. Following Paramount's release of *Every Day's a Holiday* in early 1938, the actress/author who had brought millions of dollars into the movie industry and the company that had most shaped and sold her image severed all contractual relations.

Against popular claims about the effects of reform lobbying, Production Code enforcement, and the 1936 Hearst campaign, however, no immediate connection obtains between West's box-office value and her changed relationship with Paramount. Instead, the evidence points to a surprising development: the film industry—encompassing Paramount and other major studios, the MPPDA, the trade press, and also the Hearst media empire—itself undermined West's commodity value, beginning actively around *Klondike Annie*'s release.[22] The shift in West's contractual status with Paramount for reasons other than short-term business interests bespoke complex developments in Hollywood's economic and political practices in the mid-1930s. Clearly, Paramount took more than West's box-office draw into account in figuring her reduced commodity value.

Movie Reform as Industry Policy

Two related circumstances in the film industry determined the shift in Mae West's value between 1933 and 1938: first, Paramount's impending bankruptcy in 1932-33, when the company hired and promoted West as a film star; and second, from 1936 on, Paramount leaders' increased concern with the company's appearing to support dominant cultural values of family life, moral fairness, and community control. These successive business circumstances echoed the competing middle-class interests in capitalist exploitation and moral restraint; they unspooled as Paramount first participated in building an oligopoly among the major movie companies and then responded to legal challenges to their trade practices. Thus, although "Mae West" initially worked to the film industry's advantage in all these struggles, by the late 1930s, opposing economic and social interests managed to usurp much of Mae West's iconographic power in support of their own issues, against the major movie companies' early 1930s practices.

Paramount had lost $21 million in 1932 before, in January 1933, a bankruptcy court placed the corporation in the hands of receivers for reorganization. In July 1935, the reorganization plan set John Otterson as Paramount's president. Less than a year later, the corporation again faced financial crisis, primarily through its production branch, even though Otterson had replaced the fiscally inefficient Lubitsch with the more responsible LeBaron. Paramount's board of directors commissioned Joseph P. Kennedy to evaluate the situation and, wanting to avoid going back into receivership, followed his recommendation to fire Otterson. Kennedy's report criticized Otterson, who had spent much of his tenure in Hollywood, for allowing production schedules to fall behind and for failing to retain stars.[23]

Both factors arose around Klondike Annie, and organizational and financial circumstances no doubt played a part in West's losing favor. Paramount's administration may well have been too disorganized in the second half of 1935 to manage West's star power, particularly in view of her conflicts with Lubitsch and Lubitsch's own conflicts with Otterson.[24] In his cost accounting approach to management, Otterson likely considered West's high salary and unusual degree of control over her projects unjustifiable despite her box-office draw, particularly when Klondike Annie ran over budget.[25] Some popular accounts of West's career assert that Paramount released West from her contract because of the battles with the PCA that each West film brought, which made the star more trouble to the studio than she was worth.[26] This seems plausible reasoning, but it overlooks the star's continued strong marketability, for although none of her films surpassed the financial success of I'm No Angel, West held her place as Paramount's top box-office attraction through 1936.[27]

Thus, although mismanagement may figure as a partial explanation for West's (and other stars') diminished standing at Paramount in 1936, it does not suffice as explanation, for records do not spell out what may lie behind "mismanagement." The focus on personality conflicts, difficulties with the PCA, and cost overruns ignores how such "causes" may serve as foils. For example, cost overruns occasioned by PCA-mandated retakes and revisions may have worked to harass recalcitrant producers and stars.[28] Cost overruns may also have offered studio management de facto justification for policy changes made on other than strictly financial grounds. Circumstances surrounding the production and reception of Klondike Annie strongly suggest that factors other than short-term financial considerations determined West's value to Paramount and in the industry as a whole.[29]

Precisely West's emblematic status in the morality debate codetermined her value to Paramount along with her box-office appeal.

Congressional records from February and March 1936 document West's critical positioning at the crux of an expanded political-economic debate involving the film industry. Concurrent with *Klondike Annie*'s release, subcommittees of the U.S. Senate and House of Representatives Committees on Interstate and Foreign Commerce held hearings on a proposed bill to abolish the practice of compulsory block booking and blind buying. Following this practice, major distributors required exhibitors to rent entire sets of films, usually in advance of their production and often filling many of their playdates. Independent exhibitors (those operating movie houses that the major film corporations did not own) argued that Congress should eliminate the practice as unfair restraint of trade. Paramount and other major distributors defended it as a legal and fiscally necessary operation enabling rationalized mass production and sale of movies.[30]

The independents countered that the decisive issue was community control over what films their theaters might exhibit, given their locations in smaller cities and rural regions. Social film historian Garth Jowett situates this argument within the social changes that occurred in the United States between 1890 and 1930, caused by the growing dominance of urban over rural life and the rising influence of mass media, which contributed to the undercutting of traditional power structures.[31] In the block-booking debate, the independent exhibitors, who dealt with local financial constraints, wanted to gain comparative economic advantage against the Hollywood movie corporations, which wanted to maintain their control.

West's name recurred at the 1936 hearings in testimony from independent exhibitors and reform group representatives, who presented the star as personifying the movie immorality that the block-booking system forced exhibitors to promote, against community objections.[32] Movie trade journals and other publications reported in detail the frequent mention of West in the hearings. The *Motion Picture Herald* gave the following account:

> Mae West was the real issue last week in the arguments at Washington before a sub-committee hearing of U.S. Senate on the Neely-Pettengill bill to abolish block booking. Minority exhibitor interest and club women and other "outside" supporters contended that compulsory block booking forces exhibitors to play "Mae West pictures" symbolizing a type—or else, pay and not play, which, they added, they could not afford to do.
>
> The distributors submitted evidence that there had not been a single

cancellation by an exhibitor on a Mae West picture, even during the
height of the Legion of Decency boycott movement in 1934, whereas
"high standard" pictures (Alice in Wonderland, Abraham Lincoln) were
cancelled by theaters by the hundreds.[33]

Paramount spokesmen in effect refuted the independents' claim that
blind buying of West's pictures violated community moral control by arguing that West remained a major box-office draw despite the reform
movement.[34] The revelation contradicts assertions in mid-1930s reviews
of West's films and in later film histories that the star's popularity had declined substantially prior to Klondike Annie's release. In fact, West's appeal
evidently remained strong through 1936 not only in the major urban markets and in the less populous eastern, midwestern, and southern cities
where Paramount operated its almost thirteen hundred theaters in the
United States, but also, if one accepts the distributors' logic, in the towns
where independent exhibitors ran theaters.[35] West's precipitous drop from
her position as Paramount's top box-office draw in 1936 to eighth position
in 1937 (incorporating distribution of Go West, Young Man) clearly followed rather than preceded West's departure from the production wing of
the company.

Although even Hearst's campaign against West did not reduce her box-
office appeal, instead enhancing public interest, his intervention may have
had less tangible or immediate effects. A possible indication of the campaign's eventual results appeared when in May 1938 the Hollywood Reporter named West among a number of stars (including Joan Crawford,
Greta Garbo, and Katharine Hepburn) independent theater owners had
designated "box office poison."[36] The iconographic use of West's name in
the 1936 congressional hearings, however, makes it evident that unsub-
stantiated claims from independent exhibitors (or any other group) about
public response to West (and other stars) cannot stand as disinterested sta-
tistical reports. The Hollywood Reporter's survey and its dissemination
through other news organs require analysis to reveal how exhibitors' condemnations may have contributed to diminishing certain stars' popularity.

Rather than necessarily reflecting box-office figures, the trade press's
May 1938 dismissal of West may have signaled residual outrage over her
appearance six months earlier on the "Chase and Sanborn" radio program,
where she performed a burlesque of Eve in the biblical story of Eden and
exchanged sexual repartee with ventriloquist Edgar Bergen's dummy Charlie McCarthy. A number of national papers in the Hearst chain as well as

the Hollywood trade press reported that the program had caused church and reform group members to call for tighter regulation of radio content. A month later, the Federal Communications Commission rebuked the National Broadcasting Corporation (NBC) and the fifty-nine subscribing stations that aired the program for violating the ethics of decency.[37] But Mae West herself bore the brunt of the press's criticism, while the show's sponsors received mild scolding and program star Bergen and program regular Don Ameche, who played Adam to West's Eve, escaped censure altogether.

Two days after West's radio performance on 12 December (which I discuss further in the next chapter), the *Motion Picture Daily* condemned the program and its guest star in a front-page editorial signed by Martin Quigley, the trade paper's publisher and editor. Quigley was, of course, a key promoter of the 1930 Production Code. Under the headline "Radio Begs Trouble," Quigley scolded as ignorant fools and West's pawns the radio and advertising companies that had arranged her appearance:

> The broadcast was a nice salvaging operation for Miss West because it gave her an opportunity to use certain other material for which in Hollywood there is no longer a market for reasons which it has been assumed were quite well known to all persons with a trace of knowledge of recent developments in the amusement business.[38]

Quigley's obscure mention of developments precluding a market for West's style of entertainment probably referred to the movie reform movement over the previous five years. It may also have referred to ongoing attempts by independent exhibitors, among them *Motion Picture Daily* subscribers, to win federal legislation against the major film companies' dominance in film distribution and exhibition. Certainly, *Motion Picture Daily* readers would have recognized the argument that the majors' business practices circumvented community opposition to West's movies, thereby undermining local standards of morality, whether they shared that opinion or not.

Quigley's assertion concerning the conclusion the movie industry had reached about West's low commodity value contradicted the economic facts even in 1937. Her films continued to draw large audiences; there indeed *was* still a market for West's material.[39] Six weeks after Quigley's declaration (and after the national controversy over West's radio appearance, which had promoted *Every Day's a Holiday*), the newest West vehicle again proved a financial success.[40] *Variety* suggested that Paramount, releasing the Major Pictures production, knew to turn the controversy to its advantage.[41]

But Quigley's editorial in effect argued that the movie industry now recognized that West's *iconographic* function in the reform discourse bore negatively on Hollywood interests. Paradoxically, Quigley's own weekly *Motion Picture Herald* had pointed out that the emblematic use of West's image in 1936 to oppose block booking only perpetuated a convenient fiction. In the two-year interval, that fiction had evidently gained sufficient rhetorical power to move industry leaders like Quigley to oppose West publicly.[42]

Also paradoxically, two weeks after Quigley denounced West in the *Motion Picture Daily*, an unsigned *Motion Picture Herald* editorial emphatically blamed members of the entertainment industry other than the star for the radio show's effect and for West's popularity on stage and screen. The essay's first three paragraphs appeared in bold italics:

> *The producers of Miss West's plays knew what they were trying to do.*
> *The motion picture producers of Miss West's screen drama knew what they were trying to do, and who they were doing it with.*
> *The radio sponsors of Miss West's Adam-and-Eve on the air knew who they were presenting and why.*
> . . .
> At each step, stage, screen, radio, the abandoned pursuit of attention regardless, has achieved a large disservice to the art and industry concerned.[43]

The editorial argues in favor of an unnamed "code" and concludes, "The popular arts have a contract with a public which professes a common decency as its norm." The masthead above the unsigned full-page editorial announces only Quigley's name as "Editor-in-Chief and Publisher." Readers no doubt understood that Quigley had authored or at least approved the editorial.

Although the essay calls for producers to accept responsibility for West's harmful effects on the entertainment industry, it casts those producers not in the second, but in the third person, "*They* Sent for Her." The article directly addresses film exhibitors, probably the weekly's primary readers, exhorting them to pressure producers to repudiate West and what she represented—in the words of the editorial: "attainable sex."

When these editorials appeared in late 1937, the major film companies faced an imminent antitrust suit, which the U.S. Department of Justice filed seven months later in response to independent exhibitors' charges against the majors' monopolistic trade practices.[44] The federal lawsuit, which supplanted the drive to get regulatory legislation through Congress, seriously challenged the majors' control of the industry and, twelve years later, forced them to divest exhibition outlets. We have seen that independent exhibitors wielded moral objections to "Mae West pictures" in congressional hearings to support their economic struggles with the majors. West's full significance to the film industry emerges in closer analysis of the majors' trade practices and the threat to those that the antitrust suit embodied.

In part because acute reform pressure gave the major corporations a useful pretext for strengthening industry self-regulation in the early 1930s, acquiescence in West's emblematic function in the moral discourse initially served industry's interests. Besides enhancing her value as a box-office commodity, West's status as a controversial cultural icon tested the boundaries of allowable sexual representation while deflecting attention from the majors' drive for oligopolistic power, which Code enforcement both masked and helped to achieve. A second self-regulatory code, the Motion Picture Industry Code, adopted in December 1933 to bring the film industry into compliance with the National Recovery Act (NRA), also eventually proved a boon for the major movie corporations. As industry leaders resisted its adoption during negotiations in fall 1933, the NRA Code became intertwined with MPPDA administration of the *Production* Code.[45] But, however reluctant industry leaders initially were to accept these codes, by 1935 they supported the overall guidelines of both.[46] The two codes jointly secured MPPDA member companies' domination of the industry by the mid-1930s, as the trade organization dealt as an exclusive body with the reform movement and deployed its influence in Washington.[47]

The recurrence of West's name in the congressional hearings indicates, however, that her role in public discourse no longer brought unalloyed advantages to Paramount or the other majors. The reformers who had used "Mae West" primarily as a rallying cry for censorship now joined independent exhibitors in wielding the star's emblematic power more threateningly, as justification for antitrust action. By 1937, the less immediately manageable and measurable costs of West's public image had evidently begun to outweigh its benefits as box-office commodity.

The reevaluation of West's *composite value*, encompassing her box-office and emblematic worth, accompanied the managerial and fiscal reorganization at Paramount in 1935-36. Barney Balaban, who had made a fortune with a chain of luxurious movie theaters in the Midwest, emerged in July 1938 as head of Paramount and remained in active control until 1964. His appointment coincided with a further development at Paramount and industrywide: the overt reaffirmation in movie productions and publicity of conventional American middle-class values.

At Paramount, the status reduction and departure in 1935-37 of former leading Paramount directors Ernst Lubitsch and Josef von Sternberg and stars including Marlene Dietrich and the Marx Brothers as well as West marked a shift away from an emphasis in the studio's productions and publicity image on European sophistication and anarchistic and sexually provocative comedy. Around the same time, the Hollywood press was celebrating the industry's revived financial stability and the cooperation of its leaders in strengthening the Hays Office. These mid-1930s developments signaled the rise of a new, carefully crafted industry image.

Hays and other industry leaders knew how heavily the film industry relied on broad middle-class patronage, both in audience attendance and in the tolerance of national church organizations and government bodies, which also predominantly represented middle-class interests. By the mid-1930s, the movie morality drive had gained sufficient public legitimacy to persuade Hollywood leaders that they needed to uphold dominant social values—or at least convincingly *appear* to do so—in order to thrive or even survive. Under reform pressure, the industry as a whole had begun to shift from its dominant social stance that female sexuality might be both "displayed and repressed" over to general public affirmation, in the midst of economic and social crises, of then current "family values." The persistent star image of "Mae West" as a happily wanton woman fit poorly with Hollywood's altered image. This observation brings us back to the case of *Klondike Annie*, for that production represented a pivotal attempt to revise West's image within the film industry. The communications from Hays to Paramount in July 1935 optimistically predicting "the creation of new values for you all" and from Breen to Hays in early February 1936 noting "a new type of characterization" for West indicated the MPPDA's goal of redefining the sign "Mae West." That goal extended the trade organization's practice of working to protect its member studios' investments, by trying to help Paramount adapt West's highly profitable transgressive image to the

new political and economic circumstances.[48] But West herself proved un-
amenable to any such revisions.

The Ironic Prostitute as Political Economic Threat

Klondike Annie's censorship and reception demonstrate that West's image
exceeded acceptable representations of female sexuality in the mid-1930s
not primarily because she persistently cast herself as a prostitute, but rather
because her characters *enjoyed* and *benefited from* their own sexuality and
generally repudiated all male or institutional control. Even as her roles and
spectacular presentation followed Hollywood practices in artfully anchor-
ing the female figure as a sign of sex, her recurrent performance as an autonomous and unabashed prostitute made obvious the central but ordi-
narily disguised function of female sexuality as a commodity for economic
and cultural consumption.

West's role as prostitute in her films up to and including *Klondike Annie*
cast her doubly as consumer object: as character within the narrative and
as fetishized star of the movie. But West represented not only an object;
she also played an agent in the cycle of consumption portrayed in her film
narratives, which characterized her as an actively desiring, promiscuous
consumer of men as sexual objects who enjoyed financial advantages
through the exercise. West's films thus enunciated a persistently amoral
connection between sex and money as a means to enhanced status and
power.

West's evident "self-commodification" emanated not only from her film
roles but also from her image as a performer deeply involved in every step
of the production of her movies and public image. West's typically ironic
performance even in some dramatic scenes in *Klondike Annie* communicates a distance between herself as star and the character(s) she plays. Indeed, it is this double articulation in her performance that makes West/
Doll's disguise as a missionary *qua* settlement worker into a satire of
religion. Despite Doll's protestations of her sincerity in enacting Sister Annie, the masquerade within the story echoes the masquerade inherent in
West's role-playing, so that Doll's successful disguise as a lively missionary
equates with West's own success as performer.

Although the narrative ends with a nod to moral concerns, the evident
"Mae West" behind her character Doll undercuts her acts of relinquishing
the young policeman's love and asking Bull to take her to face charges for

murdering Chan Lo. West's ironic demeanor and well-established image precluded most critics and probably many audience members from believing her character's apparent change of heart and impulse to account legally and morally for her actions.

Notwithstanding its rigorous censorship, Klondike Annie only augmented West's prevalent function as an emblem of transgressive sexuality and power. The film's opening scenes establish West, in violation of the Code's stipulation against the depiction of "white slavery," as the unwilling mistress of "the Chinese gambler." West first appears as Doll in spectacular costume and staging, strumming and singing "An Occidental Woman in an Oriental Mood for Love" (see Figure 23). The mise-en-scène and the lyrics present West/Doll as a highly fetishized object. But after the curtain falls, Doll repudiates Chan Lo's attempts to parade her before his upper-class white guests as one of his prize possessions. She rebuffs his praise for her as his "pearl of pearls" by quipping, "This poirl of poirls is gettin' unstrung!" and suggests that he entertain the guests himself: "Do a dance or show them some card tricks!" After the opening scene excessively fetishizes West/Doll in performance, her dialogue points out that not only she, but also he (notably, the "Oriental" male) may play specular object to an audience (Figure 22).

The cinematography, costuming, lighting, sets, and dialogue in Klondike Annie's opening scenes clearly mark Chan Lo as a sexual spectacle, with emphasis on his (supposed) racial "otherness." Chan Lo's death early in the film literally eliminates the threat of transgressive sex between the two. Although West's character effects his demise, her act of retribution goes unseen due to internal film censorship. Dialogue and narrative elements retained in the film suggest what PCA correspondence confirms: Doll kills Chan Lo by stabbing him with an ancient Malayan knife. The film's opening scene establishes the knife as Chan Lo's favored fetish object, just before West's introduction in her "Occidental Woman" number. This scene and later verbal references to Chan Lo's death equate West with the knife as a powerful phallic instrument.

West's screenplay for Klondike Annie follows her established pattern of making her character the primary locus of action, but then shifting responsibility for that character's social and legal violations onto others. Thus, in contrast to the usual Hollywood narrative, which holds the female responsible for sexual transgressions, it is the "master" rather than West as the "mistress" who ultimately suffers from their relationship. Still, this master's punishment remains a Hollywood convention, given his "ethnic" identity.

The film condemns Chan Lo even as it exploits the erotic appeal of forbidden cross-racial sex that his character represents.

Although *Klondike Annie* shifts some moral reprobation away from West, its deviation from the narrative fate Hollywood traditionally assigned sexually active women has narrowed, compared with West's previous films. In *She Done Him Wrong*, West's Lady Lou escapes any consequences for stabbing a woman in apparent self-defense; in *Klondike Annie*, no longer a law unto herself, West must give lip service to standards of morality and justice. Stricter enforcement of Code guidelines on the later film can account for that closing scene, but it is worth noting that the victim for whose death West must atone is male. Although emphasis in *Klondike Annie* on racial difference and Chan Lo's despicable characterization helps narratively excuse West/Doll's symbolic castration of him, still, for the first time in this film, she must manifest regret, demonstrate a respect for institutions upholding morality and law, and, implicitly, accept the power of men over women.

By 1936, the PCA would not accept even a standard Hollywood racist displacement as adequate justification for the actions of West's character. Conceivably, PCA officials recognized the particularly erotic power of West's taboo association with racial difference, even as her character appeared to repudiate it. The scene in which Doll stabbed Chan Lo in self-defense had to be cut, and West's character had to atone, not only for killing him, but also implicitly for having accepted, however unwillingly, the relationship with him that led to her action.

It is only apparently a paradox that other prescribed cuts in *Klondike Annie*, predominantly of West's scenes with Victor McLaglen, worked to emphasize, rather than lessen, West/Doll's status as a prostitute. In conceding that her choices are strictly limited ("between two evils," as this plays out in the narrative), Doll embodies rather realistically the circumstances of a woman who must trade on her sexuality for survival. This contrasts with West's earlier characters, who, although also cast at least implicitly as prostitutes, represent glamorous fantasy figures who themselves exploit and find pleasure in an economy of prostitution. Rather than generally diminishing the star's representation of sexuality in *Klondike Annie*, the censors' alterations and cuts only reduced and controlled depictions of the pleasure and power that West's character derived from her sexuality. It is evident that West's transgression lay not in her outlaw sexuality itself, but primarily in her unlimited control and enjoyment of it.

This argument contradicts those of film historians such as Andrew Bergman who suggest that the Production Code's goal of limiting the representation of prostitution directly related to the social circumstance of increased prostitution during the Depression and aimed primarily to downplay any realistic portrayal of women's economic desperation.[49] West's image as a lower-class woman who benefits substantially from the uninhibited exercise of her sexuality but subsequently neither adopts middle-class values nor repents her earlier behavior ruptured the myth of American democratic capitalism, in which everyone aspires to and may attain middle-class values and status. West's idealized prostitute figure represented the greater ideological challenge to middle-class political and economic hegemony, independent of any actual rise in prostitution during the Depression.

But even in its carefully monitored form, West's role and performance in *Klondike Annie* only compounded her previous violation of tenets of bourgeois ideology. As Breen had feared, the mere association of West's image with religious symbols had the effect for many viewers of satirizing Christianity as a masquerade and form of entertainment. West's presence in *Klondike Annie* evoked her established image not only through the much-monitored story and dialogue, but also through her usual ironic, self-conscious acting style. It became clear prior to the film's release that the star herself refused to adjust her performance or material to conform to parameters of bourgeois morality and taste to which the film industry as a whole now seemed willing to accede. The MPPDA thus failed in its apparent attempt to alter West's star image in *Klondike Annie*.

From the perspective of an industry that increasingly strove to depict bourgeois sexual morality and to embody conservative capitalism, continued promotion of West as a transgressively sexual woman seemed a threat to long-term legal and financial interests that surpassed her tangible worth as proven box-office commodity. Breen's reaction two days prior to the release of the film—"Just so long as we have Mae West on our hands . . . we are going to have trouble"—implied that the industry could and perhaps should work to reduce West's commodity value in order to disassociate itself from her function as sign. It is in this context that Hearst's campaign takes on special significance: whatever its immediate motivations may have been, the shift of the newspaper magnate's influence from his usual support of industry policy and practice to, on this occasion, the side of the reform forces worked as a public justification of a policy change already undertaken within the industry. The production and reception of *Klondike Annie* thus at once rendered and marked Mae West a liability, despite her continued status as major box-office asset. Whoever initiated the break and however indefinite the financial risk of continued association with West's image, Paramount's release of West from her contract in 1936 was an act of the studio's cutting its losses.

As an integral part of a capitalist economy under duress in the 1930s, the industry eagerly maximized its profits. But it also had a vested interest in maintaining the cultural norms that supported its hegemony. However assiduously it might exploit sex, Hollywood's own long-term interest did not lie in violating received notions of sexuality. Despite their apparently different aims, both the reform movement and the film industry simultaneously circumscribed and exploited female sexuality as a sign, and both worked to repress the resulting ideological contradictions. The primary opposition between the two perspectives lay in the proposed means and agents of control over female sexual representations, whether through industry self-regulation or state suppression. The challenge to Hollywood in the mid-1930s was thus to represent sexuality to economic advantage without offending fundamental precepts of the prevailing ideology.

By 1936, the film industry had joined the reform groups in believing that West's evident repudiation of sexual morality endangered their already weakened cultural and economic positions. Altered financial and managerial circumstances as well as public relations strategies in the film industry between 1932 and 1936 had resulted in changes in major studios' perception of how female sexuality might best be marketed. In contrast to Paramount's initial eager exploitation of West, by the time of the release of *Klondike Annie* in February 1936, not only her characteristic film roles but also her composite image and presence seemed too hedonistic, too narcissistic, too uncontrollable, too powerful, too expensive, altogether "too much" for the industry's long-term benefits. "Mae West" had initially proven a handy political icon as well as a profitable product, but the performer Mae West, who resisted attempts to curb both her real and iconographic power, now exceeded her usefulness to the leading media institutions that had helped create her as a sign.

4

Comedic Performance from Social
Satire to Self-Parody

Mae West's image provoked—and acted as a lightning rod for—cultural controversy in the 1930s because it articulated with broad ongoing public debates about social propriety and sexual representation. West's status as a *comedienne* heightened the controversies surrounding her films and other performances. Although social and genre conventions allow comedy a degree of deviance, media enterprises, government agencies, religious bodies, and educational organizations repeatedly disagreed over the permissible breadth of West's comedic license.

Representatives of these influential institutions made widely divergent assessments of West's comedy, from thinking it lighthearted, harmless spoofery to warning that its bawdiness seriously threatened public morals and social custom. The contradictory responses to West's performances exemplify a persistent fundamental disagreement about comedy's effects between those who believe that comedy permits social transgressions for collective psychic release, yet blunts the edge of such transgressions by casting them as "only a joke," and those who think that comedy can violate cultural or political norms to the point of effectively subverting such strictures.[1]

Dr. James Wingate evidently subscribed to the former position when, in 1932, as head of the MPPDA Studio Relations Committee, he emphasized that Paramount should ensure that *She Done Him Wrong* came across as a comedy, so that caricature would render West's potentially taboo material socially acceptable. Wingate prefaced his written response to Paramount's initial script for *She Done Him Wrong* with a cautionary remark:

> I am assuming that in making a picture of such a period and with such a background, you will develop the comedy elements, so that the treatment will invest the picture with such exaggerated qualities as automatically to take care of possible offensiveness.[2]

West herself claimed to have adopted her style of sexually suggestive humor early in her career to circumvent censorship of dramatic sexual material in her vaudeville acts and plays.[3] But Production Code Administration head Joseph Breen did not share his predecessor Wingate's or West's own opinion that comedic expression automatically excused or diffused social offense—at least not in her case. After witnessing censor board and public responses to West's vehicles from *She Done Him Wrong* to *Klondike Annie*, Breen concluded that the star's comedic performance exacerbated rather than ameliorated her potential to offend. As he noted in an internal PCA memo after *Klondike Annie* met a controversial reception despite his careful monitoring, West's verbal delivery and gesticulation could make any apparently innocent dialogue lubricious.[4] Breen's observation targeted West's primary verbal technique: double entendre, a style of punning that through context or voice tone imparts a sexual meaning to apparently neutral words. West's utterance of the word *loving* in *Klondike Annie* is an example: "I found him a good loving man on the trip." Several state censor boards eliminated the word or the entire line before approving the film's exhibition.

Reactions to West's 1937 performance on Edgar Bergen's radio program confirmed the star's ability to offend through verbal intonation alone. One newspaper article began its report on public response to the program with the line, "It wasn't what she said—it was the way she said it."[5] The program announcer introduced the "Adam and Eve" sketch as a "lighthearted travesty" by radio author Arch Oboler. Although other actors had previously performed the skit for national broadcast without objections, West's portrayal of Eve, as we have seen, provoked widespread public censure.[6]

In the skit, Eve/West appeals unsuccessfully to a languid and boring Adam (Don Ameche) to leave the Garden of Eden, which she finds a "dismal dump" that deprives her of opportunities to "develop [her] personality." She does, however, convince the reluctant serpent (Bergen) to wriggle up the forbidden tree to fetch an apple, which she artfully cooks into applesauce for Adam's supper. When after one bite the pair suddenly lands outside the Garden, Adam awakens to more than his previous interest in holding hands. The sound of kissing segues to a dramatic orchestral crescendo. "That," declares West, getting the skit's last word, "was the original *kiss*."

The ending replaces the story's usual moral, that Eve instigated the original *sin* by violating a divine edict against (sexual) knowledge, which led to all women's punishment through pain in childbirth and subjugation to men. Instead, West's Eve shows relief at escaping from an asexual "paradise" and gains adventure and sexual pleasure through her actions.

Telegrams and calls objecting to the program reportedly deluged radio stations and activist organizations, including the Legion of Decency; the National Council of Catholic Women threatened to boycott the show's sponsor, Chase and Sanborn coffee.[7] The broadcast's Sunday scheduling exacerbated the perceived offense: that the skit ridiculed the Bible and religious sentiment, even committed sacrilege. The reproach focused on West's performance as Eve; her sexually suggestive comedic exchange earlier in the program with dummy Charlie McCarthy (Bergen) elicited only mild criticism. The charges echoed and extended Hearst's condemnation of West's missionary disguise in *Klondike Annie*. But just as Hearst's denunciation had enhanced box office for that film, Bergen's program ratings rose due to West's appearance.[8]

The critical dilemma implicit in Breen's and Wingate's divergent assessments of West's comedic impact in the 1930s remains an issue in retroactive evaluations of the star's cultural functions: Just how socially or politically radical was West's comedy at any given time? Or, by contrast, how thoroughly entrenched in American entertainment conventions? To the extent that West's comedy offers satire or parody, what, or whom, might it satirize or parody? And what are the effects of the star's parodying herself?

Censorship history documents social concerns about West's comedic performances in specific contexts, but it cannot account for her comedy's more felicitous reception or for shifts in her performances and in audience responses to those over the course of her career. Censorship of West's radio and later television performances eased as sexual mores and broadcast standards changed in the United States. West's guest appearance in 1964 on the CBS situation comedy *Mister Ed*, broadcast Sunday evenings, roused no censorship despite its hinting at sexual transgressions, including West's prurient interest in the program's title character, a horse.

This chapter demonstrates that the effects of West's comedy shifted with its dominant mode and media, from the social satire in her 1930s films to her radio parodies to her self-parodic television performances such as that on *Mister Ed*. I argue that no single approach to comedy, but only a synthesis of perspectives—genre specific, historical, psychoanalytic, and feminist—can adequately elucidate how West's comedy contributed to her variable functions as an American cultural icon. An initial analysis of West's comedic techniques brings insight to the variable social impact and potential psychoanalytic force of her comedy.

The Impact of Verbal Humor

The scandal around West's Eve led to a long-standing unofficial ban against the star on network radio. It was a dozen years before she next appeared on NBC, in January 1950 on Perry Como's *Chesterfield Supper Club*, playing a parodic Juliet to the host's "Comeo." A report in *Newsweek* emphasized that her guest appearance was West's first "crack" at network radio since her performance on Bergen's show had "created a furor the likes of which have never since disturbed the airways." The article noted that West had been at her best on the Como program in a script "with all possible blue bleached out" but, "had she overstepped, there was the saving grace of tape recording" enabling censorship of the program before its broadcast.[9] Her appearance drew such popular response that Como's show scheduled her again within the year. On her second visit she played an assertive, smart-talking "Little Red Riding Hood" to the host's wolf.[10]

West's comedic performances enjoyed sustained popularity and also long retained the capacity to shock portions of her audiences. Much of West's comedic appeal—like that of comedy more generally—derived precisely from her violating social mores in performance, even to the point of inviting censorship. Audience knowledge that West's performances had provoked censorship augmented her comic reception, for it alerted listeners and viewers to expect and catch possible sexual implications in almost every line and gesture. The threat of censorship enhanced, even yielded, the joke.

West adeptly exploited her reputation for "censorability." A musical number West recorded around 1935 titled "That's All, Brother" has a chorus of rhymed variations on the line "It's not what I say, it's the way that I say it" (that both leads to censorship *and* gets the laughs).[11] The song's opening verse, which West speaks in cabaret style to a jazzy accompaniment, wittily reprises West's reputation for evoking censorship:

> I've the tiniest confession
> I distinctly loathe suppression
> Since I only have one life, I wanna live it
> While I've clowned around a lot
> Well, I've found what hits the spot
> If I've something good to give,
> I wanna give it.
> Now those censors say I'm naughty and no dice
> But I've heard it said what's naughty *can* be nice.

The innuendo-laden lyrics go on to recount how West might elicit censorship for enacting Snow White, Red Riding Hood, and other traditional
female characters. West sings, for example, about how she might play Cin-
derella: "If they think a fairy prince can play games with me—that's all,
brother, that's all!" The final verse sets West's comedic performance
counter to conventional melodrama:

> They'd have me portray that maiden so sweet,
> That girlie with the mortgage due and little to eat
> But should I call the butcher boy to bring me some meat
> That's all, brother, that's all.[12]

For all its carnal implications, West's song was clearly "not all, brother," at
all, for West reaped many further stage, radio, recording, film and television engagements. She made her TV debut in a surprise vignette on the
1957 Academy Awards presentation show (in spring 1958); she and Rock
Hudson sang a duet of "Baby, It's Cold Outside" in a two-minute finale to
a musical medley.[13] West's first announced television role came a year
later, in May 1959 on NBC's Dean Martin Show. She engaged in witty repartee with Martin and fellow guest Bob Hope and sang with the host a duet
in "point style" (making spoken asides to lyrics). West was next scheduled
to open the 1959 season of the CBS television news series Person to Person.
Charles Collingwood conducted a fifteen-minute interview in West's Hollywood apartment that focused on the star's newly published autobiography, but the day before the scheduled airing, CBS executives in New York
"summarily jerked" the tape, which they found too risqué.[14] Daily and
trade press writers who had previewed the program argued that West's performance typified her style and would not have harmed viewers, particularly given its planned 10:30 p.m. broadcast. Cecil Smith, Los Angeles
Times entertainment editor, cited extensive passages from the interview:

> Asked about her new book, "Goodness Had Nothing to Do With It," the
> 64-year-old actress answered: "It's about my private transgressions—that's a
> long word for sin." Asked if she is interested in foreign affairs, she said:
> "I've always had a weakness for foreign affairs." Asked if she had any
> advice for teen-agers, she said, "Mmm—grow up."
>   Asked if her famous line "Come up and see me sometime," had brought
> a rash of visitors, she said, "I'll say. I had to install two steel doors. Now I
> suppose someone will come up with a blowtorch."
>   And she repeated a number of maxims that she has made famous, such
> as "it's not the men in my life that count, but the life in my men."[15]

West showed up on CBS six months later, on 1 March 1960 on *The Red Skelton Show*.[16] The program's dialogue made humorous reference to the canceled *Person to Person* episode, and West enacted an extended parody of the banned interview. Some of West's remarks in the mock interview seem rather outrageous for U.S. prime time network broadcasting even now:

INTERVIEWER: How about a real exclusive for our television audience. Could we hear about the men who *don't* appear in your book?
MAE WEST: You mean the men that was taken out of the book? Ooh, stand by, we're about to start a telethon.
[Audience laughter]
INTERVIEWER: Miss West, I simply meant we'd like to hear about some of the unusual men—the men who were offbeat.
WEST: Well, a smart girl never beats off any man.
[Audience laughter]

In a paradox typical of American mass entertainment, the *Person to Person* spoof appeared on the very network that refused to broadcast the original interview, within months of the cancellation and at an earlier hour of transmission. Judging from the entertainment writers' reports, the canceled interview contained no Westian pun as vivid or raunchy as her quip on *Red Skelton* about women "beating off" men. CBS producers—who could have pulled or censored the pre-recorded program—likely found that Skelton's status as comedian justified a latitude in social decorum for his program not considered appropriate on the interview show.

West's comedy thus rested squarely on an institutional base and drew on well-established cinematic and comedic techniques, including the mark of "censorability." On Skelton's program, the host made frequent jokes about "the censor," addressing him as an off-screen character. At program's end, a man's desperate yelp offstage, followed by a thud at his apparent collapse, confirmed the character's hovering but ineffectual presence. Yet despite the circumscription of West's comedic performances within genre conventions, they—and she—did repeatedly offend social and religious sensibilities beyond the degree allowed in American movies and radio in the 1930s and 1940s and on television in the 1950s.[17] The unusual narrative and visual structuring of West's films, compared with other Hollywood-produced comedies of the period, can begin to account for her comedy's impact, both its popularity and its capacity to offend.

Straight Men and Comedic Butts

Acting styles, dialogue, and humorous visual and aural juxtapositions in West's 1930s films marked them generically as comedies. In keeping with her dual roles as star and author, West always clearly holds the position of central comedic figure. West delivers virtually all of the punch lines in the dialogue and also perpetrates a range of physical and other visual gags in her films. West's exaggerated stride and her gesture of rolling her eyes upward, often while patting her hair with one hand, are characteristic (and subsequently much-caricatured) techniques in her physical comedy. A few films feature West performing a physical comedy style that approaches slapstick. In *Goin' to Town* (1935), West shoots the hat off a man whose attention her character is seeking, but who has been disdainful of her, aristocrat Edward Carrington (Paul Cavanagh). When the ploy fails to evoke the desired response, West/Borden lassoes Carrington from astride her horse and pulls him to her, releasing him only when she is satisfied that she has sufficiently impressed him.

Visual comedy created through cinematography and editing in West's films also centers on the star. In a montage between narrative sequences in *I'm No Angel*, a medium shot opens on West's bejeweled hands patting a photograph of her character Tira's most recent male conquest. The camera pans to follow her arm placing the photo next to a deer figurine, then tilts down to reveal further shelves laden with figurines and correlated portraits. A framed picture of the boss of the carnival for which she has worked, who has been revealed to be stingy and sneaky, stands adjacent to a glass skunk; that of Tira's jealous former lover, a pickpocket, is paired with a porcelain snake. Carnivalesque music featuring a tuba accompanies the sequence. The scene bears a double comedic suggestion: first, that West has collected the men in the pictures en route to attaining her current monied status, just as she has collected the glass menagerie that typifies them; second, that those men are all readily reducible to beasts.

One might conclude that this visual joke makes West/Tira the object or "butt" of humor as a heartless gold digger, tantamount to a prostitute, who promiscuously exercises her sexual appeal and performance for financial gain. But another potential reading of the scene construes West's behavior as a satiric challenge to the social bias against women's frequently changing sexual partners. From this perspective, the cinematic joke ridicules not primarily West, but rather the men depicted as animals, whom she has adroitly exploited. Given West's central, sympathetic role in the film's nar-

rative and her powerful star image, the joke arguably targets the men pic-
tured for their arrogance and naïveté in attempting to possess West by
showering her with money and goods—only to be displaced by the next
higher bidder.

In delivering almost all of the visual as well as the verbal jokes in her
films, West in effect narrates her comedies. Biographers George Eells and
Stanley Musgrove describe how West successfully prevented director
Henry Hathaway from making her figure the literal butt of visual jokes in
Go West, Young Man (1936). Adapted from a popular Broadway play of the
period, *Personal Appearance*, this film differed from previous West vehicles
in extensively developing secondary characters and in making West's character, a temperamental movie star called Mavis Arden, unsympathetically
vain and egocentric. Hathaway had planned a sequence that intercut shots
of West's swaying walk with shots of jiggling tassels on a lamp shade and
another that called for West to walk away from the camera leading a bull
dog, to be followed with a cutaway to the dog's behind. In interviews,
Hathaway reported West's response: "Nobody gets laughs in my pictures
but me, see?" The shots were not taken.[18]

As the flush of West's first movie successes faded, reviewers became increasingly critical of her dominance of the films' narratives and comic dialogue. Critics sometimes hinted that West was narcissistic and selfish as a
performer for claiming the star comedic position, as did the 23 April 1935
review of *Goin' to Town* in the *Hollywood Reporter*: "Madame West gives
herself the cream of the crap [sic] in lines, and what remains is left for the
others to make the best of." Such criticism targets West's use of a dominant comedic pattern: a dialogue exchange between two actors, often a
star and a supporting performer who plays the "straight man," setting up
jokes for the star, who delivers the punch lines.

In West's comedies, performers cast as servants or other figures who do
not sexually interest her character usually fulfill the straight-man role. In
Goin' to Town, the opportunistic and unscrupulous Russian gigolo Ivan
plays West's straight man as he tries to seduce her character, Cleo Borden,
to get at her fortune. Cleo sees through his ruse and acts dismissively toward him, which Ivan takes as an insult:

IVAN: Let me tell you I am an aristocrat and the backbone of my
family!
CLEO/WEST: Your family should see a chiropractor!

The star's retort undercuts the suitor's social boasting by twisting his backbone metaphor into a description of his crooked character. At the same time, West/Cleo displays wit in her quick thinking and wisdom in recognizing Ivan's deceit through his smooth words and manners.

This exchange typifies West's use of a straight man and also the tone of her comedic film dialogue, much of which—counter to her reputation—makes *no* sexual suggestion. Especially West's early film performances contain many puns and verbal quips that express hostility rather than sexual interest. For example, in *I'm No Angel* (1933), when the skunk of a circus boss tells West/Tira, "I've changed my mind," she retorts, "Does it work any better?" In that film's lion-taming scene, West uses her unusual straight man to aggressive rather than evidently sexual comedic effect when she remarks to an uncooperative male lion: "You'll end up a rug!" (See Figure 37 for a still from that scene.)

Among the characters who play West's straight men are Ace Lamont (John Miljan) in *Belle of the Nineties* (1934):

ACE LAMONT (embracing West/Ruby Carter as the two are framed together in a medium long shot): Ruby, I must have you! Your golden hair, your fascinating eyes, alluring smile, your lovely arms, your form divine!
WEST/RUBY (looking down his body, then pushing him away): Wait a minute, wait a minute! Is this a proposal, or are you taking inventory?

Jeff Badger (Joseph Calleia), one of West's would-be suitors in *My Little Chickadee* (1940), plays a similar role (although viewers know that in his secret role as the Masked Bandit, West/Flower Belle Lee reciprocates his interest in her):

JEFF BADGER (framed in medium close up two-shot with West/Flower Belle, whom he has just met in his saloon, speaking in a husky voice): Is there anything I can do for you?
WEST/BELLE (facing camera, looking him over): Yeah, you can get out of my way!

W. C. Fields, West's costar in *My Little Chickadee*, also plays straight man to her in the few scenes the two share. In one scene, Fields's character, Cuthbert J. Twillie, has insinuated himself into her hotel suite:

FIELDS/TWILLIE: There's something sweet and dainty about a lady's boudoir.

WEST/BELLE: How do you know? . . .

FIELDS/TWILLIE: Why, the latest etiquette books are just full of such knowledge!

WEST/BELLE: Oh, for a second I thought I heard the voice of experience.

Female characters also serve as West's "straight men." In *Klondike Annie*, the character Tess (Lucille Webster Gleason) sets up West's line, "When choosing between two evils, I generally pick the one I've never tried before." Frequently, actors playing maids to West's characters double as straight men. By the end of *I'm No Angel*, West/Tira has gained four maids, all African American (see Figure 20). As they tend to her toilet, she engages in witty repartee with them, comparing her own and their interests in men. In one scene, two of the maids sing and dance along in chorus to West's lead. The maids deviate from Hollywood's stereotype of the "mammy" through the suggestion in that burst of energy and in comedic dialogue with West that they are sexual and have autonomous lives beyond grooming white people. The maid played by Libby Taylor (and called Libby in the film) exchanges the following lines with West:

LIBBY: I've been married four times!

WEST/TIRA: You ought to do well in the wholesale business!

West's interactions with minor African American and other characters marked as "not white" exceeded that of other white stars in early 1930s films, both in the length of the star's exchanges with the supporting actors and in the subjects the dialogue addressed. But these comedic exchanges fall far short of realizing a progressive racial politics. As I discussed in chapter 1, the maids clearly augment West's featured—and fetishized— status, enhancing the star's aura of power and sexual allure through their roles as servants and through their vividly contrasting visual presence, their dark skin, hair, and costumes setting off West's shimmering bleached-blonde whiteness. Playing "straight men" fits within these black female actors' services for West.

Furthermore, some of West's lines in banter between mistress and maid take the African American characters as the butts of jokes, implying, in keeping with racial stereotypes in other 1930s Hollywood films, that they are lazy, ignorant, and untrustworthy. Several of West's joking remarks especially to Pearl (Louise Beavers) in *She Done Him Wrong* and Jasmine

(Libby Taylor) in *Belle of the Nineties* belittle those characters' level of education or sense of responsibility, as in the following exchange from the latter film:

JASMINE: Wasn't you just a little nervous when [Mr. Brooks] gave you
all those presents?
WEST/RUBY: Why no. I was calm and collected. [Jasmine laughs.] There
was no reason for 'im giving me all those wonderful presents. I don't
know him much better than I know Shakespeare.
JASMINE: Shakespeare . . . I don't remember any Mr. Shakespeare
calling on you.
WEST/RUBY: (smiling) That was before you came with me.
JASMINE: Oh, I see.

The exchange not only sets up West's much-quoted quip, "I was
calm—and collected," but also gives her the opportunity to appear comparatively educated despite her overall working class or even *déclassé*
standing in the film. Libby Taylor/Jasmine's lines confirm the star's glow-
ing superiority and also allow her to display a liberal good nature. A production still for the film showing West and Taylor together off the set, with
a caption noting that the latter is "the blonde star's on- *and* off-screen
maid" (Figure 21), further inscribes West as white and powerful and yet
beguilingly—and amusingly—"different," through her hierarchical juxtaposition with Taylor.

But joke exchanges that ridicule the maid characters are mercifully in-
frequent in West's films. Instead, these figures generally facilitate West's
delivery of punch lines that play on words referring to her own character
("I was calm and *collected*") or that express aggression toward characters
not present in these scenes. For example, West quips to Jasmine, who has
mentioned West/Ruby Carter's villainous suitor Ace Lamont: "His mother
should have thrown him away and kept the stork!"

Indeed, in all West's films her verbal barbs are aimed predominantly at
male characters, whether these appear in the comedic scene or not. In *I'm
No Angel*, West's comically formulated verbal hostility targets an array of
male figures: a traveling businessman who responds to her character's gold-
digging ploys; the carnival boss; two former lovers; her lawyer Benny
Pinkowitz (Gregory Ratoff), played as an immigrant uncle stereotype (Jewish and possibly also gay); the lion; and a judge. The degrees of hostility
the jokes express range from mild and affectionate (for the lawyer) to quite
pronounced (against the two lovers she has left).

A snobbish upper-class woman, Alicia Hatton (Gertrude Michael), is
the only female character repeatedly made the humorous butt in that film.
Alicia goes to warn Tira away from her fiancé, who has fallen for Tira:

ALICIA: It might refresh you to know that I'm Kirk Lawrence's fiancée.
WEST/TIRA: Nothing refreshing about that!

After West/Tira has thrown Alicia out, the star calls to her maid the
much-quoted (and supposedly ad-libbed) remark, "Beulah, peel me a
grape!" In context, the apparently nonsensical remark asserts Tira's class
standing and power to command, compared with Alicia's (and also, obliquely, Beulah's). With the important exception of the African American
maids, the only female characters West ridicules are snobbish society
women (besides Alicia, society leader Mrs. Crane Brittany and friends in
Goin' to Town) and, in later films, morally righteous meddlers like Mrs.
Gideon (Margaret Hamilton) in My Little Chickadee. The jokes aimed at
the upper-class women contribute to the recurrent narrative trajectory of
West's films (and of many American films especially in the 1930s) that
celebrates the ideal of ever-increasing wealth and status while simultaneously taking a populist view criticizing the exclusivity, intolerance, and
pretentious mannerisms associated with the upper classes.

West's star status marked her as outstanding among a number of female
comedic performers in 1930s films. West's contemporaries in early sound
comedy (e.g, Fannie Brice, Winnie Lightner, Charlotte Greenwood, and
Marie Dressler from vaudeville traditions; Jean Harlow in some roles,
Claudette Colbert, and Carole Lombard as original Hollywood stars) either did not approach West's stature as a movie star (Brice et al.) or did not
appear in comedienne-centered comedy (Harlow, Colbert, and Lombard),
as West did. Dressler, a top-grossing Hollywood star in her four early 1930s
sound comedies, offers a possible exception. But generally, only decades
later did star comediennes such as Gracie Allen and Lucille Ball manage to
attain a stature in popular culture comparable to West's, and then in television rather than in film.[19]

The bawdiness of West's humor and the frequency with which her comedic quips targeted male characters further distinguished her films from
the bulk of Hollywood comedies of the period. The early sound films featuring comediennes other than West generally situated them as comedic
butts and concluded in their narrative containment or defeat.[20] Most major stars of sound comedy through at least the 1940s (e.g., W. C. Fields,
Laurel and Hardy, the Marx Brothers) were male, and their jokes and gags

frequently denigrated whatever supporting female characters appeared. The gender inversion in West's comedy determined its capacity both to entertain and to shock, for her performances at once drew on and worked against conventions of classical Hollywood cinema.

The Comedienne's Gaze

Rather than earnestly enacting a character role, Mae West always played herself. West signaled her star presence through her frequent direct address to the film audience. Derived from vaudeville and stage traditions, West's direct verbal and sometimes also visual address (looking at the camera) made her the primary narrative voice within her films. Not only does each film narrative make West's character central, but "Mae West" also relates each tale through her "trademark" dialogue and gestural style. As I have noted, some film critics disapproved of her films' using secondary characters and plot developments primarily to motivate her comedic star turns and weave them into apparent stories.

Particularly West's verbal style emphasized her star presence and central narrative position in films and other performances. Her complex, witty wordplay, the tone of her singing and speaking voice, her dominance in dialogue exchanges, and her pacing, including her "ums" and "ahs," all communicated intelligence, confidence, and control.[21] It was these verbal characteristics, in conjunction with her image as a highly sexual and powerful woman, that led film reviewers, Breen, and the star herself to assert, "It's the *way* that she says it." West's direct address communicates irony by foregrounding the presence of a performer enacting a character, as her exaggerated gestures also mark the performance as comedic. West's technique of playing to the film audience was far from unique, for direct address is a well-established convention of "comedian comedy." But in the 1930s and 1940s, West enjoyed exceptional status as a star comedienne who acted in a self-referential comedic style, repeatedly drawing attention to herself as a known performer and celebrity.[22] West's promotion in film publicity and the opening credits as author of her own stories further underscored her status as narrator of, as well as within, her films.

West's films employ devices common to classical Hollywood cinema (e.g., shot/reverse shot editing, presentation of female star as spectacle) that establish in the leading man or men a male-identified position that at least partially fixes "the male gaze."[23] As star and performer, West clearly holds the camera's and the audience's gaze; in many scenes, particularly as

Figure 1. "*Practice Safe Sex.*" *Charles Pierce impersonates Mae West on a 1987 greeting card; the punch line printed inside reads, "Call me when you're through practicing." Reprinted with permission of West Graphics, South San Francisco.*

Figure 2. Newsphoto taken on 10 February 1927, after the police raid of Sex and playwright and star Mae West's arraignment on charges of indecency. An evidently happy entourage of ten men surrounds West as she leaves the court after paying her $1,000 bail. Reprinted with special permission of King Features Syndicate.

Figure 3. *Mae West with burlesque performer Texas Guinan, ca. 1928.*

Figure 4. *Publicity still of Mae West, ca. 1932 (around the time of the production of Night after Night). After West signed a star contract with Paramount, her makeup and hairstyle changed, and soon more glittery and usually more opaque fabrics replaced the see-through net that she fleshily flashes in this photograph.*

Figure 5. Paramount publicity still of West for She Done Him Wrong (1933). The period chair lends the bejeweled figure a "touch of class," compared with the previous illustration.

Figure 6. Paramount publicity photograph of West for She Done Him Wrong, printed as cover for News-Week, 7 July 1934. Although West wears the same costume in Figure 5, her bold display of her breasts reasserts the "barroom" aura in her image. Copyright 1934, Newsweek, Inc. All rights reserved. Reprinted by permission.

Figure 7. *Publicity still of West performing her "Easy Rider" number in* She Done Him Wrong *(1933). Edith Head designed this and other of West's costumes in the film, and thereby launched her movie costume designing career.*

Figure 8. *Publicity still from* I'm No Angel *(1933). When Cary Grant's character "comes up to see" West as Tira, the lion tamer, to request she not pursue his engaged cousin, he himself falls into her web. Travis Banton designed West's "spider woman" costume.*

Figure 9. (facing page, top) *Publicity still of Mae West as spider in 1890s-style opening number, "My American Beauty," in* Belle of the Nineties *(1934).*

Figure 10. (facing page, bottom) *Publicity still of West as bat in "My American Beauty" number.*

Figure 11. (facing page) *Publicity still of West as Statue of Liberty in finale of* "My American Beauty" *number in* Bell of the Nineties. *This image, which critic George Nathan dubbed* "Statue of Libido," *circulates as a postcard.*

Figure 12. (right) *Still of West as Ruby Carter on stage in the New Orleans Sensation House, in* Belle of the Nineties.

Figure 13. Mae West in Goin' to Town (1935), *performing the role of Delilah in the opera* Samson and Delilah.

Figure 14. *Publicity still of West for* The Heat's On *(1943). West does not wear this costume in the finished film.*

Figure 15. *One of a series of Paramount photos of West in her apartment in the Ravenswood Building on Rossmore Avenue in Los Angeles, released as publicity for* Belle of the Nineties. *This photograph appeared in the* Los Angeles Times *on Sunday, 22 December 1935.*

Figure 16. *Paramount publicity shot of West in her bedroom, 1934.*

Figure 17. *West posing at home in her Ravenswood apartment, probably in the late 1960s, when she was in her mid-seventies. The framed painting above West shows her at a younger age.*

Figure 18. West as Ruby Carter performs "St. Louis Blues" *in* Belle of the Nineties, *accompanied by Duke Ellington and His Orchestra.*

Figure 19. *Frame enlargement from* Belle of the Nineties *(directed by Leo McCarey, 1934). West sings a hymnlike number as her face appears over a black church revival meeting set along the Mississippi River. The sound track mixes West's song with the African American performers' spiritual.*

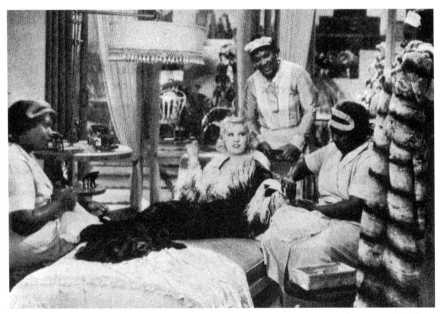

Figure 20. *Frame enlargement from* I'm No Angel *(1933). Mae West as the one-time honky-tonk queen receives the attentions of four African American maids, evidence that she's now a lady, as her primary maid, Beulah, assures her. The three women on the right are (from left to right) Libby Taylor (Libby), Hattie McDaniel (unnamed and uncredited in the film), and Gertrude Howard (Beulah). The actress on the left is not identified or credited in the film.*

Figure 21. Publicity shot of West with Libby Taylor (right) and hairdresser Maybelle McCarey, on the set of Belle of the Nineties. *The suggested caption pasted on the back of the photograph reads, in part, "Libby Taylor, the blonde star's on-and-off-the-screen maid, adds her usual joviality to the situation."*

Figure 22. West and Harold Huber (playing Chan Lo) in *Paramount publicity still for* Klondike Annie (1936).

Figure 23. *Paramount publicity still of West and men cast as Chinese musicians in Chan Lo's club in San Francisco's Chinatown, in Klondike Annie's opening number "I'm an Occidental Woman in an Oriental Mood for Love."*

Figure 24. *Paramount publicity still, dated 1936, of West standing in her wardrobe area with a woman identified as "her maid Daisy."*

Figure 25. *Press photograph of West with Chalky Wright, a boxer who worked as West's chauffeur in 1935 (and was rumored to be her lover).*

Figure 26. *Paramount publicity photo of West's chauffeur Chalky Wright with Harry Dean, impersonating West, and Jack Southard of the Los Angeles District Attorney's Office, after West had received a threat of extortion (dated 11 October 1935).*

Figure 27. *Charles Butterworth as Graves the butler in* Every Day's a Holiday *(1938).*

Figure 28. *One of a series of publicity photographs for* Belle of the Nineties *showing West holding a variety of firearms, including a machine gun. The studio's suggested caption for this photo reads:* "TAKE YOUR CHOICE: *Mae West, blonde Paramount star, getting ready for her next picture, 'It Ain't No Sin,' chooses the heavy pistol. Since she was held up and robbed, she's taking no chances and is shown here with Jack Criss, assistant chief of the gangster bureau, Los Angeles District Attorney's office, on the police rifle range."*

Figure 29. (right) *Publicity photograph of West with McCarey during the production of* Belle of the Nineties.

Figure 30. (below, right) *Publicity photograph of West with cinematographer Karl Struss during the production of* Belle of the Nineties. *The following suggested caption appears on the back of the photo:* "THE BUSINESS END—Hollywood's one-woman production staff—Mae West, the Paramount blonde siren whose box office records have established new highs in the sinema thermometer—takes a peek at a scene through one of the cameras trained on her in her new starring drama of the Naughty Nineties, 'It Ain't No Sin.' Karl Struss, one of Hollywood's ace cameramen, in charge of the photographic task of transferring Mae's action and curves on celluloid, is giving Mae a tip of the angle to put on her charms. Aside from her camera interest, Mae writes her own stories, knows her costume designing, and can do a bit of directing when necessary."

Figure 31. *Publicity still for* Belle of the Nineties, *with the following suggested caption:* "ONE-WOMAN PRODUCTION STAFF IN ACTION—*Here's Mae West, who writes her own stuff as well as transferring the lines to film, dictating some of her famous lines between scenes of her new starring drama of the Naughty Nineties, 'It Ain't No Sin.' Nesta Charles, script girl, is transcribing the Westian dialogue that will become as well-known in Chinese as Mae's native Brooklynese. Aside from her writing and acting abilities, Mae knows her camera angles, has her hand in costume designing, and can lend a directorial touch when necessary.*"

Figure 32. *Publicity still for* Belle of the Nineties. *The suggested caption reads:* "CENSORSHIP ON THE SPOT —*Mae West's Paramount pictures—representative of curves and affairs of the heart—nevertheless pack a laugh with every situation, and Mae's behind it all. She has her eye on censorship as closely as any producer and is in a huddle on one of the sequences of her new Naughty Nineties drama, 'It Ain't No Sin,' with a man whose entire duties consist of nipping objectional screen material in the bud. He is John Hammell, right, former theater owner and Paramount's censorship expert for the past seven years. On the left is Boris Petroff, Mae's dramatic advisor.*"

Figure 33. (above) *Scene from* She Done Him Wrong (1933), *with West as Lady Lou being introduced to Serge (Gilbert Roland) under the watchful eye of Russian Rita (Rafaela Ottiano) and Gus Jordan (Noah Beery Sr.).*

Figure 34. (below) *Scene from* She Done Him Wrong *where West/Lady Lou tends to the would-be suicide Sally (Rochelle Hudson), brought to her room by Spider Kane (Dewey Robinson) and Steak McGarry (Harry Wallace).*

Figure 35. (above) *Publicity still of West as "the San Francisco Doll" and Victor McLaglen as Captain Bull Brackett in* Klondike Annie *(1936).*

Figure 36. (below) *Publicity still of Mae West/Doll masquerading as "Soul-Savin' Annie," discussing the limits on her options with her friend Tess (Lucille Webster Gleason).*

Figure 37. *Publicity still of West as Tira the lion tamer in* I'm No Angel *(1933). West claims in her autobiography really to have worked with the lions, despite Paramount's anxiety about her safety.*

Figure 38. *Photo illustrating a 29 February 1964* TV Guide *article about West's guest appearance on the television situation comedy* Mister Ed. *West supervises the horse's bubble bath at the hands of two grooms. Photo by Gene Trindl, reprinted with permission.*

Figure 39. *"Mae West, Hollywood." West reenacted her pose as the "Statue of Libido" in* Belle of the Nineties *(Figure 11) for photographer Terry O'Neill in 1970. Like the 1934 image it cites, this photograph circulates as a postcard that is available in many gay-oriented memorabilia and card shops. Photo copyright Terry O'Neill, reprinted with permission.*

Figure 40. *Publicity still of West as Mavis Arden and Randolph Scott as Bud in* Go West, Young Man *(1936).*

Figure 41. *Barbershop quartet (Irving Bacon, Allan Rogers, Otto Fries, and John "Skins" Miller) performing "Flutterby, Butterfly" in the opening scene of* Every Day's a Holiday *(1938).*

Figure 42. *West as Peaches O'Day in* Every Day's a Holiday, *disguised and performing onstage as Mademoiselle Fifi.*

$25,000 PER WEEK WORTH OF SEX-APPEAL

THERE'S an old Polynesian saying which, literally translated, goes something like this: "One ounce of sex-appeal is worth a pound of beauty." How true, how true! Consider the all-time Hollywood favorites, those perennials whose names are the pass keys to the world of pure excitement: Bara, Bow, Garbo, Harlow, Turner, Gardner and possibly (only time will tell) Monroe. The ladies are remembered or are today riding high not for their acting abilities or inabilities but for their undiluted basic appeal. With the exception of Ava they are something less than beautifu With Ava included they all pack a terrif female wallop on the screen. Off the scree may or may not be a different matter. Hearsa made Cleopatra sizzle—in fact she may hav been colder than a fish head at dawn.

CONTINUED NEXT PAG

Figure 43. *"Puff piece" about West rehearsing her act at the Las Vegas Sahara Hotel with "Mr. America" Dick Dubois, in the December 1954 issue of* Nite O'Day, *a monthly "amusement parade and talent guide" published by the now-defunct Hollywood Musical and Theatrical Club.*

And so it is that Mae West of "come-up-and-see-me-some-time" fame is still able, after more years than most women will count, to command $25,000 a week and the attention of any man who prefers to wear pants.

The photographs on these pages of West and "Mr. America" Dick Dubois, were snapped during rehearsal for her now famous act at the Sahara Hotel in Las Vegas. The supporting cast included eight professional dancers, as many muscle men and Louise Beavers. Typical of the gags Mae tells as the boys crowd around her, "Take it easy—you'll blow your candelabra!"

Figure 44. Nite O'Day *photo layout of West with Dick Dubois.*

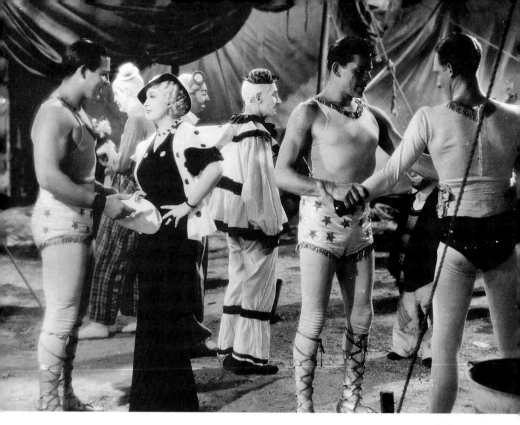

Figure 45. West as Tira, the "honky-tonk" dancer and lion tamer in I'm No Angel *(1933), conversing with the carnival's aerialists (those in star-decorated shorts are played by Nat Pendleton and Harry Schultz).*

Figure 46. Publicity photo (distributed in the late 1980s as a postcard) from Belle of the Nineties *(1934) showing West as Ruby Carter looking at the "Tiger Kid" (Roger Pryor), a former (and future) paramour to whom she gives drugged water in this scene to ensure that he loses the boxing match.*

Figure 47. *West at age eighty-six as Marlo Manners, a bride for the sixth time, in* Sextette *(1978). The chorus of men surrounding her are cast as hotel bellhops who welcome their guest by dancing and singing "Hooray for Hollywood!"*

Figure 48. *Paramount publicity photo of West with Marlene Dietrich, ca. 1936 (West wearing a costume from* Klondike Annie*).*

West performs on stage, the film's editing makes her the "object of the gaze" not only for the male characters and extras, but also for supporting female characters who regard West with rapt attention.

The opening sequence in *Belle of the Nineties* provides an example. The film cuts back and forth between West posing in the spotlight on stage and the admiring assemblage, including her current lover, the Tiger Kid. (Figures 9-11 show West on stage in this scene.) But no one male character functions through the course of the film as an identificatory position, fixing the gaze of desire. After West's character Ruby Carter leaves for New Orleans, Tiger disappears from the narrative for an extended time; when he reappears, initially to cooperate with the villain, Ace Lamont (whose point of view we do not generally experience), the film invites the audience to gaze with West's character at her lover, rather than vice versa (see Figure 46).

West's characters often narratively motivate a cinematically structured visual focus on male characters. West's character first sees the men that Cary Grant plays in *She Done Him Wrong* and *I'm No Angel* and takes an active role in pursuing romances with them. In *Goin' to Town*, West calls audience attention to the aristocrat who becomes her character's primary romantic interest by commenting, before his figure has been introduced on screen, "Ah, English, eh? I thought that body looked imported!" In her first scene with him, West wears trousers as she rides a horse out to see him working on her oil rigs. He first appears in medium shot from behind, leaning over a forge. West/Cleo calls out "Hey, handsome!" to attract his attention—unsuccessfully, for he finds her behavior crude. It is then that she ropes him and pulls him to her. Only near the end of the film, in the scene in which West performs the operatic role of Delilah, does this object of female narrative desire finally fix his own gaze on the star.

In place of a singular male gaze structured by an Oedipal narrative pattern that Laura Mulvey, Stephen Heath, and others, drawing on Roland Barthes's work, have posited dominates classical Hollywood cinema, a complex system of multiple gazes operates in West's films.[24] The effect derives both from West's central position in the films as a character continually narrating her own desire and from her ironic, excessively theatrical style. Playing directly, through the camera, to the anticipated audience in the movie theater, West in effect returns its gaze.

West also *audially* counters the gaze of the audience, positioned as voyeurs of the cinematic spectacle, from her position as recognized narrator (author/star) of each film's humorous dialogue. In frequently setting up

male characters as targets of her joking dialogue, West's performances direct aggression toward those audience members (male and female) who
might identify with those figures or who are otherwise sutured by conventions of classical Hollywood cinema into a male-identified spectator position. West's performances invert the usual gender associations in the look's
structuring in terms of sadistic and masochistic implications.[25] Despite the
star's exhibitionism—which psychonanalytic theory associates with
masochism—West expresses *aural* dominance along with the visual dominance she achieves through the excessive spectacle centered on her body,
which draws and directs the audience's vision.

West usually punctuates her gesture of looking at primary male characters (both when initiating a gaze and when returning the gazes she has
sought from them) with a comedic quip. The correlation of sight and
sound secures West's position as narrator and encourages active viewer
identification with her. In comprehending and enjoying West's comedy,
the viewer or listener must accept the female lead as speaking subject and
also perceive the predominantly male targets of her jokes as "other," a
position usually signified by the female figure. West's performance thus
structures a viewer/listener seeking active/sadistic (rather than passive/
masochistic) pleasure to identify *not* with the male object of West's desire
and/or aggression, but rather with West herself as desiring subject. The
films also invite viewer identification with the narrational process, which
I have argued inheres in West as recognized narrator/author and star. But
West's films deviate most strikingly and consistently from the classical
Hollywood narrative model in the way her comedic dialogue structures
gender identification.

Cinematic Jokes and Sexual Difference

Despite the misfit that I have begun to point out between West's films and
the Oedipal narrative model that psychoanalytic film theories discover in
classical Hollywood films, Sigmund Freud's work *Jokes and Their Relation to
the Unconscious*, first published in 1905, brings insights into the social and
psychological impact of West's comedy in the 1930s.[26] The circulation of
snippets from West's movie dialogue as colloquial jokes (repeatedly cited
in newspapers, radio, television, and books of West's witticisms) attests to
the relative narrative autonomy of these comedic quips and warrants their
analysis in terms of Freud's analysis of jokes.[27] West herself frequently cited

her film dialogue in radio and television interviews or other performances.[28] Like the vaudevillian she had been, West used material repeatedly and knew how to anchor her jokes to her image, rather than to an
individual routine that another performer might steal, just as she herself
stole many gags and lines from others and incorporated them into her performances.

Freud's analysis of the purposes and pleasures of jokes focuses on what he
calls "tendentious" jokes, those which have a specific object (90). For
Freud, the primary manifestations of tendentious jokes are *hostile* jokes,
that "serve the purpose of aggressiveness, satire or defense," and obscene or
smutty jokes, which serve the purpose of exposure (97). Freud also briefly
discusses *cynical* jokes, which disguise cynicisms about cultural institutions
(107), and a class of intellectual jokes, the *skeptical* (115), as further types
of tendentious jokes. Most comedic exchanges in West's films qualify in
Freud's terms as hostile or smutty jokes.

Freud proposes a triadic model for the psychodynamics in joke telling: a
narrator relates a joke about its *object* or butt to a *listener*, who presumably
laughs (54, 96ff). Interpreted as a paradigm for structured communication
rather than a literal description of interpersonal interactions, this triadic
model usefully elucidates how film comedies address their audiences. The
film enunciating the jokes functions as primary narrator, with the comedian or, in this case, comedienne narrating specific comedic moments. The
film spectator is the listener invited to join in the laughter at the butt(s) of
the film's (and comedic performer's) humor. Whereas the "straight men"
(and women) who facilitate West's joking narration represent onscreen listeners, the cinema audience members, whose enjoyment the film (and
West) seeks, make up the joke's actual listeners. This model can account
for the comedic impact of West's lines that qualify as hostile jokes as well
as of the smutty jokes for which she gained wider renown.

Freud asserts that a person telling a joke that takes as its butt an individual or human type (e.g., a member of a particular ethnic or other group)
expresses aggression toward that individual or group in a socially acceptable form: "Brutal hostility, forbidden by law, has been replaced by verbal
invective" (102). For Freud, social aggression arises from a "powerful in-
herited disposition to hostility" that in adults has usually become restrained through internalized social conventions; the hostile joke allows
the teller to express aggression in a form that *"will evade restrictions and
open sources of pleasure that have become inaccessible"* (102-3). The narrator

of a hostile joke simultaneously solicits a listener's compliance and plea-sure in an act of aggression; the listener becomes spectator to the aggres-sive act and can thus gain voyeuristic pleasure from the joke (97).

Discussing smutty jokes, Freud first distinguishes between those and what he calls simple smut. Rather than drawing attention to physical sexual difference or practice with an undisguised indecent remark, as smut does, the smutty joke refers to sex through allusion. And whereas the per-son whom a smutty exchange targets (and whom the narrator implicitly or explicitly wishes to seduce) is often present (e.g., a woman serving in a bar), the desired sexual object is usually absent at the telling of smutty jokes. Freud attributes the elaboration of smutty jokes out of simple smut, which only "the common people" tolerate, to the power of repressions aris-ing from "civilization and higher education" (99-101). He thus correlates the occurrence of smutty jokes with social class standing:

> [Jokes] make possible the satisfaction of an instinct (whether lustful or hostile) in the face of an obstacle that stands in its way. They circumvent this obstacle and in that way draw pleasure from a source which the obstacle had made inaccessible. The obstacle standing in the way is in reality nothing other than *women's* incapacity to tolerate undisguised sexuality, an incapacity correspondingly increased with a rise in the educational and social level. The *woman* who is thought of as having been present in the initial situation is afterwards retained as though she were still present, or in her absence her influence still has an intimidating effect on the men. (101; emphasis added)

Freud's analysis presumes not only class distinctions in the incidence of smut and smutty jokes, but also a strict delineation of gender behaviors: a sexually aggressive male and sexually submissive but repressed female, who is the original object of the smut.[29] But West's enunciation of smutty jokes clearly transgresses Freud's model of male narrator, male listener, and fe-male object of the joke. Paradoxically, the usefulness of Freud's analysis in understanding West's comedy arises precisely because her films contradict the master's assumptions about gender. The cultural significance of West's role as central subject and joke narrator lies, of course, not in its deviation from a psychiatric model, but in its violating the dominant social ideology that the model presumes. Judging from reactions to West's early film com-edies, the social strictures against women telling smutty jokes obtained as much for 1930s U.S. middle-class society as for the turn-of-the-century Vi-ennese bourgeoisie that Freud observed.

West's comedic film performances transgressed American social norms in the 1930s both because she was a woman telling smutty and hostile jokes and because those jokes took as their butts men attempting to assert their economic, physical, or sexual power over her. Women's expression of lust and social aggression, albeit masked in jokes, is no longer—if it ever was—as uncommon in industrialized Western societies as Freud apparently believed. Indeed, West's reception as a comedic performer and cultural icon has no doubt contributed to altering the patterns of middle-class social behavior that Freud noted.

Although West's performance invalidates the strict gender delineation of Freud's model, his analysis remains useful to understanding both the pleasure and the scandal her comedy occasioned, for, as Freud noted, some jokes express a will to opposition:

[T]endentious jokes are especially favored in order to make aggressiveness or criticism possible against persons in exalted positions who claim to exercise authority. The joke then represents a rebellion against that authority, a liberation from its pressure. (105)

From this perspective, West's numerous jokes against male (and occasional upper-class female) claimants to social authority may encode rebellion against the power that individual men and male-dominated institutions wield over women. This may well have been a source of pleasure in West's comedy for many viewers, particularly women and working-class audiences. But, not surprisingly, industry and state censorship targeted primarily West's *smutty* jokes, which targeted male characters (and audience members who might identify with them) as objects of her seductive powers. The conventional prerogative of males to draw attention to their sexual prowess and to make sexual overtures accompanies the "exalted position" men have categorically long enjoyed. West's smutty joking challenged this gender prerogative.

The individuals and institutions that objected to West evidently shared Freud's view that comedy can express rebellion—and believed that West's comedy could effect rebellion sufficient to undermine their social and religious values, especially the sanctity of marriage. Freud introduced the category of "cynical jokes" as a subclassification of tendentious jokes that take institutions, ideologies, and persons who represent these as objects of aggression (108-10). Marriage, Freud noted in 1905, is the institution that cynical jokes most often attack. Asserting that a single example suffices to make his point, Freud relates the following joke: "A wife is like an umbrella—sooner or later one takes a cab" (110). Freud's discussion of the

joke asserts an analogy he finds self-evident: because a man's wifely umbrella cannot repel a strong deluge of sexual desire, he on occasion under-
standably seeks shelter in a public conveyance.

One cynical joke about marriage in West's films also suffices to illustrate
how her comedy deviates from Freud's gendered model: the much-cited exchange in *She Done Him Wrong* in which Cummings (Cary Grant) asks
West/Lou, "Haven't you ever met a man that could make you happy?" and
she responds, "Sure, lots of times!" West's response takes the word "happy"
to allude to sexual rather than emotional satisfaction, and turns an apparent inquiry about her presumed search for an ideal husband into a celebration of promiscuous sexual gratification. The exchange works as a smutty
joke but also as a cynical joke in Freud's terms, with its object the institution of monogamous marriage.

The joke narrator's gender clearly influences its potential psychoanalytic and cultural impact. Freud's joke suggests "among men" that wives
eventually prove inadequate sexual partners and comedically defends married men who visit prostitutes or conduct extramarital affairs. West's quip
asserts a woman's expansive sexual appetite for multiple partners and comedically rejects the man's attempt to position her as a potential wife, restrained by vows of sexual fidelity. Both jokes violate social norms, but
West's line breaches the historically more powerful taboo. Reception of
West's joke in the 1930s as both a hilarious and an officially censorable
moment documents its transgressive power in American social history,
which arguably exceeds that of Freud's joke.[30]

Notwithstanding his own gender biases, Freud's analysis of jokes suggests
why some audiences might find West's comedy socially subversive: her ribald jokes at least momentarily undercut social inhibitions. Yet many other
viewers considered West's comedy inoffensive or may indeed have found
pleasure precisely in her comedy's power to offend. But whereas Freud's
theories explain why some people might laugh at a given joke and others
will not, his approach cannot ascertain that everyone who enjoys a joke
laughs for the same reasons. Even widely successful jokes may have ambiguous "butts," depending on circumstances of the utterance and the
identities of narrator and listener. Certainly, West's comedy has evoked
equivocal, even contradictory, responses.

The Psychiatrist and the "Red-Hot Mama"

The capacity of West's comedic dialogue to elicit diverse reactions emerged in the MPPDA employee's speculative account in 1933 (discussed in chapter 2) of a father's ambivalence toward West: a man might enjoy a ribald laugh at West's famous invitation to a dalliance, but condemn his daughter's playfully enacting the "Come up and see me" line to her male suitors. Although the employee's scenario offers no rigorous evidence of West's historical reception, it does register a concerned observer's insight that the impact of the star's joking dialogue might shift with the narrator's and listener's genders. The comedic force even of West's most widely cited and clearly attributed line of dialogue is fluid, not fixed, particularly once it has been extracted from the narrative and cinematic structures that delineated its original delivery.

While some audiences enjoy West's quips such as the "lots of times" retort as an autonomous and happily promiscuous woman's jokes about marriage, other listeners may conclude that such lines cast—and humorously castigate—West herself as a "red-hot mama," an excessively sexual female stereotype conventionally made the butt of jokes in comedic burlesque routines and blues lyrics.[31] Sophie Tucker often counts as a "hot mama," as do singers Ma Rainey and Bessie Smith, whose "dirty blues" style West adapted. The figure stands in psychoanalytic literature as a disguise degrading the lustful mother, in the service of unresolved Oedipal feelings.[32]

A remarkable essay in a 1945 issue of *Psychoanalytic Review* records West's status as "red-hot mama" for at least one consumer of popular culture at that time, while demonstrating how West's image exceeded attempts to define her as such. The essay is of historical interest for documenting revisions to Freud's theories in the United States during the 1940s and for revealing the concomitant cultural presumptions about gender within and against which "Mae West" circulated as a comedic and sexual icon. The essay's author, Ludwig Eidelberg, attempts to extend Freud's explanation for laughter at jokes. He bases his argument on a detailed analysis of a single joke told not by, but *about* Mae West:

Mae West returns home and finds ten sailors in her bedroom. She says: "I am tired, two must go."[33]

Eidelberg claims to take an empirical approach to his subject. Using the rhetorical "we," he reports at the outset an experiment he conducted, which consisted of his telling the joke to "a number of people" and then separating "those who laughed from those who did not." Eidelberg observes that among the people who did not laugh were some "who for some personal reasons could not enjoy this particular joke," but he quickly dis-

misses them as irrelevant to his study, along with those listeners who had
heard the story recently and "those without a sense of humor." Eidelberg
concentrates instead on listeners who failed to laugh because, he argues,
they did not understand the punch line's implication that eight men stay
to have sexual intercourse with West.

Eidelberg never returns to the "personal reasons" of those who failed to
appreciate the joke, nor does he specify the circumstances under which he
related the joke or the genders or other characteristics of his listeners. Yet
he clearly presumes exclusive and uncomplicated listener identification
with the men who in the joke have the prospect of sleeping with West. In
so doing, Eidelberg reveals possibly his assumption that his laughing listeners are heterosexual males, possibly his grasp of the joke as somehow
structuring a male "audial" position (analogous to that of a film spectator).
Although he systematically uses the "Mae West" joke to test the empirical
value of Freud's triadic model of narrator, listener, and object in joke exchanges, Eidelberg neglects to consider the gender assumptions in Freud's
analysis. In conducting his "research," Eidelberg was evidently himself the
narrator and West presumably the object of the joke for his listeners and
also readers, whom he implicitly casts as male.[34]

Parodies of West as a "red-hot mama" in productions like the Tex Avery
cartoon *Red Hot Riding Hood* (1943) confirm West's occasional construction during the early 1940s as the "butt" of a sexual joke. One of Tex
Avery's wartime "Red Riding Hood and the Wolf" animations, the cartoon focuses about half its length on a white-haired grandmother wearing
a slinky red dress, who reclines on a chaise longue in the penthouse of a
high-rise building that flashes the sign "Grandma's Joint: Come Up and
See Me Sometime." Rather than submit to the grandmother's sexually rav-
enous pursuit, the wolf who has come to court granddaughter Red crashes
through the wall and falls twenty stories to the street below.[35]

But Eidelberg's psychoanalytic use of West's image in his joke waxes
more bizarre than the most surreal Avery cartoon. Attempting to account
for listener pleasure in the joke, Eidelberg ventures that with her declaration "two must go," West is expressing resistance, ambivalence, and guilt
feelings about sexual intercourse! Eidelberg's assertion confounds his
search for the sources of a joke's pleasure with unfounded speculations
about the joke character's psyche. In analyzing the motives of "Mae West"
as narrator *in* the joke, he oddly obscures his own role as narrator *of* the
joke. His perspective may well be a move, not uncommon in psychoanalytic practice (nor, as we have seen, in the censorship of West's films), to

displace West's threat to men by asserting his institutional power over her as a patient suffering from unrestrained sexual impulses.

Paradoxically, Eidelberg's rhetorical move lets slip his evident grasp of West's position as *subject* rather than object in the joke's narrative: only she speaks and acts, only she expresses desire and controls the situation. Like West's films, this joke structures her character as the central identificatory figure and allows her dominance as the comedienne who delivers the punch line.

Twenty-five years later, West herself delivered this punch line in the 1970 film *Myra Breckinridge*, in which her performance is a sustained self-referential pastiche. West plays a Hollywood agent who, after strolling past a dozen young virile actors waiting in her office, turns to tell her assistant, "I'm tired. One of those guys will have to go." In incorporating a long-standing joke that West apparently did not originate, the scene appropriates comic material to assert from the star's own perspective as subject the excessive, transgressive sexuality the joke about her implied. West's version even tops Eidelberg's in the number of men she is willing to handle at once. West's delivery invalidates Eidelberg's awkward equivocation about who is the narrator, who the listener, and who the object of the smutty joke. Clearly boasting of her sexual appetite, rather than expressing any guilt or resistance, West tells the joke to us, the viewers, at the expense of the men eagerly awaiting her.

Eidelberg himself considers how the joke about West alludes to transgressive sexuality and suggests at essay's end that it gives listeners the pleasure of making fun of the sailors' "sexual tendencies" and "infantile inhibitions." But nowhere does he spell out what is laughable in the sailors' tendencies, which he ostensibly holds to be their unrestrained sexual desire for West. At one point he peevishly insists, "[A] listener who having heard [the punch line] does not laugh but inquires into the further fate of Mae West and the sailors fails to understand our joke." But just as Eidelberg's attempt to position West as the joke's butt could not efface her narrative structuring as subject, his convoluted analysis cannot obscure his implicit recognition that the joke hints at a scenario rather different from the one he is trying to enforce.

Already in 1945, West's image—and that of sailors, all the more so in wartime—bore strong male homosexual associations. For listeners who acknowledge West's gay affiliation, the joke intimates desires even more socially transgressive than an orgy in which many men try to satisfy one voraciously sexual woman: the men may eagerly anticipate an orgy with *each other*, under West's auspices and perhaps embracing her as a gay man in drag!

Even listeners who cannot admit that reading will, unlike Eidelberg, probably recognize that the joke turns on West's particular image as sexual and comedic icon. In parsing how the joke evokes laughter, Eidelberg asserts that the substitution of Marlene Dietrich's name for West's would not impair listeners' enjoyment. But his choice of Dietrich's name (and not of a contemporary star more heterosexually anchored, such as Rita Hayworth) undercuts his own argument, for, like West's, Dietrich's image has long borne sexually transgressive implications, including of homosexuality. The image that adheres to Dietrich's name from films like *Morocco* (1931) and *The Devil Is a Woman* (1935), in which she sadistically manipulates eager, then abject, male lovers, encodes not the excessive, unrepressed sexual drives that West exudes, but rather a complex masochism foreign to West's image. At least to 1990s listeners, "Marlene Dietrich comes home and finds ten men . . ." does not necessarily guarantee fun for all.

The impact of West's name in the joke also exceeds Dietrich's because the latter had no prevailing reputation as a comedienne. West's comedienne status inflects not only her delivery of the joke in 1970, but also its original construction. Even in Eidelberg's telling, the joke positions the star not as passive butt (as a joke about a purportedly humorless or dense person or ethnic group might), but rather as a clever, witty, socially and sexually powerful woman who consistently acts as a desiring—and sometimes rejecting—subject.

Like songs and dialogue that others wrote for West (even if she managed to take credit for them), the joke's structure and tenor echoes the star's well-established style and, indeed, may offer a *parody* of West. Her later cinematic rendition of the joke redoubles the parody, creating, for those previously familiar with the joke, a moment of self-parody.

West's 1970 delivery of that and other jokes in *Myra Breckinridge* struck many audiences as self-parody, a reaction her performances over the previous two decades had increasingly evoked. In previous chapters, I have argued that the extracinematic circulation of West's image—in promotion and publicity as well as through colloquial jokes—had a complex impact on her popular reception. The timing of Eidelberg's essay, appearing as West's primary comedic mode shifted from social satire to parody and self-parody, suggests a mutual dependence between the star's reception and her performance style.

Satire, Celebrity and Parody

The varying capacity to shock audiences that West's material had over the course of her career resulted in part from the performer's several changes of venue (from feature films to radio, back to the stage, and to television). Different conventions, audience expectations, and degree of comedic license inhere in each medium. West's return to theater in 1944 and her Las Vegas nightclub act a decade later marked a move away from the sphere controlled by the Production Code—and by concerns about mass marketing. On stage, West performed for audiences presumed to be urbane theatergoers or for vacationers in Las Vegas, an arena that explicitly sanctions the combined public display of sex and money in the flashy stage shows providing backdrop and enticement to the gambling machines and tables.

Gradual changes in West's reception as comedienne also relate to her increasing *celebrity* through the U.S. press, which fostered audience conviction that West's characters extended the actor's private persona. The star's guest performances on radio and TV further conflated actor and character, as West, appearing as herself, invariably cited lines or bits of stage business from her films.

The more audiences assumed that West enacted herself in performance, the more her comedy referred to her own image, rather than to social customs and circumstances. Thus, although West long remained an icon, the basis of her popularity arguably altered over the decades: West's widespread recognition as a powerful satiric performer in the 1930s transmuted by the 1960s to a sometimes ambivalent appreciation of her increasingly bawdy comedy as self-parody.

Media theorists and historians Steve Neale and Frank Krutnik, building on Linda Hutcheon's work on contemporary parody, distinguish meaningfully between cinematic parody and satire: the former "draws on—and highlights—aesthetic conventions, [whereas] satire draws on—and highlights—social ones."[36] Hutcheon herself argues that satire and parody, along with irony, each have a dominant "ethos" (an inferred intended effect), although these may overlap somewhat. For Hutcheon, the satiric ethos scorns social norms, the ironic ethos mocks, and the parodic ethos is playful or neutral ("unmarked"), but not necessarily pejorative.

Textual conventions that Hutcheon summarizes as "repetition with critical distance" qualify a work as parody. Although a parodic text always makes evident its difference from the prior text to which it refers, twentieth-century parody does not always ridicule or mock the referent text. Rather, Hutcheon argues, a parody may well stand in complicity with the "background" text, employing it as a means of criticizing conventions that circumscribe both texts. She names Woody Allen's film *Play It Again, Sam* as an example, for although it parodies *Casablanca*, it takes not that prior film, which it evidently reveres, but rather Hollywood's mythologizing traditions generally as the target of its parody. But due to parody's fundamentally ambiguous construction, juxtaposing two texts, its impact emerges only pragmatically, in its reception.[37]

West's ironic performance of institutionally defined roles (prostitute, wife, missionary) in her 1930s films functioned both as entertainment and social satire. Her exaggerated feminine display, utterance of lascivious and aggressive puns, and display of other behaviors uncharacteristic for most female performers of the period all fostered interpretations of her films as satires on gender behaviors and relations. To the extent it satirized cherished social precepts, West's comedic performance quickly met with objections from institutions and individuals defending the scorned values. As we have seen, state and industry censorship of West's films targeted primarily the star's many comedic lines satirizing ideals of female chastity and the institution of marriage.

Censors treated particularly *Goin' to Town* as a sustained satire on marriage. Early in the production, Breen warned Paramount that the screenplay read like "the boasting of a woman of loose morals who has had any number of men in her time, and has climbed over them to the top of the ladder where she has finally married respectability."[38] Later PCA censorship of the project concentrated on comedic lines in proposed "dirty blues"-style numbers that implied that West's character was happily promiscuous and regarded both sex and marriage primarily as means of social and economic advancement. State censors also focused on West's comedic quips to reduce the film's satiric presentation of marriage, for example, by cutting the word "twice" in an exchange between West/Cleo Borden and her accountant and asexual confidant Winslow (Gilbert Emery):

WINSLOW: You did consent [to marry Gonzales, a rich rancher killed while rustling cattle], didn't you?
CLEO/WEST: I certainly did—twice!

Without the word "twice," there is no joke. In eliminating West's punch line, the censors excised the suggestion that Cleo consented to premarital sex as well as to marriage.[39]

West's growing celebrity at that time sharpened the satiric impact, for the film's release in spring 1935 coincided with public revelation that West herself had cynically discarded and now refused to recognize a long-secret husband. A *Los Angeles Times* columnist noted on 4 May that the news had "chased Hitler, the N.R.A., and the quintuplets off the front page of every newspaper in America for the period of two weeks."

Five years later, Breen was still cautioning Universal that *My Little Chickadee* should avoid making a joke of marriage.[40] In that film, West as Flower Belle agrees to marry Cuthbert J. Twillie (W. C. Fields) in clear anticipation of financial gain; only she and the gambler who conducts the wedding in the guise of a clergyman know that the ritual is a sham. Breen warned on reading the first draft of the screenplay that "there should be no comedy in the performance of the marriage ceremony." No one could address the gambler as "Pastor," nor could he dress like a minister. In the film, characters physically point to the gambler as someone who can perform the service without voicing their presumptions about his profession, and he tries to deny that he is a preacher until Flower Belle hints that she will share Twillie's money with him.

The film avoids directly parodying a marriage ceremony through an audio technique: all dialogue is masked by a loud train whistle beginning after the gambler's preface, "Of course you're both acquainted with the rules of the game—I mean the requirements of matrimony," through his pronouncement of their union. (Producers ignored Breen's suggestion that the "rules of the game" line be changed.) But the audial joke still obliquely parodies a wedding. And West's performance throughout the film continues her pattern of satirizing marriage and other socially condoned institutions. Pinch-hitting as a teacher, for example, West/Flower Belle undertakes to give an arithmetic lesson that turns into coaching on gambling techniques: "Two and two is four and five will get you ten if you know how to work it!" But unlike West's performances in *Goin' to Town* and her 1937 radio rendition of Eve, West's Flower Belle evoked little controversy. The wedding parody came across as acceptably comic rather than offensive and West's scorn of her fake marriage to Fields's character apparently did not effectively satirize the institution to the point of eliciting condemnation.[41]

West's appearance in the Eden skit had marked a turn in her dominant comedic mode from satire to parody, in her critically refunctioning a culturally recognized text. West's enacting Delilah in *Goin' to Town* had been an earlier brief act of parody, and her subsequent portrayals of Czarina Catherine, Juliet, and Red Riding Hood on stage, radio, and TV parodied further mythic female figures. West reportedly proposed to expand the range of historic women she enacted. In the early 1950s, she and her long-time producer, William LeBaron, planned a TV series titled *It Ain't History, It's Herstory*, featuring West each week as an (in)famous woman. Josephine, Marie Antoinette, George Sand, Lola Montez, Helen of Troy, Pocahontas, and Beatrice, each paired with her historically appropriate male partner, were among the roles projected for the never-produced series.[42] But whatever traditional female figures she portrayed, West always played herself. By the late 1930s, West's variously celebrated and reviled image exceeded every script and suffused every new character she might play.

The comedy in West's parodies arose largely from the incongruities between the star's image and the original text West was enacting (e.g., the Bible). Advance publicity about West's appearances on radio and TV emphasized her star identity and celebrity status, rather than the material she was to perform, and press reviews often attributed the impact of a program, positive or negative, entirely to West's brief guest turn, as occurred following her performance on Bergen's show. The broader the distinctions between West's image and the parodied text, and the more culturally hallowed the text, the louder the social reverberations. But no Westian parody generated the controversy that met her Eve. Depictions of Shakespearean characters and fairy-tale and Russian historical figures did not threaten sacrilege, certainly, and the conduct of the Second World War soon wrought changes in dominant U.S. social values and institutions. By war's end, West had lost much of her movie star status, although she remained very much a celebrity.

After about 1959, West made only celebrity appearances on radio and television, exaggeratedly—and comedically—enacting herself. Indeed, West's performances as an imperious movie actress in *Go West, Young Man*, based on a play said to parody Mary Pickford, and as a high-strung stage star in *The Heat's On* (1943) had come across to some critics as parodies of West herself.[43] West's 1940s stage performances received primarily negative reviews from theater critics, who found the plays tired reenactments of old material. But although the critics sought originality, audiences apparently did not, for West's plays drew strong popular response through the 1940s and 1950s.[44] The continuing marketability of West's 1930s image justified her extensively reprising musical numbers, gestures, and comedic lines from her films.

Although West scarcely modified her self-presentation over the decades as a highly desirable and powerful sexual being, she could not prevent her body's gradual altering or dictate responses to her appearance and manner from critics and audiences who closely associated sexuality with youthfulness and found its display in an aging body disgusting. West's standard bawdy quips, when uttered by a septuagenarian, elicited a different reaction from that she had gotten as a forty-year-old presumed younger. Her advancing age evidently supplied "critical distance" to the familiar material, and West's late-career acts seemed increasingly to parody herself. Especially those who believed West unaware of her aging demeanor's impact considered her appearance lamentable self-parody.

Recent criticism of West frequently validates her early comedy as socially subversive but dismisses her later self-parodic performances as aesthetically tasteless and denigrating to women. Such dichotomous evaluation ignores both the varied reception that West always had among different audiences and the relevance of West's *comedienne* status for evaluations of her late-career image. West's performance as herself on *Mister Ed* dynamically illustrates the complex workings of her self-parodic act. Read in the context of that weekly series and other TV programming of the period, as well as against West's sustained image, the "Mae West Meets Ed" episode offers provocative material that complicates any ready assessment of the star's late-career appearances as only self-denigrating display.

The Politics of Self-Parody

Broadcast on CBS from 1961 to 1965, *Mister Ed* centered on the adventures of a talking horse and his owner, Wilbur Post, an architect.[45] The episode featuring West first aired in March 1964; Zsa Zsa Gabor, George Burns, Clint Eastwood, and Los Angeles Dodger Leo Durocher had made previous celebrity appearances on the series. West's performance upholds her image as a sexy, smart-talking businesswoman who knows what she wants and goes after it. West commissions Wilbur (Alan Young) to design a stable for her French horses and also attempts to secure the services of his "deep-voiced associate," whom she has talked with by telephone; Wilbur and the audience know that this associate is the horse. For his part, Mister Ed imagines the luxurious treatment that West affords her horses to be an attractive alternative to Wilbur's continually nagging him to clean up his stall. He presents himself at West's door as an abandoned baby horse, but after discovering the feminizing nature of her indulgent treatment (bubble bath, perfume, beribboned mane) at the hands of two hypermasculine grooms, runs back home to Wilbur, protesting to him, "My name is Ed, not Edwina!" In a final phone conversation with West, Ed as the "deep-voiced associate" explains that he cannot "come up and see her" because he has been drafted into the Army. West expresses disappointment but gets the last word before the credits: "I'll just have to start my own draft board!"

As the synopsis suggests, West's bawdy image and flashy performance in satin evening gown, blonde wig, and furs infused the popular family program with distinct sexual undertones. Then as now, many adult viewers may have recognized references in the episode to homosexuality and other sexual and gender behaviors violating social norms. West's performance emphasizes her own long-standing association with gender impersonation and involves the program regulars, especially Mister Ed and Wilbur, in suggestively transgressive gender play. West's presence reveals especially the "person"-able beast Ed as a figure that exceeds categories conventionally distinguishing not only animal from human, but also child from adult, female from male, and homosexual from heterosexual.

A strain of torchy jazz music and the arrival of a black limousine herald West's entrance five minutes into the program. Three large male figures in tuxedos stand at attention as the star glides to the door of the Posts' suburban home. The scene visually and aurally cites West's first arrival on a movie screen thirty-two years previously in *Night after Night*, although there, West's character, Maudie Triplett, has to talk her way into her former lover's new mansion.[46] In the 1964 replay, West arrives as a star and celebrity eagerly awaited by the Posts and their equally starstruck neighbors, the Kirkwoods. Inside, West presents her "card"—the queen of hearts, a bit of business she had performed in *The Heat's On*.

West basks in the assembled regular characters' admiration and dispenses advice about how to stay young and beautiful, "Like I'm going to tell the ladies at the PTA . . . [pause for laughter] you've got to be feminine. . . ." She makes markedly feminine gestures with her gloved hand and tightly sheathed hip as she delivers the lines in a long shot. The camera cuts to a facial close-up as she adds, "dress like a woman, look like a woman, act like a woman, *feel* like a woman." West gives her famous leer with upwardly rolling eyes as she concludes, "It's what separates the men from the *girls*!"

West's ironic verbal delivery and exaggerated physical and facial gestures cast doubt on the meaning of her words as she utters them, for they suggest that gender distinctions have no *natural* basis: it's all in what one looks and feels like. The reference to the Parent-Teacher Association works as a joke because of the incongruity of West's speaking about femininity or any other issue before the members of such a presumably staid institution, which upholds middle-class values and attempts to shield youth from corruption. The cut to a facial close-up of West, one of only three in the program, privileges her gesture and dialogue at that point as a punch line, so that West's emphasis on "girls" comes across as a pun implying cross-dressing or "camping" men. West's excessive display of conventional marks of femininity in that scene makes her appear nothing so much as a female impersonator who is parodying her(him)self.

Two "studly" grooms who bathe and curry Mister Ed under West's supervision lend a further aura of sexual and gender deviance to the episode. Draped in white satin and fur, West leans against a stable post and self-parodically tosses her hips and pats her piled blonde hair as she utters such lines as, "Brush him a little harder, boys! I want him to look like a full-length mink!" While such vaguely risqué dialogue, suggesting mild sadism and an odd intimacy with the horse as fur coat, echoes West's standard performance, other quips and visual gags in the scene bear all-but-overt male homosexual implications. The two musclebound grooms seem butch male pinups performing masculinity. A medium shot shows one groom close to Ed's glistening rump, braiding his tail. Instructed by West to take the horse's temperature, the other groom feigns innocence about the procedure (the suggestion is that the thermometer should be inserted rectally) and prepares to inject a large needle full of vitamins into Ed's haunches. Adult viewers who recognize West's stance and gestures in this scene as seductive or who associate West with Catherine the Great (who, popular legend maintains, kept male horses for her sexual pleasure) discover hints of bestiality in the scene. Paradoxically, West's and her employees' implicitly sexual actions toward the humanlike Mister Ed also communicate male homosexuality, with West sharing the grooms' male persona. But, as the animal's stamping and pulling away suggests and the narrative soon confirms, Mister Ed, never a very butch horse, fears transformation into "Edwina."

A production still from this scene illustrated an article announcing the program in TV Guide shortly before the broadcast (see Figure 38). The text asserts that West was treated like royalty on the Mister Ed set, "as befitted her station as one of the greats of show business," and notes that she insisted on bringing her own canopied bed from her private apartment for her "boudoir" set. It also hints at the contents of the program: "The episode itself is chock-full of what [director Arthur] Lubin likes to call the

'Mae West flavor.' " The phrasing of the article, headlined "Mister Ed
Barges into a Boudoir," presumed that *TV Guide* readers knew West's
bawdy comedic style and that it would attract them to watch the episode.[47] Unusually high ratings for the episode suggest that the publicity
struck a chord among prospective viewers. West's performance apparently
drew such favorable response that several months later the producers announced (precipitously) that she would return in another episode early in
the fall 1964 season.[48]

The dearth of interpretive reviews following the broadcast complicates
attempts to reconstruct the basis of the episode's popularity. It is not clear
to what extent adult viewers discerned the program's innuendo and visually encoded references to homosexuality, or whether they perceived
West's appearance as a denigrating self-parody or as an over-the-top parody
of *Mister Ed* series. But cultural critic Susan Sontag's discussion of West in
her essay "Notes on 'Camp,' " published the year of West's guest appearance, documents the star's urban cult (read: gay) reception at the time as a
camp figure, enacting "Being-as-Playing-a-Role." Sontag notes "the delicate relation between parody and self-parody in Camp" in relation to West
and asserts that although West's active camping (her *playing at* "Being-as-
Playing-a-Role) sometimes reveals self-parody, it also always reeks of self-
love.[49]

Subsequent analyses have argued that the parodic attitude characterizing camp does not ridicule female performers such as Carmen Miranda and
Joan Crawford, even if these performers are unwitting camps. These figures' camp reception may mock not the stars but rather the oppressive gender roles to which their exaggerated performances draw attention.[50] Parodies of such stars' performances (like those of female impersonators) only
magnify the original performers' parody of femininity, and thus do not necessarily denigrate those stars. West's *self*-parodic performance in *Mister Ed*
emphasizes her own long-standing image as a female impersonator who
loves herself and appreciates other women but who also mockingly repudiates strictly prescribed gender behaviors.

Many 1990s viewers of *Mister Ed* in cable or local market reruns consider not just the occasionally glimpsed "West Meets Ed" episode but the
entire program campy, due to Wilbur and Ed's clearly homosocial relationship.[51] Although ostensibly these characters are man and pet, or "just
pals," the dialogue, narrative development, shot composition, and editing
in the series always present the pair as a conventional sitcom married
couple. The two frequently appear together in camera shots ("two shots")

and trade dialogue in extended shot/reverse shot sequences. These scenes consist primarily of argumentative exchanges culminating in affectionate reconciliations that by each episode's end reassert the primacy of their male bond. Even Wilbur's wife, Carol, does not fathom the depth or basis of the pair's relationship, for only the master—and the audience—knows that the horse can talk.

Mister Ed's name and his deep voice overdetermine his male identity, yet he is a neutered figure, both narratively and literally: the trained palomino is a gelding, not a stallion. Character relations and visual structuring of space on the program make the talking horse a feminine figure who functions in place of women (e.g., Ed as "mistress" of the barn) and often competes with them, notably Carol.[52] Her secondary character overlaps with Mister Ed's in their both suffering unfulfilled desires that fuel the narrative week after week. In "West Meets Ed," the horse childishly resists cleaning his room and seeks motherly indulgence and a luxuriously decorated stall. In all episodes, he yearns for more attention from Wilbur, and behaves in both childish and conventionally feminine ways, making him resemble Carol more than Wilbur.[53]

The dual definition of Wilbur and Ed as pals and spouses bears the homoerotic implications of many "buddy movies," including comedies such as The Odd Couple, which similarly inscribe femininity on male figures. But West's sexually transgressive presence on the program, along with her feminizing treatment of the horse, unmasks the homoeroticism underlying the lead characters' relationship. West's performance makes the episode into a parody of the ostensibly socially conservative sitcom itself.

Still, audiences may conclude that even as West's performance ridicules Mister Ed and other program regulars, Mister Ed also makes fun of "Mae West." The episode's narrative treats West in part as comedic butt. Unlike the radio and TV parodies in which West as Eve, Juliet, and Red Riding Hood triumphs in "getting her man" (altering thereby the original tales), Mister Ed makes West's seductive ploys misdirected and unsuccessful. Of course, the conventions of situation comedy dictate West's failure and Ed's relieved return to Wilbur, for the series format uses West's presence and desires as that week's narrative disruption and resolves it by program's end in a return to the status quo.[54] But the episode excessively justifies West's dismissal by suggesting that the guest star's indulgence portends emasculation.

Near program's end, Wilbur himself bathes Ed to remove the signs (ribbons) and smells (perfume) of femininity that the horse's dalliance with

West had led to. Despite verbal praise for West early on, the program similarly effaces the appeal of the feminine indulgence that West in part represents. On the face of it, the *Mister Ed* episode casts West as spectacular
star whom the regular characters acclaim in dialogue as a feminine ideal.
After meeting West, Wilbur and his neighbor Gordon suggest to Carol and
Winnie (Gordon's wife) that the women should be more like the star:
"The way *she* dresses, now *that's* my idea of a real woman!" declares Gordon (Leon Ames). But developments in the narrative undercut these
claims. Many of the comedy's (canned) laughs come at the women's expense as they attempt to emulate West, though it is not clear whether the
mockery comes for their failing at their goal or for their patterning themselves after such an exaggerated figure to begin with. Viewers who regard
West as an aging red-hot mama may conclude the latter. But that judgment arises from viewers' social conventions rather than from West's performance per se, for there is nothing inherently laughable in a seventy-
year-old woman acting sexual.

It is precisely West's self-presentation as a randy sexual woman (or cross-
dressed man) that calls the show's apparently conservative representation
of gender and sex appeal into question. The comedienne is complicit in
the comedy: she plays all her scenes in her accustomed self-referential,
ironic manner and enjoys the usual support from the cast playing "straight
men." For example, neighbor Gordon, a retired army colonel, has donned
his uniform to meet West. When she sees him, West gushes, "I've always
admired men in uniform—I even choke up when I see the Good Humor
man!" Her comment, implying the equivalence of all uniforms and their
wearers, deflates Gordon's masculine pretensions and undercuts a symbol
of authority.

West's performance ensures that her yet powerful image, rather than the
role she performs, permeates the episode. Thus, despite her failure in the
narrative, West clearly succeeds *performatively* in the episode, as the prospective invitation for her return indicates.[55] And she enacts *not* a conventional woman like Carol and Winnie, whom the series regularly mocks,
but rather an exceptional female performer long recognized for parodying
conventional femininity. West's evident age in 1964 is an element of her
performance, not its target. Rather than mocking herself, West's self-
parody renews and heightens her capacity to satirize conventional gender
roles and prescribed sexual behaviors.

Although *Mister Ed* obliquely made West's age a topic of discussion, her
self-aware performance, enduring star stature, and control of dialogue pre-

cluded the stock characters from ridiculing either her age or her behavior. Just as in her forties West had prevented a director from making her figure a literal butt of cinematic jokes, she refused to allow other directors to parody her image as she aged. Such parody would likely have resulted had she accepted the roles for which Billy Wilder, Federico Fellini, and other directors tried to win her when she was in her fifties, sixties, and seventies: as Norma Desmond in Wilder's *Sunset Boulevard* (1950) and as secondary characters in Fellini's *Juliet of the Spirits* (1965) and *Satyricon* (1969).[56] Biographers and critics who fault West for refusing those opportunities ignore both her avoidance of roles that might ridicule her persona and her self-nurtured identity as a *comedic* star. Although West partially fit the cultural stereotype of the denigrated red-hot mama, her image never suggested the desperation and anxiety about rejection implicit in that stereotype. Precisely such anxieties were embedded in the roles that Wilder and Fellini offered her.

I have argued that West's comedic performances evoked a diverse and often contradictory reception over the course of her career. Even readings that incorporate documented audience responses cannot claim to be exclusive or exhaustive. Knowledge of West's previous cultural impact may inform, but cannot fully determine, what diverse contemporary audiences may make of her persona and performances. Thus, comedic lines in West's mid-1930s performances that struck audiences as transgressive may, some decades later, support rather than offend audiences' dominant social values. West's opening lines in *Goin' to Town* (1934) about not being ashamed of how she lived (implicitly, as a prostitute) lose their subversive edge when delivered in 1971 to a radio audience of U.S. soldiers in Vietnam. The workings of comedy are always historically inscribed in its reception.

Audience and institutional responses to West had continual influence on both the performer's comedic style and the icon's cultural functions. By 1964, when West appeared on *Mister Ed*, her comedic performance had become predominantly self-parodic and her reception placed increasing emphasis on her characterization as a rather unique media phenomenon: a female female impersonator. Yet, as analysis of her appearance on *Mister Ed* reveals, her self-parodic performance was not necessarily self-denigrating, but rather could effect a parody of the media forms in which she appeared. It could also renew the satire of social constraints on gender and sex that her performance had previously offered.

Some popular cultural critics writing in the last decade of West's life, while she was still performing, vehemently disagreed with that assessment. The capacity of West's image to provoke controversy had receded in the 1940s, but returned with new vigor in the early 1970s as viewers began to contest her comedic performance of gender from fresh political perspectives.

5

The Female Impersonator
in Gender Politics

The well-publicized release in 1970 of the Twentieth Century-Fox production *Myra Breckinridge* revitalized public discussion of Mae West. Two
emerging groups of critics and consumers boosted West's status as a political icon in the last decade of her life: gay men and feminists. West's image
offered a complex emblem of sex and gender that self-identified gay and
feminist media critics rhetorically deployed to achieve sometimes counter-
posed political aims.

West's 1970s gay reception emphasized the transgressive sexual practices
and ambiguities in *Myra Breckinridge* and in her last film, *Sextette* (1978).
Gay male audiences also appreciated the star's evident gender play in her
1930s films, which some urban movie houses were reviving. Emboldened
by the gay rights movement, critics such as longtime New York essayist
Parker Tyler began to reveal their gay identities in writing about West.
Tyler and other more or less "out" gay critics in the late 1960s and early
1970s recognized parodic female impersonation in West's performances
and valorized her "camping." As Susan Sontag had observed in 1964,
West's self-parodic performance style, especially in her later career, acknowledged and addressed her large gay male following. Even as segments
of the early gay rights movement began to condemn camp as a politically
ineffectual and self-stigmatizing subcultural practice, and even as West
aged, the star retained a treasured status among those who viewed theatrical excess and playful masquerade as a means of surviving in a society
that oppresses any deviations from the "norm" in gender identity and
sexual relations (see Figure 39).

Among feminist media critics during the same period, West roused more
ambivalent and variable reactions. The feminist project to rewrite *history*
as "*herstory*," recognizing women's historical agency, fueled interest in
West for being an exceptional performer and writer. But most contributors
to early feminist media discourses in the 1970s concluded that the movie
star failed as a model for alternative female behavior or representation, and

instead embodied conventional media exploitation of women. Indeed, several feminist critics found West's performance and appearance a misogynistic travesty. Writing mostly from the perspective of middle-class, straight white women, they argued variously that West's female impersonation parodied real women, that her acting style and persona were age and gender inappropriate, and that the cinematic spectacle of her body and performance was intrinsically sexist.[1] Only years after West's death did feminist media critics begin to find common cause with gay men in understanding the sign "Mae West" as a masquerade parodying the social construction of gender.

Gay male and feminist media critics contributed to an evolving discourse in the 1970s about alternative cultural practices. Even as these critics sometimes took antagonistic positions, they—and the audiences they addressed—jointly renewed "Mae West" as a site of political contestation over gender and sexuality. West's politicized reception in turn influenced her figure's treatment in mainstream media during the decade before she died in 1980, and beyond, occasioning further shifts in her image and its iconographic functions.

Camping Out with West

The ease and authority of Miss West as a homosexual camp symbol speaks aloud of her unique privilege: she is, after all, a woman. In many respects she behaves like a homo with a lifelong dedication to putting on the ritz, while undeniably being a good fellow through it all. (Parker Tyler, 1972)[2]

It was primarily gay male critics and audiences who revived West's image in 1969-70. Long a champion of West, Parker Tyler acclaimed the star in his 1969 book *Sex Psyche Etcetera in the Film* for having introduced "the screen's first sterling brand of conscious sex camp." Apparently unaware of George Davis's 1934 *Vanity Fair* essay, Tyler also took credit for first (in 1944) discussing West in print as a female impersonator.[3]

Thoughtful responses to Sontag's signal essay have productively critiqued and complicated its analysis of camp as an attitude in enacting and consuming culture. Nevertheless, Sontag's observations bring insights into West's camp appeal in the 1960s and 1970s. Sontag argues that camp taste involves appreciation for both the androgynous figure and "the exaggeration of sexual characteristics and personality mannerisms" (a style, she notes, that only appears to differ from androgyny). Movie stars like West provide ready figures of exaggeration, for, in Sontag's words, camp is the farthest extension, in sensibility, of the metaphor of life as theater.[4] In the years since Sontag's essay was first published, as mainstream cultural producers and media have taken up the term and the sensibility it describes, West's image and films have received broad recognition for their "camp" style.

Another groundbreaking work on camp, Esther Newton's 1960s study of professional female impersonators, *Mother Camp*, also documents West's early gay subcultural reception. Newton argues that three recurrent techniques characterize camp: incongruity, theatricality, and humor. "Incongruity is the subject matter of camp, theatricality its style, and humor its strategy."[5] Newton observes the following incongruous juxtapositions in camp:

> Masculine-feminine juxtapositions are, of course, the most characteristic form of camp, but any incongruous contrast can be campy. For instance, juxtapositions of high and low status, youth and old age, profane and sacred functions or symbols, cheap and expensive articles are frequently used for camp purposes.[6]

Newton writes of camp, more explicitly than Sontag and from an insider perspective, as a style deriving from urban gay culture. Her study of gay clubs in Chicago, St. Louis, and Kansas City reveals the popularity of Mae West impersonations around 1965. One accomplished impersonator whom Newton observed, Lynne Carter, performed a West-style number about the Statue of Liberty, "Miss Liberty's Gonna be Liberal from Now On." Carter's song lamented "the boredom of standing in water not having any kicks, with side remarks about how hard it is anyway for a big girl to have any fun." Newton found Carter's act an "incredibly accurate imitation of distinctive bodily movements, voice, and expression of Mae West."[7]

Except for one or two characteristics ("slender" and "youthful"), West's own appearance throughout her career matched the definition of ideal feminine glamour that Newton gleaned from female impersonators in the 1960s:

> ideally, a slender body with the appearance of large breasts and wide hips, a youthful face with "good" bone structure, skin that seems soft but is heavily and dramatically made-up, jewelry (especially earrings), a long-haired wig (preferably blond and in a sophisticated style . . .), a gown (preferably low-cut and floor length), and, *invariably*, high-heeled shoes.[8]

West knew that female impersonators frequently enacted her persona; indeed, she even claimed that such performers originally learned their craft

from her![9] Given that female impersonation acts appeared on stage decades before West's debut performance, her assertion is clearly more egocentric than accurate. But both as the producer of the plays The Drag and
Pleasure Man and in her own performances, West made sexual innuendo a
more visible feature of female impersonation than before.[10] Female impersonators who "camped" in New York's gay subcultures of the late 1920s
and early 1930s considered West a model.[11] And at least one famous female impersonator of the 1960s-80s, Craig Russell, made West literally his
mentor. Russell met West and was her houseguest in the late 1960s. Later
commenting on his featured West performances in the film Too Outrageous! (1987), he proclaimed, "She taught me everything I know."[12]

The figures of performers who currently do Mae West indicate that the
star's deviating from the "slender and young" ideal has proven a boon for
some. West's ample figure and aging face in her late career offer an expansive role for female impersonators who have broad shoulders, thickening
waists, or mature demeanor, for such body features do not preclude a convincing West impersonation.[13]

Parker Tyler notes West's boast about setting the pattern for campy female impersonation on the opening page of his 1972 book Screening the
Sexes: Homosexuality in the Movies, but argues that whether or not she de-
served that credit, "Miss West's style as a woman fully qualifies her—as it
always did—to be a Mother Superior of the Faggots." Tyler's aside, "as it
always did," refers to and augments his previously published appreciations
of West's performances as cross-gendered identity play. Tyler further asserts
his insider position in celebrating West's gay cult status by observing on
the same page, "Once I spent several years among the fairies, e.g., those
homosexuals unafraid to advertise themselves socially." Here, a critic who
had written only obliquely as a gay man takes West's image both as a point
of departure for the first English-language book on homosexuality in film
and as a rhetorical strategy for coming out to his readers.[14]

Tyler argues in Screening the Sexes that West's long-standing iconographic standing among homosexuals determined her casting in Myra
Breckinridge. Based on Gore Vidal's controversial best-selling novel about a
male-to-female transsexual, that film had its world premiere in New York's
Criterion Theater on 24 June 1970, just five days short of the first anniversary of the Stonewall rebellion, the uprising in a New York gay bar that
has become a historical marker in the gay rights movement.[15] Although
West plays only a supporting character, she receives top billing above Rex

Reed (Myron), Raquel Welch (Myra), and John Huston (Buck, Myron/ Myra's lascivious uncle).[16] And although West herself did not play the main role, Tyler notes, her performance and image make her character the film's primary identificatory figure for gay men.[17] Eric Braun made a similar assertion in a lengthy overview of West's career that appeared in two fall 1970 issues of the gay-oriented British publication *Films and Filming*.[18]

West's character, Leticia Van Allen, is a sexually assertive Hollywood talent agent who specializes in virile young actors. According to *Look* magazine, West rewrote the dialogue in her scenes and altered her character, "completely changing the book's Letitia Van Allen from a masochistic victim of men to a Mae Westian all-conqueror." West also changed the spelling of her character's first name because, she announced in an interview, "the other spelling might give people ideas."[19] West's comment was typically sly, for her declaration, made appropriately enough to *Look*, guaranteed that no one would miss envisioning the "tit" that the name change presumably masked. Tyler and Braun both point out other differences in the film's Leticia and attribute the changes to West. Many reviewers found West's performance the film's primary appeal. General identification of West with the film and the issues it addressed often led to the assumption that she played the title role of the transsexual.[20]

The "X" rating that *Myra Breckinridge* received for U.S. distribution limited the film's audience but enhanced the controversy over its depiction of a transsexual operation and over scenes involving masturbation and female nudity, as well as many allusions to homosexuality and male sexual performance.[21] Film critics considered Hollywood's representing these taboo subjects to be symptomatic of ongoing social changes the press had dubbed a "sexual revolution."[22] One scene that qualified the film for an "X" rating showed Myra (Welch) wielding a medical instrument as a dildo behind a male character, Rusty (Roger Herren).

Critics found implications of anal intercourse in one of West's scenes even more outrageous. As the scene opens, West, dressed in a lacy boudoir gown, ends a telephone conversation, turns to Rusty, who sprawls on her bed nude but for a draped towel, and asks him, "How about another trip around the world?" Tyler points out that the scene's dialogue, blocking, and costuming suggest that West/Leticia Van Allen has anally penetrated Rusty, even without benefit of a medical device, and proposes to do so again. This scene spells out in what Tyler calls "sexual vernacular" the implications of the *Mister Ed* bubble-bath scene: West is a drag queen who has both the inclination and the capacity to ravish man and beast. This scene not only fostered West's long-standing reception as a female impersonator, but also fed rumors that West was in fact a gay man.[23]

West's campy role in Myra Breckinridge validated and encouraged retrospective readings of the star's 1930s films as implying sexual practices or orientations other than the conventional heterosexual—if promiscuous—mode that dominated the plots. In The Celluloid Closet (1981), a pioneering overview of homosexuality in movies, Vito Russo discovers references to male homosexual desire in West's She Done Him Wrong dialogue. One involves Cary Grant's character, who, resisting West/Lou's seductive ploys, insists, "I'd better be getting back to the mission now. Sally's father is waiting for me." West retorts, "Yeah, well that ought to be interestin'!" Russo discerns that West's response acknowledges "the possibilities of such an encounter."[24]

Finding gay reference in West and Grant's exchange presumes a counterhegemonic perspective that seeks subtexts and thrives on the subcultural "gossip" that has long provided an oppositional viewing strategy.[25] West's bold, original inclusion of gay male characters in her 1920s Broadway plays, often noted in 1970s biographies of West, lent support to Russo's reading, as did rumors that Grant himself was gay or bisexual. Some of Grant's later roles also encode that implication, notably in Howard Hawks's Bringing Up Baby (1938), in which Grant dons a fur-trimmed negligee and makes a playful leap while declaring, "I just went gay—all of a sudden!"[26]

West's symbolic positioning as a gay male in drag, which Myra Breckinridge disseminated to a broader public, further nourished retroactive readings of Grant's characters in She Done Him Wrong and I'm No Angel as potentially gay. Even some of Grant's lines that do not hint particularly at homosexuality do suggest unconventional gender relations and also Grant's possible sexual masochism, under West's playfully sadistic control. For example, in the closing scene of I'm No Angel, Grant's character declares to West's, "I could be your slave!" West/Tira's response: "That could be arranged!" After Grant's death in 1986, printed reports confirmed rumors about his bisexual orientation. A 1989 biography offers especially strong evidence of his long-term romance with Randolph Scott, the male lead in West's independently produced 1936 film Go West, Young Man.[27] That the two best-known romantic male leads in West's star vehicles should have been lovers while appearing in West's films is a striking coincidence that, through its colloquial circulation, strengthens the cogency and pleasure of subcultural readings.

Indeed, *Go West, Young Man* encodes Scott's character as gay more overtly than West's 1933 vehicles did Grant's roles. Scott plays a good-looking young mechanic called Bud, who remains oblivious to the seductive feminine wiles of West's character, Mavis Arden. The film presents Scott's body as a sexual object through Hollywood techniques that commonly specularize the *female* body. A shot from West/Mavis's point of view introduces Bud in the film: she watches him from behind while he rises from his bent-over position, then turns around to hoist up a car, leaning back with his legs spread apart, the light playing across his crotch in center frame. "What large and sinewy muscles!" West murmurs.

Even as the narrative makes Scott the focus of West's presumably female admiration, the film's cinematography, editing, and dialogue fashion him as a potential erotic object also for male viewers. In other scenes, West directs attention to Scott's exposed chest and even beats musical rhythms on his buttocks. (See Figure 40.) Scott's stance in the introductory scene and his overall presentation resemble gay male pinups, which became widely visible and recognizable as such in the 1970s.

Perception of Bud (or Scott himself) as a closeted gay, conjoined with West's image as a gay male in drag, lends a queer twist even to the title *Go West, Young Man*. The phrase puns on the star's name and also on Horace Greeley's mid-nineteenth-century call to geographic expansion and conquest of new worlds. In the film "West" represents Hollywood, the place West/Mavis dangles as a lure to Scott's character. But "go" is also a pun, meaning "become" ("Go wild!"). Thus construed, the film title sounds a call to campy female impersonation: "Become like West" or, even, "Come out!"[28]

West's films displayed stereotypically effeminate as well as exaggeratedly masculine supporting characters. In *I'm No Angel*, several beefy male trapeze artists in West's circus come across as butch (Figure 45), but Gregory Ratoff plays a lawyer, Benny Pinkowitz, as an effeminate gay. One of only two men (the other is the skunky circus boss) in the film whom West/Tira does not seduce, Pinkowitz sleeps alone in a richly textured bed and gown and mothers his client, clucking understandingly at her problems. Before Pinkowitz first appears on screen, West calls him by long-distance telephone, spelling his name out for the operator: " 'P,' like in pansy . . . ."

Every Day's a Holiday (1938), the West vehicle Emanuel Cohen produced after *Go West, Young Man*, has a butler character, Graves (Charles Butterworth), whose effeminacy hints at homosexuality. Although other suggestively queer characters appear in minor roles in other West vehicles, Graves stands alone in West's 1932-43 films as an implicitly gay female impersonator (other than West herself, of course.)[29] I noted in chapter 1 that Paramount made a publicity photograph of Butterworth in female drag (see Figure 27). That photograph and the scene it comes from seem to be what Sontag has called "conscious camp." The advertising campaign for the film included a photograph of a barbershop quartet, comically mismatched in height, that sings a number in the film's opening scene, "Flutterby, Butterfly" (Figure 41). Female dancers in diaphanous winged costumes ascend on guy wires to circle, fluttering, above the quartet onstage. This scene also comes across as camp, due to the gender and genus incongruities and the exaggerated aural and visual spectacle it offers, as the quartet of men croon in unison about butterflies while lepidopterous women swoop about. Tellingly, Joseph Breen, always alert to screenplay depictions of men as "nances," recognized that the scene transgressed conventions of strictly binary gender representation. He proposed to Cohen that the male singers be replaced by women,[30] but the PCA head's attempt to efface the scene's gay overtones went unheeded.

The opening number in *Every Day's a Holiday* and the scene of Graves stealing and posing in women's clothes introduce the motifs of visual excess, playacting, and masquerade that become the film's primary themes. Exiled from New York for her repeated con games (including selling the Brooklyn Bridge), West's character, Peaches, assumes a French accent and a brunette wig to appear as "Mademoiselle Fifi," the star of a musical show on Broadway (see Figure 42). The "Flutterby" number and the butler's playful cross-dressing enhance West's own characterization as a mistress of disguise.

West's Las Vegas act in the 1950s built on her excessive presentation as Mademoiselle Fifi and on her other films. For those alert to the implications, the stage show all but announced West as a campy female impersonator by incorporating a pronounced *male* masquerade: eight young muscle men dressed only in tight bathing suits who carried West onstage and played, along with Louise Beavers in a maid's role, "straight men" to the star's raunchy comedic dialogue and song lyrics (see Figures 43-44).[31]

The muscle men functioned on stage as West's admirers and erotic objects; their presence visually supported legends of the star's insatiable sexual appetite and her own endless desirability to men, young and old.

West publicly accounted for their inclusion as a gesture to please female patrons.[32] The assertion presumes, no doubt with some justification, that some women would want to look at such men and fantasize about receiving their sexual attentions. And presumably the heterosexual men watching the performance could find the muscular male models a visual idealization with whom they might identify in any fantasized interactions with West. Some straight men in the 1950s did evidently take enjoyment from West's sexual presentation.[33]

Yet the muscle men also offered male impersonations. In Newton's words: "The muscleman and the drag queen are true Gemini: the make-believe man and the make-believe woman."[34] West's inscription as a camp figure, a female drag queen, embraced also the all-but-naked muscle men who paraded around West in excessively virile display. These men enacted their apparent gender as emphatically and self-consciously as the star did hers.

Despite the campy theatrical excess in West's presentation, her subject positioning and featured performance in the stage act, like in her films, structured audience identification primarily with her figure. Fantasy association with West as the act's powerful star and dominant character might thus yield narcissistic gratification for all, male *and* female viewers, of any conscious or unconscious sexual orientation. But audience recognition of West as female impersonator and of her muscled companions as butch gay men fostered transgendered identifications. Particularly men who appreciated West's act as cross-gender drag or who, like the star, desired hypermasculine male partners might enjoy the homoerotic fantasies that unconscious identifications with West along with the muscle men facilitated.

Of all her performances, West's last film, *Sextette*, released in November 1978 by Crown International, most openly addressed gay males through its construction throughout as self-conscious camp. Based on a play West authored and took on tour in the early 1950s, the film presents an elaborate pastiche of lines and scenes from West's previous performances, generally summarizing the star's career and image. Indeed, it offers a camp homage to the then eighty-five-year-old star. West plays Marlo Manners, a long-time Hollywood star and beauty queen getting married for the sixth time. A young Timothy Dalton plays her new groom, Sir Michael Barrington (recalling Lord Carrington from *Goin' to Town*); his secondary characterization as a debonair British secret agent prefigures his short-lived "James Bond" persona.

Among the actors playing Marlo Manners's former husbands, all still enamored of her, are Tony Curtis, Ringo Starr, and George Hamilton. George Raft and Walter Pidgeon and various media celebrities such as Regis Philbin appear in cameo roles. Short dialogue scenes and comedic turns by Dom DeLuise, who plays Marlo's manager, interweave the thin plot of recurrent chance meetings and unlikely political intrigues. Between having hysterical fits and dancing a solo soft-shoe number, DeLuise's character promotes Marlo's latest production, *Catherine Was Great*: "It's in Technicolor!" Glitter-rock performer Alice Cooper, a short curly wig hiding his usual long tresses, shows up in the guise of a waiter to deliver a telegram and serenade West on the piano. Keith Moon, drummer for the rock group the Who, dashes in as a frenetic high-fashion dress designer. He assures West of his enthusiasm for his creations by telling her, "That dress is so fantastic that even I would wear it—in fact, I have!"

In keeping with the star's standard opening in all media, the first scene in *Sextette* builds up to West's regal entrance in a full-skirted antebellum-style white wedding gown. Carefully shot in soft focus, she descends from a limousine at the luxurious London hotel where she and Dalton/Barrington will spend their honeymoon. An elaborately choreographed number reminiscent of Hollywood backstage musicals greets the newlyweds, with high-stepping bellboys singing "Hooray for Hollywood!" in place of the usual chorus line of "girls." (See Figure 47.)

A later scene between West and the U.S. Olympic team staying at the hotel recalls a musical number in Hawks's film *Gentlemen Prefer Blondes* (1953), which itself has gay cult status: Jane Russell sings "Is There Anyone Here for Love?" at ocean liner poolside while a bevy of nearly nude male athletes flex and dance around her. However, the citation differs from the original scene, in which the Olympic team totally ignores Russell as she sings and leaves her frustrated and dripping in the pool. By contrast, the bounding athletes in *Sextette* enthusiastically surround West/Manners as she makes ribald jokes about their bodies and then herself departs to return to her handsome and presumably sexually voracious groom.

Sextette contains a number of openly gay jokes, chiefly in a sequence in which television personality Rona Barrett interviews Dalton's character and reveals him to be a "closet queen." (A sample naive remark by Sir Barrington about his years at school and love of sports: "Ah, the camaraderie of the field, the jolly give-and-take in the shower—oh, we all pulled together at Eton!") Many reviews described *Sextette* as camp and implied that the film's two twenty-three-year-old producers, Daniel Briggs and

Robert Sullivan, both heirs to British business fortunes, were gay. Although the mainstream U.S. press panned the film, it played for a period in New York at weekend midnight shows to mostly gay audiences.[35]

One critic who liked the film, Dean Billanti, argued in *Films in Review* that mainstream reviewers rejected *Sextette* because they lacked appreciation for West's style of self-parody and also held sexist presumptions about gender- and age-appropriate behaviors:

> [T]his enjoyable little movie has been quite badly received by critics and for several reasons. Firstly, reviewers seemed to have expected a straight situation comedy from West. But *Sextette* is a vehicle that traffics in the mystique of Mae West, a legend that has been supported and nourished for 50 years. The second possible excuse for this nasty reception goes deeper and its roots are somewhat chauvinistic. Male critics were especially repelled by the film; they seemed angered and baffled by West's image as a sexy octogenarian. Would they react as adversely, if say, George Burns were on screen making naughty quips while being pawed by a bevy of obliging young female cuties?[36]

Billanti implies that the (presumably straight) male critics who condemned West's aging image failed to comprehend *Sextette* as camp. But even some viewers who recognized the film's camp status rejected it, for ten years after Stonewall, many activists had come to consider camp either thoroughly self-denigrating or, as Sontag has argued, "disengaged, depoliticized, or at least apolitical." Even Newton added footnotes to the 1979 edition of *Mother Camp* explaining that in the decade since her sympathetic analysis she had come to consider camp a "pre- or proto-political phenomenon" that "undercuts rage and therefore rebellion by ridiculing serious and concentrated bitterness."[37]

Yet many gay-identified critics continued to acclaim camp's political potential. Film scholar Richard Dyer argued lucidly in a 1976 article that appeared in the British and Canadian gay press that camp can build unity among gay men by demystifying masculinity and undercutting sex roles and a worldview that admits to only two sharply delineated genders.[38] However, like Newton, Dyer pointed to camp's ambiguities and limitations in its making a joke of the consequences of gay men and women's oppression, rather than addressing those through political action. He compared camp to the role of "soul" in black culture as a source of identity but potentially also of repressive stereotyping and political inefficacy. But he argued that the context of camp determines its effect and that gay men can build on "camp's anti-butch legacy of fun and wit":

> [C]amp is not masculine. By definition, camping about is not butch. It is a way of being human and vital (for the whole camp stance is full of vitality) without conforming to the drabness and rigidity of the male role.[39]

While conceding that camp has equivocal meanings rather than any intrinsically subversive effects on dominant culture, Dyer called for the activation of camp's positive attributes as a form of resistance: "You know those clenched fists you sometimes see on political badges (including women's liberation and GLF)? Well, why shouldn't it be a clenched fist on a limp wrist?"[40]

In *Gays and Film*, an anthology Dyer edited in 1977, Jack Babuscio argued that gay audiences who perceive camp in the performances of Tallulah Bankhead, Edward Everett Horton, and Mae West see these figures as "poking fun at the whole cosmology of restrictive sex roles and sexual identifications." For Babuscio, the camp attitude criticizes gender roles even when those who appreciate camp are not "politically aware." "The [camp] response is mainly instinctive; there is something of the shock of recognition in . . . seeing on screen the absurdity of those roles that each of us is urged to play with such a deadly seriousness."[41]

Babuscio and other 1970s critics considered West an active, conscious participant in the social critique of gender roles that they found in the camp aesthetic. But neither Babuscio nor Dyer, nor Sontag nor Newton, satisfactorily addressed a paradox: while camp's theatrical and ironic exaggerations are most frequently associated with *female* masquerade, it is gay men, rather than women of any sexual orientation, who have primarily generated and appreciated camp traditions.[42] For many early feminist critics, precisely West's gay cult status detracted from her potential to offer an alternative to dominant, oppressive representations of women. For these feminists, West's cult male following confirmed her function as a female stereotype, even as a fetish object, that had little to offer women viewers.

Critiquing the Cinematic Spectacle

In one of the first books of explicitly feminist media criticism, *Women and Their Sexuality in the New Film* (1973), Joan Mellen obliquely makes West's popularity with gay men a basis for women's rejecting the figure:

Those who applaud West's performances at the re-run houses on St. Marks Place do not differentiate the Mae West of *She Done Him Wrong* from the West of *Myra Breckinridge*. She is cheered there primarily by some men perhaps because she seems to them to represent the ultimate of sexual degradation in a woman. In her aggressiveness West imparts at times an aura of the transvestite, making a mockery of female sexuality by flaunting what are no more than ordinary female attributes.[43]

Mellen's assumption that male-to-female transvestism always denigrates and ridicules women presupposes an essentialist view of gender: West violates the essence of being female by approximating a male's necessarily failed attempt to pass as a woman. Mellen's further assumption, that the pleasure gay men (the audiences frequenting St. Marks Place) take in West necessarily derives from misogyny, itself smacks of homophobia.

Certainly gay men—and the cultural forms they create—are not exempt from the sexism that permeates U.S. society, and misogyny may indeed color drag queens' reception, also among gay men, as risible or pitiable spectacle. The most gender-deviant gays, drag queens, have historically received the brunt not only of dominant society's abhorrence, but also of the self-hatred that many homosexuals, like other long-oppressed groups, may have internalized, especially prior to the gay rights movement.[44] Thus, even an identity-affirming gay subcultural ritual like jointly hooting over a queen's performance may draw on unresolved anxieties over gender deviance and self-loathing. But to presume, as Mellen does, that some gays' evident delight in West automatically entails misogyny much oversimplifies a complex phenomenon and entirely ignores how drag and other forms of camp have served historically as a survival technique, not of men against women, but of gay men in a society where primarily straight men set and enforce the rules.[45]

Mellen's book evinces the tendency of popular U.S. media criticism to evaluate "positive" and "negative" images with reference to a political or social ideal, rather than to examine closely an image's possibly diverse and complex historical impact. Thus, Mellen adjudges only the suitability of West's image as a role model for women, instead of assessing its potential for audiences as a source of unbridled fantasy, visual pleasure, or social subversion:

The Mae West who at 77 appears in *Myra Breckinridge* as a lascivious Hollywood agent collecting well-endowed young boys, like the West who appears at interviews with a collection of studs, is embarrassing when she does not offend. . . . *Myra Breckinridge* shows us West as merely a distortion of the female, a travesty of self-parody which convinces us of the truth of its opposite, that compulsive sex is neither desirable nor pleasurable, that despite her bravura, West did women less a favor than a disservice.[46]

For Mellen, the sexual display of the aging female body violated not only representational but also appropriate social practice. Her evaluation of West's performance in terms of social propriety recalls the position of moral reformists in the 1930s, who argued that impressionable moviegoers copied behaviors represented on the screen and that the depiction of hap-pily transgressive women would promote social disorder, even prostitution. Mellen's condemnation of West for depicting a sexually active older woman renews this censorious stance. Just as censorship of West's early films resulted from social movements that believed the star a threat to the established order that restrained female sexuality, Mellen's criticisms arose out of an emergent feminist discourse that addressed how media repre-sented women in relation to traditional gender roles, comparative social power, and the potential for political change.

Most early feminist critiques of West's image avoided Mellen's thor-oughgoing gender essentialism and evident homophobia, but the concerns she voiced also found expression in other evaluations of the star. Other U.S. feminist media critics writing in the early 1970s, such as Marjorie Rosen and Molly Haskell, also compared West with other female stars of the 1930s, contrasted her earlier image to that projected by more recent performances, and evaluated the effects of her image on contemporary viewers, especially women.

West's widely documented accomplishments as author, producer, per-former, and celebrity into her old age made her a ready historical subject to reclaim and celebrate from feminist perspectives. Alone on the basis of her central narrative roles in star vehicles, enhanced by reports of her many run-ins with censors, she appeared a strong and independent female type and a historical mover and shaker. But precisely therein also lay the rub: feminist critics like Mellen and Rosen found the star's literal moving and shaking in performance much more problematic than her role in Holly-wood history as an unusually accomplished professional woman. For some, the spectacle of West's body came suspiciously close to a phallic symbol, in the colloquial sense of the term, penile shaped. Such critics found the tight encasement of West's body in shiny materials, her upswept blonde hair crowned with an elaborate hat, and the canes, whips, and umbrellas she carried in performance evidence of the sexist figure she cut.[47]

Rosen, for example, struggles to reconcile her admiration for West's narrative roles with the star's visual manifestations, especially her exaggerated feminine artifice:

> While she embodied certain aspects of the strong, independent female, this is a comforting delusion more than a clear-cut reality. . . . Mae West was uncomfortable with her femininity. She girdled and minced and pouted and purred, posturing and gesticulating so that she did in fact mirror the transvestites whom she had studied thoroughly. . . . while all females suffer and starve to some extent for fashion, Mae's was an unnecessarily masochistic kind of extreme vanity which she overworked as her trademark.[48]

Rosen perceives West's construction as a female impersonator, but fails to discern any irony or play in West's style or to consider that comedic or other genre conventions might circumscribe the performance and its reception. Instead, she criticizes West's film costuming and performance for offering inappropriate models for female behavior.

Not only West's artifice, but also her mixed embodiment of feminine and masculine characteristics gave some early feminist critics difficulty, as another passage from Rosen illustrates:

> Audiences knew that West would provide a gutsy, robust show. She had balls. But never for one moment would a man take her eccentric character seriously as a *real woman*; never would a woman fantasize about *becoming* Mae West, though she might well copy her dramatic cartwheel hats and plumes, her boas and diamonds.[49]

After describing West's masculine, even *male*, traits ("balls"), Rosen retreats from the complexity of her insight. Her contradictory rhetoric at once acknowledges and denies that viewers' enjoyment of West may involve fantasy and gender play. Like Mellen's, Rosen's approach to West in 1973 bespeaks a cultural feminism that valorizes intrinsic female qualities, considers women victims of sexual exploitation more than of sexual repression, and, in Alice Echols's words, aims at "preserving rather than annihilating gender distinctions."[50]

By contrast, New York film critic Molly Haskell has analyzed West from a feminist position informed by a more radical analysis of gender practice and representation and by a more gay-positive perspective. Haskell argues that the complexity of West's image defies ready dismissal by feminist viewers:

> [S]o complete was West's androgyny, that one hardly knows into which sex she belongs, and by any sexual-ideological standards, she is an anomaly, too masculine to be a female impersonator, too gay in her tastes to be a

woman. She was a composite of sexual types: the female impersonator that
Parker Tyler has discerned (in which the mother and gay son are
reconciled); a hypothetical, sexually aggressive woman; and woman as sex
object turned subject. . . .
    . . . In her size, her voice, her boisterous one-liners, and her swagger,
there was something decidedly, if parodistically, masculine. But she was a
woman and she thus stretched the definition of her sex. Those who object
that in her masculinity (and her maternalism) she reinforced the myth of
male supremacy (phallic, imperialist, sexist) in the cinema fail to see that
it is the valuation of the sex itself, male over female, rather than their
inherent qualities, which is the basis of structural inequality.[51]

Haskell's analysis of West, published in 1974, obliquely responds to an
influential essay that British film theorist Claire Johnston had published
the previous year. Johnston's essay, "Women's Cinema as Counter-
Cinema," was an early attempt to adapt Jacques Lacan's psychoanalytic
theories to feminist analysis of media. Johnston argues that West's representation of excessive, wanton sexuality did not counter, but rather reinforced sexist myths, particularly through her costuming and cinematic presentation as fetishized spectacle. Pointing to "traces of phallic replacement
in [West's] persona," Johnston employs West's image to illustrate her central point that all female stars support "the collective fantasy of phallo-
centrism":

[T]he voice itself is strongly masculine, suggesting the absence of the male,
and establishes a male/non-male dichotomy. The characteristic phallic dress
possesses elements of the fetish. The female element which is introduced,
the mother image, expresses male oedipal fantasy. In other words, at the
unconscious level, the persona of Mae West is entirely consistent with
sexist ideology; it in no way subverts existing myths, but reinforces them.[52]

Johnston's cursory analysis of West is predicated on her assumption, following Lacan, that the dichotomy male/not-male offers the single appropriate model for analyzing classically constructed cinema. Discovering in
West's body a literal embodiment of the phallus, Johnston concludes that
the star's performance and persona contribute to the phallocentric denial
of sexual difference. Following its rigorously feminist psychoanalytic perspective, Johnston's analysis entails rejection of West's image for eradicat-
ing female presence.
    Due largely to Johnston's status as a founding mother of feminist film
theory, her view that West and other female stars were inescapably constructed within phallogocentric modes of representation has had an endur-

ing impact on how feminist scholars approach these figures. But although Johnston's argument may bring insights into West's impact as an isolated, fetishized spectacle in photographs and to the extent that visual, aural, and narrative conventions of classical Hollywood cinema shape her presentation, it inadequately accounts for the complex workings of West's films and star image. Johnston purports to analyze cinematic spectacle, but she does so only by addressing the spectacle of the cinematic star abstracted from all specific film performances. Her approach is also ahistorical, leaving entirely out of consideration the documented cultural functions of West's image, which formed the contexts for audience reception of her films. Johnston also fails to recognize West's identity as a *comedienne* and to consider the impact of West's comedic (satiric and parodic) mode on viewer interpretations of her performance.

Despite their divergent evaluations of West, Johnston and Haskell both recognized that viewers' consumption of West involved fantasy. The authors differed in their analysis of *whose* fantasies West's image might evoke or fulfill. Notwithstanding Johnston's theoretical sophistication, she shared Rosen's and Mellen's premise that West's image could satisfy only masculinist fantasies. Among film scholars, only Haskell—and Linda Williams, writing a short article in a university journal in 1975, while a graduate student—asserted in print during this period that West's image might offer a site of cultural engagement in the ongoing social redefinition of "woman."[53]

The limited response to West among feminists after the first burst of criticism around 1973-74 suggests that her image did not readily speak to primary feminist political agendas of the period: solidarity in defense against rape and other forms of male violence; control over reproductive rights; improved pay, educational, and career opportunities; and more egalitarian gender relations, defined and realized in other than sexual terms. For many committed feminists, West generally represented not the new but the "old"-style, highly sexualized woman. West's evident pleasure in continuing to play the type as an eighty-year-old appeared to many a travesty of female dignity rather than a convincing parody of gender distinctions.

West's death at age eighty-seven in 1980 received wide press and occasioned numerous summaries of the star's accomplishments and persona. Obituaries and feature articles generally celebrated the star's long career, but many also expressed disapproval over her personal qualities and habits and asserted that she was overly vain and self-centered, especially in her later years. Los Angeles papers reported with barely concealed outrage that West left nothing in her will to her longtime companion (lover, body-guard, chauffeur, friend) Paul Novak, a former Mr. California thirty or so years the star's junior who had taken up residence with her soon after be-coming a member of her Las Vegas ensemble.

These evaluations and those that followed through the mid-1980s often referred superficially to feminist issues that West's image had evoked and sometimes admiringly deemed West a "liberated woman."[54] Despite earlier feminist dismissals of West, the tide in reception of West's image and per-formances began to turn within a few years of her death. The posthumous February 1984 publication in Ms. magazine of an interview with West sig-naled her growing validation as a popular feminist figure.[55] But just as more feminists began to embrace West's transgressive persona as a histori-cally exceptional instance of "gender bending" in American popular cul-ture, mainstream media worked to redefine and market the star as a con-ventional modern woman. A 1982 made-for-TV biographical movie titled Mae West presented its subject, in the words of West biographer Carol Ward, "as a model liberated woman who faced the now-stereotypical prob-lem of balancing romance and career."[56]

Straightening the Record

Mae West, featuring Ann Jillian in the title role, is a fictionalized biogra-phy on film, a "biopic" in industry parlance.[57] Like most Hollywood bio-pics, Mae West integrates accepted details of its subject's life into the genre's conventional narrative pattern, that of the American "myth of suc-cess." Movie star biopics are in a sense tautological, for such films confirm the myth of success that their subjects' stardom already represents.[58] Re-lating how an icon of success became successful, a biopic like Mae West offers a metamyth.

In keeping with its genre, the biopic Mae West incorporates numerous publicized elements of West's life and career, within a chronology that ex-ercises fictional license. But it also proposes revisions to the star's image by characterizing West as having been long and, unbeknownst to herself, deeply in love with one man, James Timony (West's manager for many years), portrayed by James Brolin. The biopic does suggest that West func-tioned as a cultural icon of transgressive female sexuality and nominally associates her with two implicitly gay male characters: Mr. Elsner, the di-rector of West's first produced play, Sex, and Val (played by Roddy Mc-

Dowall), West's fellow vaudeville trouper. (Val seems patterned after the acclaimed turn-of-the-century female impersonator Julian Eltinge, who reportedly helped West develop her style.) But the film effaces or renegotiates the elements that had come to dominate West's image in the previous two decades: her personal autonomy, her unabashed pleasure in multiple sexual partners, and her gay cult status as a campy female impersonator. It also almost completely erases West's long-standing professional and personal association with African Americans and indeed performers of any races or ethnic groups besides the European American.

As the film opens, Mae West awaits judgment of a suit against her 1926 play *Sex* for being salacious. Extended flashbacks cued by West's musings while gazing at herself in a mirror fill in the story of her childhood and early career, before the narrative returns to depict later episodes in her life from 1926 through about 1944. The film exaggerates West's reportedly tepid reception in vaudeville to suggest that she enjoyed tremendous success thanks to her exceptional talent, her personal determination, and an original, daringly sexy act she developed under the tutelage of James Timony and Val, West's faithful confidant throughout the film. The film makes Timony a handsome, powerful, rich young finance lawyer who helps mold West's stage and screen career and gives her legal advice and moral support for more than three decades. West's mother, a seamstress who aspires to better for the daughter she considers so special, also figures importantly in the emergence of West's winning persona.

The biopic adheres to the star's autobiography in showing her mother's influence on West's relations with men: her early interest in a number of men and her steadfast refusal, even after a secret marriage to Frank Wallace in 1911, to settle down with any one. In this she follows her mother's advice to avoid the social and professional limitations that a woman necessarily falls prey to in loving one man. But the film deviates sharply from the autobiography and other previous tales of West's life in depicting the consequences of West's persistent sexual promiscuity. As the film ends, West sits alone in a Broadway dressing room, following her triumphant stage comeback in *Diamond Lil*. Despite the dismal failure of *The Heat's On* (1943), West has again become a rollicking success, notably with female theater patrons, but only after her hesitant, tearful start on stage. And West has ventured back to the theater only at the ever-loyal Timony's urging. The film shows Timony leaving West for a time after years of jealous anguish over her refusal to marry him. But he returns to California for an emotional reunion, and West finally admits that her career and personal well-being suffered without him. Tragically, Timony soon suffers a debilitating heart attack, so West must share her *Diamond Lil* triumph with him by long-distance telephone. West recognizes the importance of romantic love and her great need and longing for a husband only when her would-be spouse lies dying in the Malibu sunset.

The biopic structures West's life and career as a romantic melodrama, complete with a dashing male romantic hero and antagonists who are individualized, such as the Paramount producer "Al Kaufman"; Mr. Abbey, an anxious representative of the Production Code Administration; and several Protestant ministers. The film thus reinterprets West's dominant image as an irrepressibly promiscuous woman who persisted to her death in resisting attachments to any one man. *That* Mae West is said to have withdrawn from a sexual relationship with Timony as he grew older and kept him on until his death in 1954 only as her business manager and old friend, while she enjoyed sexual relationships with numerous other men.[59] Writing in the late 1980s from a feminist perspective, biographer Ward dismisses the film as "embarrassingly inaccurate" and argues that especially the casting of Brolin was a "major distortion," for "the real Timony was an overweight, relatively unattractive Irishman."

Also in contrast to most previous West biographies, the biopic assigns power over its subject to parental figures (the motherly Val, the fatherly Timony), sentimentalizes her character, and shows her professional ambitions to have negative consequences. The film achieves these revisions not only through its narrative, but also in its *mise-en-scène* and cinematography, which combine to create a Mae West with private motivations quite distinct from those of the characters she portrayed in a dozen films. According to the biopic, this "real" Mae West, in marked contrast to her film persona, needed and eventually also *wanted* not just sexual satisfaction and personal and economic power, but also romantic love and emotional security with one man. The film's depiction of the star as uncertain and dependent in her private and professional lives, quite unlike her bold screen characters, inverts standard claims that West offscreen was even less sentimental, more independent, and more personally and financially powerful than her 1930s film roles allowed.

Like most biopics, *Mae West* emphasizes the importance of the subject's talents and capacity for hard work and professionalism, qualities that the key men in her life much encourage. But the film simultaneously represents what Richard Dyer, analyzing what stars signify, calls the "failure of the [American] dream."[60] The biopic shows West's professional success to interfere with her potential *personal* success in a monogamous relationship. Notably, however, it is not West's film or stage career, but rather her faithless sexual conduct, extending her professional image, that drives Timony away, leaving her lonely, unfulfilled, and now indifferent to other men. West's personal loss forbodes a sharp downturn in her professional success; Timony's return signals her career's revival.

Mae West thus expresses not a direct failure of the myth of success, but rather the limitations of another myth that Dyer identifies as a component of stardom: the ideology of conspicuous consumption. Some American movie stars, such as Judy Garland, represent the failure of this myth, for their stories relate the personally debilitating effects of high living. But, again significantly, it is *not* West's celebrity or wealth, manifested in the film in her luxurious clothes, cars, and jewels, or any stress-induced consumption of alcohol or drugs that interferes with her true happiness. Instead, the biopic attributes West's unhappiness to her compulsive consumption of sex partners.

The representational convention associating sexual liaisons with consumer items such as jewelry receives emphasis only in West's relationship with Timony, who gives her a diamond necklace. Lighting, camera work, and music make Timony's seducing West with the gift a romantic scene. The film makes this crucial exchange of goods (Timony's diamonds for West's sexual favors) entirely unproblematic; West's accepting the diamonds—the conspicuous consumption that stardom fosters—leads only to love and success. But West violates the terms of the exchange by pursuing other men not for diamonds, but for pleasure alone.

Mae West thus makes its subject embody the myth of success, but also to suffer its rupture due to excessive sexual consumption. In this the biopic promotes a version of "Mae West" resembling Marilyn Monroe, whose image reveals that success can lead to destruction through excessive sexuality. Unlike Monroe, however, West is shown to be suffering not because others sexually exploit her, but because she sexually exploits herself and others. Also unlike Monroe, West in this film fails only temporarily: instead of dying, desperate and alone, at her own hand at age thirty-six, West suffers a professional and psychological setback for several years, but overcomes this through her belated insight into the importance of romantic, emotional commitment to one man. Although the melodramatic conventions that shape the film anticipate a more punitive end for the heroine, West's fame as a long-lived successful career woman beyond the period depicted obviously constrained the screenplay from subjecting her to a tragic fate.

Thus, even though *Mae West* portrays excessive career ambitions and sexual promiscuity as impeding personal happiness, West's professional revival constitutes the film's narrative climax and colors its brief denouement and close. "Mae, you've done it," Timony congratulates her from his invalid's bed. "You're here to stay!" The final scene fades out to melancholy music over a wiser and lonely, but still young and glamorous Mae West, shot in silhouette at her dressing room window. This shot cuts to closing credits scrolling over a medium close-up freeze frame of a smiling Ann Jillian/West in Gay Nineties costume. The shot, culled from an earlier scene in the film depicting West's appearance in *Every Day's a Holiday*, approximates widely reproduced stills of West in similar poses and costume and so recalls West's historical movie star status.

Mae West gains authority by initially adhering to established parameters of the star's image: that she was both happily promiscuous *and* a professional success. But within those parameters, the biopic rewrites West's persona. As Ward notes, the film establishes the false dichotomy prevalent in much discourse in the United States, which assumes that a woman's career must preclude her achieving stable intimate relationships. Paradoxically, the film represents West's multiple sexual partners as a facet of her *professional* life, manifesting her narcissistic career drive. The biopic narratively reconciles the star's purported personal failures with her prevailing successful reputation in Timony's projected death.

The film's take on the supposed dilemma—affirming a woman's need for a man while characterizing the ideal husband as supportive of his spouse's career—echoes a centrist feminist position on gender roles current in 1982. The TV film seems directed particularly toward women and, indeed, molds West into the kind of figure that Rosen and Mellen had sought the previous decade. In its refiguring West's image within a superficially updated but fundamentally conservative sexual ideology, *Mae West* seems an effort by the entertainment industry to reclaim the star posthumously for contemporary mainstream consumption.[61]

But just as Paramount's mid-1930s efforts to sanitize West's image to meet altered social circumstances had failed, the biopic's flattened characterization of West scarcely affected her dominant star image a half century later. By the mid-1980s, West's campy drag queen persona had become a basis not only for her sustained popularity among gay men, but also for many feminists' growing interest in her image as a cultural sign worthy of renewal and celebration.

6

Merging Interests

The renewed attention that feminist critics began to pay West in the mid-
to late 1980s has several probable sources. One is a continuing popular interest in West as an exceptional historical figure: a successful female cinematic author whose self-directed performance, screenplay writing, and
brash sexual, emotional, and financial autonomy yet remain uncommon
onscreen and off. The gradual shift in feminist media theory over the past
fifteen years, away from a primary critical focus on a theorized male spectator's perceptions and uses of female representations to more concerted
study of what pleasures actual women spectators derive from popular cultural forms, has also provoked reevaluation of West's image and recorded
performances.

This critical shift, which has crystallized in academia as feminist-inflected cultural studies, expanded ethnic studies, queer studies, and identity politics, accompanies a growing awareness of how racial, gender, and
class identities may codetermine media reception. It has become evident
that neither of two dominant feminist critical approaches to media (the
sociological and the psychoanalytic) developed in the 1970s and early
1980s can sufficiently account for the persistent pleasures that female audiences continue to find in the very media icons and texts (from romance
novels and soap operas to Mae West) that many early feminist theorists
summarily dismissed.[1]

Both factors—West's protofeminist persona and a concern with how diverse audiences, but especially women, consume popular culture—evoked
my own interest in the figure. My initial reappraisals of what pleasures female consumers might glean from West's image resonated with other feminist essays that began to appear in both scholarly and popular publications,
sometimes with an implicit address to lesbian consumers.[2] But current
feminist acclaim of West does not indicate that either the star's critical
academic or broader public reception has satisfactorily answered earlier
feminist objections to her performances and image. Rather, ongoing de-

bates about representations of the excessively sexual and gender-transgressive woman—for failing as a positive model for female viewers, for focusing
excessively on the sexual display of the body, and for parodying women
from misogynist perspectives—have been displaced onto another figure:
Madonna. Audiences and critics in the 1980s and early 1990s vilified,
praised, and elaborated that performer as an emblem of contested sociopolitical issues to an extent comparable to West's reception among audiences
and media institutions in the 1930s.

Just as declared feminists and openly gay men determined West's dominant reception over the past three decades, these two sets of critics and
consumers have largely shaped Madonna's sustained cultural impact. But
unlike 1970s criticism of West, feminist analysis of Madonna has generally
not taken that star's appeal to gay men to indicate misogyny in her image.
Nor do most current feminist critiques of *West* reiterate the homophobic
attitudes in 1970s writing. An exception occurs, surprisingly, in an August
1993 *New York Times* essay by Molly Haskell, where she asserts, "[West]
made [the unfortunate] *Myra Breckinridge* and *Sextette* at a time when she
was much too old and her gay constituency had become more explicit and
obtrusive."[3]

Despite Haskell's apparent loss of sympathy since 1974 for gay perspectives on West, most current feminist writing on the star implicitly accepts
as unproblematic her continuing status as a gay icon, if one now secondary
to Madonna, Bette Midler, and other figures. A more confident feminist
focus on women's responses to West may have led to the change in tone,
possibly also some self-censorship of potentially offensive or socially inappropriate observations. But I think the change may also be due to a growing political rapprochement, often on a microsocial level, between gay
men and feminists of all sexual orientations, in conjunction with the
broadening of both the gay and the women's movements and the commitment of both to a concerted response in the AIDS crisis. Still, West's feminist and gay male evaluation has remained largely disparate, isolated in
separate essays and books. No study before 1990 explicitly addressed what
joint interests feminists and gay men might have in West's image as a cultural icon.[4]

As Madonna's controversial reception has attested, the issues that
West's image evokes remain vital in feminist approaches to media as well
as in developing queer analytic approaches. But feminist and gay reception
and analysis need not stand in isolation, contrast, or contestation. In this
chapter's analysis, summarizing critical issues surrounding "Mae West," I

argue that feminist and gay male interests in the figure may be comple-
mentary rather than antithetical.

Several Mae West jokes and quips in recent circulation structure the argument yielding that conclusion. I consider the range of possible readings
each joke invites or enables as a textual form within the larger nexus "Mae
West," and discuss what is at stake in various responses to Westian jokes,
and to her stage, film, or other appearances. Just as class position, gender
identity, and institutional affiliations influenced responses to West in the
1930s, whether a 1990s consumer *qua* popular producer of West discovers
in her performances and jokes a negative feminine image, a sexist phallic
spectacle, or a playfully campy queen may correlate to a high degree with
the gender and class politics of the cultural participant passing judgment.

A Positively Negative Image?

MAE WEST: I'm the girl that works at Paramount all day and Fox all
night.

West utters this punning joke in the 1978 independently produced film
Sextette. She addresses the audience directly, standing next to a triple mirror in a shimmering black beaded dress with white fur trim and a high-
arching black feather headdress. Her appearance here, even to her long
blonde wig and thickened waist, anticipates (and may have been a model
for) that of impersonator Charles Pierce on the front of the "Call me when
you're through practicing" greeting card I discuss in the Introduction (see
Figure 1). West's line comes as the last in a series of short star turns: she
models a sequence of elaborate gowns and verbally punctuates each vignette with a smutty quip. Keith Moon, playing a screaming queen dress
designer, provides over-the-top commentary on the joys of female fashion
to connect the short scenes.

Like much of West's film dialogue, the quip has circulated colloquially
as a joke. And, as Freudian psychiatrist Eidelberg observed in 1945 of the
"Mae West and ten sailors" joke, some people laugh when they hear it,
some people don't. The joke may shock or disconcert the people who don't
laugh (and perhaps some who do), probably depending on who relates the
joke to them (and utters the "f-word" thereby), as well as on what prior
view the listeners have of "Mae West."

In the film, the joke's narrator is, of course, a heavily made-up and glam-
orously dressed octogenarian woman playing bride to a young Timothy
Dalton, who a few scenes before has serenaded West about her continuing

youth and beauty. Like much dialogue in *Sextette*'s pastiched homage, West's line refers to the star's familiar associations, specifically her work at Paramount Studios in the 1930s and with Twentieth Century Fox for *Myra Breckinridge*. But the joke listener's response probably relies less on the pleasure of recognizing those citations than on her or his attitude about West as a woman who even as an eighty-six-year-old exhibitionistically celebrates how she "fox/fucks" at will.

West long maintained her status as a cultural icon signifying transgression precisely by continually offending presumptions about what sexual behaviors (or claims about those) are socially appropriate—for whom and in what contexts. The power of West's "Fox all night" line to amuse or shock or both arises in part from her taking—even in a pun—the yet somewhat taboo word *fuck* to describe her own sexual activity. West's uttering the word as an expletive or intensifier ("Fuck!"; "That fucking . . .") would probably shock even more than her using it as a verb. Although West's pronouncing the verb may strike some viewers as vulgar or anachronistic to her image, it (unlike cursing) expresses her long-standing association with unrestrained sex in the terms of a linguistically freer era.

The quip's potential to offend many listeners no doubt lies less in West's words or their attribution to her in the joke's retelling than in their conjunction in *Sextette* with the spectacle of her aging body. Most feminist critics who currently praise West focus only on her earlier image, ignoring the later productions altogether or briefly condemning them as "unfortunate valedictory films," as Haskell does in her 1993 essay. Haskell also now condemns West's late image as a "grotesque parody of a parody." Another contemporary author, Pamela Robertson, who otherwise lauds the feminist import of West's visual and audial excesses and social transgressions on screen, dismisses her late image in passing as "a one-dimensional misogynist joke."[5]

Yet the star's ultimate transgression may well be her most radical representation, for her late image violates the strong proscription against clearly postmenopausal women displaying sexual vanity and lust—and their alleged desirability to men forty or more years their junior. The intragenerational sexual relations that West enacts may offend so deeply because the pairing of the older woman with the much younger man implicitly breaks the strongest incest taboo: between mother and son. It may also yet offend some feminist critics and consumers because West's masculine associations—the presumably gay male behind the female impersonator that her late-career appearance and behavior strongly encodes—may seem to displace a positive, womanly identity.[6]

The conclusion that West's masquerade effaces womanliness or that her sexy octogenarian image is intrinsically misogynist presupposes an ideal femininity that the star fails to realize. Further, concern that West (whether at age forty or eighty) presents a negative image for women presumes that viewers recognize the star sign as a model they might wish to emulate, or as a realistic type whose treatment of and by others is a template for social relations. There may be some slight merit to this argument with reference to the ten-year-old "wannabes" who emerged around Madonna in the mid-1980s. But although children have impersonated West (as did, for example, a twelve-year-old Mickey Rooney in 1932 and a six-year-old Shirley Temple in 1934), their acts, like those of Charles Pierce and other Westian performers on club stages and at Halloween balls, never worshipfully emulated West.[7] Rather, in comedically enacting the star's own clearly exaggerated style, Mae West impersonators have always addressed and compounded the gender-transgressive implications in her own performance.

With the exception, perhaps, of Beverly West, the star's look-alike sister, who made a living for a time as a Mae West impersonator, women and men have "played" "Mae West" only as a fantasy figure. As in the PCA employee's imagined scenario (discussed in chapter 2) in which a young woman, to her father's dismay, teasingly invites her suitors to "come up," women who have witnessed West may perform a gesture, utter a phrase, tell a joke, briefly feel empowered.[8] But there is no evidence that audiences ever construed West's image as realistic or that the image has had any sustained impact on viewers' behaviors. Given the extent to which West's image is inscribed—and consumed—as illusion, it is illogical to fault the performer for exaggerating or exceeding some "realistic" social norm.

This is the case also for claims that West's late-career appearances are grotesque, disgusting, or pathetic, largely, so goes the rhetoric, because West as a highly narcissistic person had begun to take herself seriously as she aged and thereby lost the ironic edge many valued in her earlier performances. A viewer may well conclude that West was earnestly trying to embody a sexual glamour queen despite her age, rather than intending a parody of such a figure. But from either perspective, West's late-career appearance and performances extend the excesses—of bodily adornment, of evident narcissism, of bold sexual speech—that always constituted her image as a sign. Her evident age only intensifies the social incongruity, the outrageousness, the excess that always characterized her performance.

Indeed, West's positioning as a subject speaking excessive, transgressive desire has been the primary basis of her functions as a gay icon *and* of feminist readings of her performance. Critics who valorize the early but condemn the late image reveal more about their own biases against certain kinds of excesses, in favor of others, than anything about West's performance or iconographic functioning. This observation applies as well to Madonna's ambivalent critics, for the workings of spectacular excess are central to the impact of both cultural icons.

Coming Up, Going West?

MAE WEST/LADY LOU (in *She Done Him Wrong*): Why don't you come up sometime and see me? I'm home every evening.

Many feminist media critics and consumers no longer accept as self-evident the argument that Claire Johnston made about West: that her visual presentation illustrates how all female stars operate as fetishistic phallic signs. Yet none of the challenges and revisions to Johnston's and other feminist theorists' psychoanalytic approaches to date have satisfactorily countered her pronouncement about West, or cogently demonstrated how the spectacular excess in West's image relates to her status as cultural icon. Although West's image is exceptional in ways demonstrated in previous chapters, it offers a productive site for exploring how female cinema stars that become celebrities or even icons may signify something besides a phallic sign, in Lacanian terms.

In recent years, Johnston's work has been put aside (some of it quite undeservedly, I think), but both scholarly and popular feminist media discourses continue to address—and sometimes hotly contest—the effects of a female star's construction as fetishistic spectacle, now often in reference to Madonna. In Freud's writings and in much media analysis drawing directly or indirectly on Freud, the fetish enables the male user or cinematic viewer to deny sexual difference (the "lack" of the female) by symbolically replacing the missing penis of the female/mother, thereby assuaging castration anxiety. From this perspective, West's body, elaborately adorned in furs, feathers, highly tactile fabrics, jewels, and other signs of luxury, represents not a woman but only a projection of male narcissistic fantasy, Johnston's "phallic replacement."[9]

Although a grasp of West's filmic image as "phallic" is apt, the much-used term provides insights only when freshly theorized. Moving beyond psychoanalytic approaches that implicitly correlate the phallus with the penis or with the social category "male," one can conceptualize the term as a historically and culturally determined sign of power only conventionally correlated with biological sex.[10] Rather than comprehending "woman" exclusively as a mark of difference, as "nonmale," one can recognize the representation of *a woman*, a member of a historically determined and politically relevant social category, as a sign of presence. In this view, Mae West appears *not* as nonmale, but as a female asserting in her costuming and performance a claim to the phallus as a sign of power. From this perspective, "Mae West" represents a phallic woman.

Psychoanalytic discussions of representation have sometimes considered figures such as the snake-haired Medusa and the witch, "adorned with manifold symbols of masculinity," as examples of "the phallic woman."[11] This use of the concept "phallic" fits West. Her body is in fact doubly fetishized: first, in its associations with conventional phallic representations of power (such as the gold-crested riding crop she wields while singing "Easy Rider" in *She Done Him Wrong* and the Malay knife that was largely censored out of *Klondike Annie*); second, in the Marxist sense of fetishism, in being marked as an overvalued commodity. But the phrase *phallic woman* is not equivalent to *phallic sign*, for the former term assumes conscious recognition of the operative social gender of the signifying figure, in conjunction with a perhaps unconscious reading of the phallus as a symbol of sexual power. So understood, phallic woman represents a *powerfully sexual female*, who possesses the potential to give and to withhold what she *has*, rather than what she presumably lacks. The concept "phallic woman" thus expands rather than effaces the gendered term *female* by refuting any presumed biological imperative in relation to power and negating conventional role ascriptions.

In chapter 4, I suggested that audiences may respond to West's cinematic performance through a masochistic dynamic: the powerful sexual woman may offer a viewer not unpleasurably threatened with castration anxiety the pleasures of relinquishing power to a dominant counterpart. Given West's presence as phallic woman and her exceptional narrative positioning on screen and stage, her performance may, in a variation of the paradigmatic male-centered Oedipal narrative, elicit pleasures of *female* control: to *be* a powerful woman, or, alternately, and perhaps simultaneously, even for female viewers, to *possess* the powerful woman. West's spectacular image may engage male and female spectators in a fantasy of being potential objects as well as viewing subjects of the star's display. Particularly, West's iconographic depiction of the prostitute with the heart of gold—the lustful, loving mother—may evoke the erotic appeal of being passive, under the control of a powerful, indulgent maternal figure, "the phallic mother."[12]

A plenitudinous female form such as West's—with her full breasts and ample hips—may embody the powerful, sensual, engulfing mother for female and male consumers alike. Indeed, in 1934 an engaging article in *Photoplay*, a movie fan magazine marketed to women, analyzed West's appeal as a powerful—and powerfully loving—mother.[13] A feature the same year in *Esquire*—"The Magazine for Men"—also suggested, albeit less directly, that men's pleasure in West arose from their imagined helplessness in her ever-open, loving arms.[14] The 1964 *Mister Ed* episode discussed in chapter 4 made its theme the title character's desire for precisely such maternal indulgence from West. West enacts the phallic mother, who, within the program's narrative operations, threatens castration. Ed's initially strong desire in seeking West as a mother figure transforms into an impulse to flee when he becomes aware of the sexual power underpinning West's mothering.

Thus, a reassessed psychoanalytic approach to narrative and cinematic suture can account for the masochistic pleasures that the excessive spectacle of West may offer to *all* viewers, not only to female spectators, as Mulveyan feminist psychoanalytic theory, positing a narrow, gender-aligned process of identification, would have it. Indeed, West's broad and lasting appeal may reside in her exceptional potential to elicit masochistic as well as sadistic fantasies, however unconscious. Certainly, the promise embedded in West's much-quoted line from *She Done Him Wrong* seems enticingly double-edged. "Come up and see me," as the offer has been reiterated thousands of times, may well gloss as "Come up and subject yourself *to* me."

West's (as well as Madonna's) functioning imagistically as a powerful maternal figure has no doubt influenced her popularity among gay men as a camp icon, in relation to her status as (female) female impersonator. As Esther Newton notes in explaining the title of her book,

"Mother Camp" as an honorific implies something about the relationship of the female impersonator to his gay audience. A female impersonator will sometimes refer to himself as "mother," as in "Your mother's gonna explain all these dirty words to you." . . . [The] drag queen . . . is a magical dream figure: the fusion of mother and son.[15]

Newton argues that although all female impersonators in the gay world are drag queens, not all are "camps." The drag queen engages in a masculine-feminine transformation that expresses incongruities, but the camp presents a "*philosophy* of transformations and incongruity," through the *comedic* performance of gender as a matter of style and artifice.[16] Many other feminists, straight and lesbian, have over the past twenty years come to appreciate camp's aesthetic, emotional, or political potential, including that of cross-gender impersonation, a central instance of camp.

Parker Tyler argues in his discussion of West's import as "Mother Superior" of female impersonators, "[I]f the female impersonator has one serious moral function, it is to inform the world that sex is a sense of style, a predilection of the mind and senses, and is not answerable to nature's dually blunt decision about gender."[17] West's designation as a female impersonator has always, in gay male subculture, signaled recognition not only of "Mae West" as camp, but of Mae West herself as *a* camp.[18] Although some feminist critics have dismissed West precisely on that account, others have come to value the camp impact of her image. These feminists, myself among them, find common cause with gay male audiences in understanding the sign "Mae West" as a welcome parody of the social dictates maintaining conventional gender boundaries.

However serious West's function as a campy female impersonator, the construction of her performance *as camp* relies crucially on the verbal comedy continually inflecting her exaggeratedly feminine costume and gesture. The broad dissemination of West's comedic quips has largely borne her iconographic status over decades, even when her films received only very limited exhibition. This is not to say that everyone who enjoys Westian jokes has always consumed her as camp. The much-quoted "Is that a pistol in your pocket" line is pretty straightforward ribaldry when related by a straight woman to a presumably straight man. West's line asserts its narrator's ability to elicit sexual reactions from men and, when the narrator is a woman, her sass in speaking freely and publicly of the spectacle of the male body, pointing to the erect penis as a potential source of social embarrassment to men. A woman uttering the line momentarily s(e)izes and plays with the phallus in that form. But there is no philosophy of gender incongruities behind the play. Such may arise if one man utters the line to another—or to a woman. The line also works as camp when the male pistol is transformed into a female puddle (significantly *not* the realistic source of women's potential social embarrassment, a puddle of menstrual blood). What makes that joke camp is the hyperbole, the excess—in volume and visibility—of female lubricity, along with the incongruity (in terms of social norms but also with reference to West's heterosexual/gay male image) of West's sexual desirability to a woman watching her.

The puddle joke related in the introduction distills three recurrent elements in West's star image: sex, power, and gender ambiguity/ transgression. Their joint comedic enactment—whether performed by or attributed to West—expresses the gender impersonation and creates the camp moment. Feminists' appreciation of that and other outrageous Westian jokes—and of West's image altogether—may turn on acceptance of campy impersonation as a performative and interpretive strategy that deconstructs and displaces rather than heralds the masculine phallic spectacle.[19] Feminist appreciation of West also depends on a comprehension of camp practice not as a parody of the female, but rather as a humorous critique of a repressive binary gender system that constrains women—straight and lesbian—as much as or more than gay men.

Who's Wa(s)tching Which Hair?

In the early 1930s, Marlene Dietrich and Mae West were both leading stars at Paramount. In interviews, a newspaper reporter tried to elicit evidence of a catty feud between them. West refused to criticize Dietrich, saying, "Why, Marlene and I are the greatest of friends. She likes to cook and I like to eat, so we're both happy. We're such good friends that the other day she offered to wash my hair. I wouldn't let her, though, because I wasn't sure which hair she meant!"

This narrative joke, a version of which circulated at least a decade before the pistol became a puddle, suggests the complexity of "Mae West's" associations with lesbian desire.[20] Enjoyment of the joke depends on listener recognition not only of West's but also of Dietrich's star image, which, as I have noted, has long circulated as both a gay and a lesbian icon. Response also depends on the listener's own attitude toward those stars and the sexual transgressions each represents. Thus, some listeners may think the joke a put-down of Dietrich as a known bisexual and conclude that it expresses general hostility toward women desiring women. Others may hear and enjoy its articulating the option of lesbian sexuality, for, as a lesbian friend remarked, "West doesn't say which hair she *wanted* washed!" (This is not to suggest, of course, that lesbians wouldn't also enjoy washing each other's *head* hair!)[21]

Any presumably straight female speaker in the joke but West would probably make the ambiguous joke seem hostile. But West's sexually transgressive nature supports comprehension of it as a smutty joke hinting at lesbian sex, even though her own image itself is generally construed as that of a heterosexual woman. Just as West's interracial associations earlier enhanced her aura of sexual transgression (as Madonna's also do), West's presumed tabooed sexual practices readily transmute. To construe West in the joke as wishing Dietrich to wash her pubic hair is not to assert that West was lesbian, nor to claim that any lesbian would want to bathe or otherwise would seriously desire West. Rather, it is to enunciate a grasp of both West and Dietrich as transgressing a restrictive heterosexual norm. From such a perspective, the joke conjures up a playful polymorphous scene suggesting the gender bending that a Paramount publicity photograph of the two stars together already hinted at: a gay man impersonating a woman coupled with a gay woman impersonating a man (see Figure 48). A gay couple, indeed!

By no means have all viewers taken the pronounced feminine excess in West's appearance as cross-gender impersonation or as any sort of disguise. In the early years of her movie stardom, as I have documented in chapter 1, West was earnestly promoted and regarded by some as a glamorous, stylish woman. But West's generally anachronistic dress and exaggerated manner, onscreen and off, have always suggested to some observers that she was performing a feminine masquerade. Feminist media critics, including Claire Johnston and Mary Ann Doane, have discussed the possible effects of gender masquerade in cinema. Departing from observations made by psychoanalyst Joan Riviere in 1929, Doane argued in 1982,

> The masquerade, in flaunting femininity, holds it at a distance. . . . The masquerade's resistance to patriarchal positioning would therefore lie in its denial of the production of femininity as closeness, as presence-to-itself, as, precisely, imagistic. . . . By destabilizing the image, the masquerade confounds th[e] masculine structure of the look. It effects a defamiliarization of female iconography.[22]

Doane names Dietrich and the *femme fatale* type as examples of Hollywood figures enacting such a masquerade. My analysis of both West's performance and her long-standing reception has revealed how vividly "Mae

West" creates the effects that Doane describes. Doane's analysis, which ex-plores the possibilities for female film spectatorship, can also account for most feminist critics' rejection of West's late-career image, for "[t]he effec-tivity of masquerade lies precisely in its potential to manufacture a dis-tance from the image, to generate a problematic within which the image is manipulable, producible and readable by the woman."[23]

Viewers who think that West was seriously presenting herself as glam-orous in *Sextette* miss any distance between West's self-presentation and her persona, through which she (and they) might manipulate, produce, or read her image as a gender parody. The older West got, the more she was held to be vain, narcissistic, and deluded about her own sexual appeal. These characteristics, considered negative in any woman but entirely un-acceptable in an eighty-year-old, contributed for some consumers to the collapse of distance between the aging actress and celebrity Mae West and her performative image. A camp reading discerns such distance also in West's late image.

West's reception as a camp figure thus parallels but also counters her consumption as fetishized spectacle. Feminist as well as queer camp per-spectives can discover in her image a critique not only of what Doane calls feminine iconography, but also fundamentally of gender—femininity *and* masculinity—as a social construct. "Dietrich" may do so as well, given her alternating appearance in both male and female attire and widely accepted bisexuality. West's construction and reception as a *female* female imperson-ator yields her capacity to reveal both femininity and masculinity as a fa-cade, for the implied masculinity behind the feminine masquerade is also only an act. As I argued in chapters 4 and 5, the muscle men and other exaggeratedly masculine figures that surrounded West throughout her ca-reer, but particularly in her nightclub and late-career film performances, augmented the parody of masculinity suggested in West's own swaggering image.

My argument detailing how West's image *may* be considered camp does not, of course, require that it always is or *should* be so read. My analysis maintains that "Mae West" has always operated as a multivalent image, and that not every aspect of the image is equally available to all consumers. I have also argued that West's image has lent itself to sometimes contra-dictory readings and uses, due largely to the often ambiguous impact of her comedic performances. A case in point is the interpretation I offer in chap-ter 4 of West's appearance on *Mister Ed*. I myself perceive West as gender impersonator in that episode, whether it is seen against the show's original promotion and reception, or within the series as it now circulates in cable reruns, in part to a camp-happy audience. But my interpretation admittedly relies on reading strategies not widely accessible to many viewers in 1964 and still not available to some, especially to children. "Camp" is certainly not an exclusive way of understanding or enjoying the program; West's image can come across to some more as self-ridicule than as parodic gender impersonation. An analysis of a final citation illustrates the diverse interpretations that contemporary references to West may provoke, and what these might reveal about the icon's contribution to the politics of personal identity.

Do You Scream for Ice Cream?

When I'm caught between two evils, I always like to take the one I've never tried.

In the late 1980s, the interiors of buses in the Chicago transit system featured a poster emblazoned with this much-cited Westian quip from *Klondike Annie*. Two stylized drawings of ice cream sundaes, one in a tall parfait glass, one in a low boat dish used for banana splits, illustrated the saying. The poster mentioned neither a brand of ice cream nor any shop where one might make the proffered choice. And West's name appeared nowhere: the quip ran without attribution. Small print indicated only that the poster was part of a series by a San Franciso graphics company. Ah—its purpose, indirect as it was, emerges: to promote the use of interior bus advertising space, which had much fallen off.

The range of possible interpretations a bus rider might give this poster confirms the importance of spectator position in discerning what is at stake in reading "Mae West." At first glance, the bus poster seems to sell nothing, instead offering a pleasant amusement amid urban mundanity. Readers who do not recognize its association with West might take it as a mild joke: the thought of choosing between two "evils," rather than between good and evil, may seem funny (if not morally obscene) when melded with the idea that an ice cream menu encompasses all evil, and that indulging a sweet tooth is a sin. In a surfeited economy, food may become eroticized—as ice cream and bananas, together or separately, often are. Many readers may thus find the poster a vaguely *sexual* joke. Those who recognize the citation as deriving from West are almost certain to do so.

In West's original utterance, the phrase suggests a choice between sexual partners. Its humor lies in casting as "evil" a desired sexual adventure that the speaker clearly plans to pursue, and just as clearly holds for "good," not evil. The poster's connecting word and picture casts the graphics as sexual symbols, though the gender correlation of the illustrations remains a matter of taste. If the tall parfait seems conventionally phallic, its V shape also evokes vaginal imagery. And the low boat dish offers a banana split topped with whipped cream and a cherry: make of that what you will. I see in its two lips and horizontality hints at vulvularity and other banana-enveloping orifices.

For those who recognize West behind the quotation, the ice cream sundaes may evoke her choosing, as she often does in films, between two or more eager male lovers. But those who also acknowledge West's broad gay associations may discover in the poster more transgressive options than West's own apparently heterosexual choices. Inflected through West's image, the delectables offer a variety of flavors: What kind of ice cream haven't *you* tried—which gender, race, or sexual style?

Neither the juxtaposition of a parfait and a banana split nor the "choosing between two evils" inscription entails the poster's seeming an affront to monogamous heterosexuality. But that was also the case when West spoke the words in *Klondike Annie*. It was "not what she said, but how she said it"—even more to the point, *who* said it, and who heard it. West's powerful but playfully transgressive star image invites the reader to join her in choosing an untried sexual object or fantasy. Pleasure in—and perhaps also displeasure at—the poster may arise from perceiving that it articulates inhibited desire. Especially recognition of West's image behind the poster may, at the moment of reading it (as while watching a film or other Westian performance), temporarily alleviate—but possibly aggravate—the sociopsychic repression of a viewer's polymorphously sexual impulses.

The bus poster also documents the absorption of a formerly distinctive symbol into the anonymous pastiche of postmodernist commodity culture. It neither marks the "author" of its tag line nor sells any product: not ice cream, not a movie, not even a cigar, as West's image was once, against her own wishes, used to do.[24] West's uncredited line here doesn't even sell the poster displaying it, as greeting cards and anthologies of her sayings do; rather, it sells only the patch of undervalued promotional space that the poster covers. The poster producers may have thereby achieved what the PCA's editing of *Klondike Annie* and ABC's broadcast of the *Mae West* biopic could not: a flattening of "Mae West," reducing it from its persistent cultural function—and its equally persistent economic value—as a challenging sign of social transgression to an odd declaration about junk food.

Still, to judge from television commercials and other media forms in a secular, health-conscious, 1990s North American culture, eating fatty sweets may have become the ultimate popular sin, with transgressive power practically tantamount to that of switching lovers when West first spoke the line. "Mae West" does yet entice, delight, challenge, and sell. As expansive and adaptable and profitable as the image has proven over most of the twentieth century, it is likely that "Mae West" will continue to circulate as an emblem of what is both forbidden and accessible. But its specific historical functions and meanings will shift further, as in the image's use as a rhetorical trope to promote Madonna as West's successor icon and commodity.

Beyond exploring "Mae West" as a particular formation, I have argued in this book for combining critical methodologies to elucidate how popular culture operates as a source and site of social meanings. I have thus endeavored to synthesize a range of productive approaches to media: star studies, close textual interpretation, discursive analysis of cultural phenomena, industrial and social history, modified feminist psychoanalytic media criticism, and genre analysis. I believe that the compound theoretical apparatus the book demonstrates using the case "Mae West" may prove a fruitful method of analysis for other star images and cultural signifiers.

Besides unpacking my fascination with "Mae West" while developing critical approaches to popular culture, this book has, I trust, revealed another of my interests and intellectual projects: helping to decenter the still highly visible, universalized generic (and implicitly heterosexual) male spectator who has long dominated media studies, even prior to "his" theorization through feminist psychoanalytic criticism. I have also sought to challenge an ongoing scholarly *and* popular feminist concern with women's suffering from the dominance of that male spectator/producer/consumer in and through media. In doing so, I by no means underestimate the ideological power of the male-dominated institutional and material bases of popular culture. Nor do I undervalue the crucial contributions psychoanalytic feminist theorists have made to the profound analysis of the en-gendered address that obtains within media and that can imbricate the consumer.

But while recognizing the historical constraints structuring media consumption, I have worked to displace the male spectator/reader who may bring the unconscious arrogance of a socially privileged position to cultural icons, and thus approach Mae West exclusively, without comprehension of alternative views, as a "red-hot mama" awaiting his pleasure or ridicule. MPPDA staff member Ray Norr, who in 1933 imagined a father who himself enjoyed West's performance but objected to his daughter's enjoying the same, was focusing on the father's reaction and acceding to that man's power to determine the dollars and sense that West signified. There are probably readers who share Norr's, or even the father's, concerns. I acknowledge those readings, but do not privilege them. Instead, I have attempted to reconstruct the historical reception of a cultural sign, "Mae West," in all its diversity and variability. I have aimed to demonstrate particularly how feminist-minded women and gay men and others who are engaged in some degree of sociopolitical and psychological opposition to the status quo may produce alternative cultural representations that foster their interests out of the materials of dominant popular culture. Although "Mae West" was and is such a dominant cultural product, that performer and icon has also offered rich source material and complex multiple pleasures to a wide array of "coproducing" consumers.

Notes

Introduction: Posthumous Citings from Pistol to Puddle

1. Bob Thomas (AP, Los Angeles), "Mae West Remains Hot Number," *Champaign-Urbana News-Gazette*, 15 August 1993, F2.

2. Molly Haskell, "Mae West's Bawdy Spirit Spans the Gay 90s," *New York Times*, 15 August 1993, 14. Previously, the only West films available on video had been her first star vehicle, *She Done Him Wrong* (1933); her film with costar W. C. Fields, *My Little Chicadee* (1940); and her late-career films *Myra Breckinridge* (1970) and *Sextette* (1978). Otherwise, West's films have been available in 16mm and 35mm rental prints for retrospective screenings or classroom use, and also play occasionally on late-night local television or cable TV; for example, *Klondike Annie* (1936) ran on the American Movie Classics cable channel in 1991. Many U.S. cultural consumers who have never seen an entire West film may recognize her from photographs or from brief clips of her films integrated into documentaries about Hollywood film.

3. Carl Anthony, "The Mae in Madonna," *Los Angeles Times*, 10 January 1993, 22. I suggested in my essay "Madonna from Marilyn to Marlene: Pastiche and/or Parody?" *Journal of Film and Video*, 42, no. 2 (1990): 28, that West's exaggerated female impersonation may have served Madonna as a prototype. For extensive critical discussion of Madonna's book *Sex*, see Lisa Frank and Paul Smith, eds., *Madonnarama: Essays on Sex and Popular Culture* (Pittsburgh: Cleiss, 1993).

4. A sampling of popular Westian citations or formulations that have appeared in recent years includes the following. The *Chicago Tribune Magazine*, 15 March 1990, 10, cites West in a filler item: "To catch a husband is an art; to hold him is a job." *TV Guide*, 15-21 April 1989 obliquely equates Joan Collins and West (whose second starring feature was titled *I'm No Angel*) in a headline accompanying Collins's cover photo: " 'I'm No Angel': Joan Collins' Parting Shots at Dynasty." A 1989 Ben Sargent political cartoon captioned "Dubious Conversations" suggests that then Vice President Dan Quayle's claim to having discussed human rights with Central American politicians was as likely as "Mae West discuss[ing] chastity with a grapefruit." Press discussions around the time of the death of Muppets creator Jim Henson in May 1990 noted that he had based the character of Miss Piggy on West. And African American actor Jackee Harry noted that she had based her performance of the character Sandra on the NBC television show *227* on West. See Kathleen Mackay, "Jackee Harry's High-Tack Style Enlivens '227,' " *Chicago Tribune TV Week*. The *Texas Monthly*, August 1990, 111, featured a large

color ad for a Dallas bar called Nana that had as its headline: "Why don't you come up and see Nana sometime?" John Darnton reported in "Political Correctness: A Quirk the British Can Do Without," *New York Times*, 13 March 1994, E4, that in spring 1994 London was studded with billboards for the Wonderbra bearing the tag line "Or are you just glad to see me?" below a photograph of a "giggling, scantily clad model." Another citation of that line appeared on page H14 in the same issue of the *New York Times*, in an advertisement for *Naked Gun 33⅓: The Final Insult*. The banner headline on the ad read "Mostly All New Jokes."

Further: A friend who carries a key chain with an attached plaque that reads "Too much of a good thing is wonderful" recounted to me in the late 1980s how a man whom she did not know noticed the key chain in her hand while they were both waiting in a shop and remarked, "I've always wanted to meet a woman who thinks like Mae West!" A local restaurant in my university community advertised itself in 1992 as "a natural cafe, where too much of a good thing can be wonderful." West's image had of course sold products through movie tie-ins, such as hats for May's Department Store in Los Angeles, in a Paramount publicity campaign for *Goin' to Town* (1935). Late in her life, West herself did radio commercials for Poland Spring Water. See Kevin Thomas, "Mae West—Testing Commercial Waters," *Los Angeles Times*, 29 August 1979, IV 26.

5. To give one contemporary citation besides the Texas bar ad cited above: in an episode of the television sitcom *Night Court* that ran in the late 1980s, a female character attempting to be seductive purrs, "Why don't you come up and see me?" with a bold toss of the head and hips.

6. These variations, which I have not seen in print, may indicate gender nuance in the dissemination of popular culture. In conversation, a number of my female acquaintances have insisted that "banana" belongs in place of "gun." A forty-year-old friend who participated as an adolescent in homemaking and crafts clubs in her home state, Indiana, recognizes only the "pickle" version as correct, for she recalls its gleeful communication among her girlfriends at club meetings, as they learned to conserve garden produce. The squishy edible, in place of the hard steel weapon, makes the bulging object palatable even as it deprives it of any power to wound.

7. The biographies are George Eells and Stanley Musgrove's *Mae West: A Biography* (New York: William Morrow, 1982); Carol Ward's *Mae West: A Bio-bibliography* (Westport, Conn.: Greenwood, 1989); Maurice Leonard's *Mae West: Empress of Sex* (New York: Carol, 1992); and June Sochen's *Mae West: She Who Laughs, Lasts* (Arlington Heights, Ill.: Harlan Davidson, 1992). The biographical film is *Mae West*, directed by Lee Philips (Hill-Mandelker Productions), first broadcast on the ABC television network on 2 May 1982. The documentary is *Mae West and the Men Who Knew Her*, directed by Gene Feldman; this film was aired as part of the series *Biography* on the Arts & Entertainment cable TV channel in 1994–95.

8. Stuart Kaminsky, *He Done Her Wrong* (New York: St. Martin's, 1983); George Baxt, *The Mae West Murder Case* (New York: St. Martin's, 1993).

9. For sample references to Mae West impersonations in gay-identified settings in recent years, see David MacLean, "Resurrecting Russell," *Epicene*, October 1987, 4-7, 52; "Masquerade Follies," *Windy City Times*, 19 January 1989, 19; Kevin

Thaddeus Paulson, "Mae West Goes Out West," *San Francisco Sentinel*, 13 April 1994, 32. See also the full-page advertisement for *Too Outrageous* in the *Village Voice*, 20 October 1987, 62, which features an image of the film's star, Craig Russell, costumed as West, his specialty act. *The Rose* (1979), with Bette Midler, and *Torch Song Trilogy* (1988), with Harvey Fierstein, have scenes in which impersonators perform West acts. A female impersonation club in New Orleans' French Quarter that plays to tourist audiences had a Mae West act in February 1993.

For reports of impersonations of West in gay-frequented locales or stage shows attended by a broad public before 1970, see Kenneth Marlowe, *Mr. Madam: Confessions of a Male Madam* (Los Angeles: Sherbourne, 1964), 28, 74; Esther Newton, *Mother Camp: Female Impersonators in America* (Chicago: University of Chicago Press, 1968), 46, 48, 93-94; Roger Baker, *Drag: A History of Female Impersonation on the Stage* (London: Triton, 1968), 194, 207, 221; and Peter Underwood, *Life's a Drag! Danny La Rue and the Drag Scene* (London: Leslie Frewin, 1974). (La Rue was a very broadly popular British female impersonator during the 1960s and early 1970s.) Some reviewers found Barbra Streisand's performance in *Hello, Dolly!* (1969) a Mae West impersonation. For a recent fictional account of West impersonations at a variety of Los Angeles venues, see Baxt's mystery novel, cited in note 8, above. Set in 1936, it involves the serial murders of female as well as male impersonators of West. Historian George Chauncey solidly documents the existence of gay male impersonations of West in the 1930s in *Gay New York: Gender, Urban Culture, and the Making of the Gay Male World 1890-1940* (New York: Basic Books, 1994).

10. French decorator Jean Michel Franck constructed the pink velvet sofa for Dalí in 1936-37; Green and Abbott of London made two other versions of *Mae West's Lips Sofa* for Dalí's patron, Edward James. See Dawn Ades, *Dalí* (London: Thames & Hudson, 1982), 164, ill. 134. Photographs of the Mae West room in the Teatro Museo Dalí at the artist's birthplace, Figueras, Spain, appear in Ramon Gomez de La Serna, *Dalí* (New York: Park Lane, 1978), 190, 192-93. Dalí himself oversaw the construction of the museum, inaugurated in 1974.

11. The cover illustration derives from a postcard, which alert friends have sent me on at least four different occasions during my research on Mae West. Among the art historical works that have reproduced the image is Conroy Maddox's *Salvador Dalí, 1904-1989* (Cologne: Benedikt Taschen, 1990), 43. For an instance of a newspaper reproduction of the image, see art critic Alan G. Artner's piece, "Pssst! There Are Hidden Treasures at the Art Institute. Take a Peek," *Chicago Tribune*, 31 October 1993, 13: 4-6. A curator interviewed for that piece, Douglas Druick, commented on the fragility of the Mae West gouache, "Because of the flaking it cannot be shown vertically. It is safe only when lying on its back, which may be appropriate considering the subject."

12. British film scholar Richard Dyer's stimulating and original critical work on stars has profoundly influenced my thinking in this area. Dyer's pioneering monograph *Stars* (London: British Film Institute, 1979) takes issue with what he calls "sociological theories of stars" for presuming a generalized, homogeneous collectivity as audience; he specifically calls for serious attention to the common observation that adolescents and women engage particularly intensely with the star

phenomenon. Dyer also called for analysis of potential differences in the star-audience relationship according to class and race as well as gender, and himself undertakes such research in *Heavenly Bodies: Film Stars and Society* (New York: St. Martin's, 1986), where he discusses Marilyn Monroe as an embodiment of "whiteness" and Paul Robeson as an embodiment of "blackness," and both stars in relation to the representation of gender. That book also examines Judy Garland's status as a gay icon. My own approach extends beyond Dyer's in that I demonstrate that a given star image is a historically specific, though changeable, social formation that diverse publics consume and deploy in variable and sometimes contradictory ways.

13. Research on Mae West is complicated by the inaccessibility of many financial records, correspondence, and other historical data from Paramount, the studio at which West first established her career, making six films from 1932 to 1936. Unlike other major studios, such as Warner Bros. and Universal, Paramount Corporation has not made its legal files and other archival material available to scholars through research library collections or directly. As I was unable to obtain cost accounting records for individual West films, I have had to rely on reports of the profitability of the films in trade journals such as *Variety* and also on somewhat impressionistic and anecdotal accounts of public reception of the films and their star by individual critics writing in urban newspapers. The case files of the Production Code Administration (PCA) on West's films, available in the Margaret Herrick Library of the Academy of Motion Picture Arts and Sciences in Beverly Hills, California, are quite extensive and revealing, as I discuss in chapters 2 and 3. These are consequently invaluable sources for reconstructing issues in the production and reception of West's films. The collections of Paramount stills and promotional materials, as well as biographical files, available through the Margaret Herrick Library are also very useful. However, even these detailed records cannot be taken to document every negotiation that affected the form of the Mae West films or other representations of the star distributed to the public. See Lea Jacobs's essay "The Censorship of *Blonde Venus*: Textual Analysis and Historical Method," *Cinema Journal* 27, no. 3 (1988): 21-22, for a discussion of the practical limitations in interpreting the PCA files.

14. I shall not belabor the point by adhering to a strict typographical designation of this sign as "Mae West," but rather primarily use—and ask that the reader associate—the sign Mae West, without quotation marks, as a reference to the image rather than the historical person, to whom I shall usually refer, after a first mention in each chapter, only as West. I sometimes use quotation marks around the full name for emphasis or to clarify meaning in a sentence.

1. The Sex "Queen"

1. See "Mae West and 2 Men in Jail for Play 'Sex,' " *New York Herald Tribune*, 20 April 1927, 1; "Mae West Jailed with 2 Producers," *New York Times*, 20 April 1927, 1; "Author-Star of 'Sex' Taken to Workhouse," *Chicago Daily News*, 20 April 1927, 3; and "Principals in Play 'Sex' Go to Jail in Cleanup," *Chicago Tribune*, 20 April 1927, 17. See also Kaier Curtin, *"We Can Always Call Them Bulgarians": The*

Emergence of Lesbians and Gay Men on the American Stage (Boston: Alyson, 1987), 68-104, esp. 96-98. Curtin argues that the closing of *Sex* came in a clampdown on sexual (especially homosexual) representations in New York theater precipitated in part by West's proposed Broadway production of another of her original plays, *The Drag*, featuring evidently gay female impersonators. Newspaper magnate William Randolph Hearst helped to initiate and lead the political drive in New York focused on theater censorship that came to a peak in *Sex's* closing in 1927. See Curtin, 60-62, 70, 87, 155. Hearst's evident disapproval of West's plays anticipated a role he would play a decade later in Hollywood, discussed in chapter 3.

2. See George Eells and Stanley Musgrove, *Mae West: A Biography* (New York: William Morrow, 1982), 23-28; and Carol Ward, *Mae West: A Bio-bibliography* (Westport, Conn.: Greenwood, 1989), 6-9.

3. On West's relation to burlesque and vaudeville, see Ward, *Mae West*, 6-7; Robert C. Allen, *Horrible Prettiness: Burlesque and American Culture* (Chapel Hill: University of North Carolina Press, 1991), 274-75, 282-83; and Joe Laurie Jr., *Vaudeville: From the Honky-Tonks to the Palace* (New York: Henry Holt, 1953), 53-60. Eells and Musgrove suggest (as does Allen) that West's bawdy performance style resembles burlesque more than vaudeville: "Her undulating hips and shoulders invariably stirred memories of the burlesque 'talking woman' whose perpetual gyrations traditionally led the comic to call out, 'Hey, honey, you left your motor running' " (*Mae West*, 26). These authors maintain that West appeared in at least one New York burlesque theater. Ward (*Mae West*, 6) asserts that acts with risqué humor and vulgarity also characterized vaudeville. See Douglas Gilbert, *American Vaudeville—Its Life and Times* (New York: McGraw-Hill, 1940), 5, 9-10; as well as Allen, *Horrible Prettiness*, for a discussion of historical relations and differences between vaudeville and burlesque. For a historical overview of women's performance in burlesque in the late nineteenth century, see Irving Zeidman, *The American Burlesque Show* (New York: Hawthorne, 1967), 20-32. On West's relation to Texas Guinan, see Maurice Leonard, *Mae West: Empress of Sex* (New York: Carol, 1992), 53, 110, 135, 410; and Louise Berliner, *Texas Guinan: Queen of the Night Clubs* (Austin: University of Texas Press, 1995). The 1994 documentary *Mae West and the Men Who Knew Her*, directed by Gene Feldman, contains a newsreel clip of West with Texas Guinan in the late 1920s.

4. Mae West, *Goodness Had Nothing to Do with It*, 2d ed. (New York: Macfadden-Bartell, 1970 [1959]), 65-66; Eells and Musgrove, *Mae West*, 46; Ward, *Mae West*, 9; and Ethan Mordden, *Movie Star: A Look at the Women Who Made Hollywood* (New York: St. Martin's, 1983), 116-17. Allen (*Horrible Prettiness*, 275) notes that burlesque dancers across the United States had integrated the "shimmy" into their routines by 1918, the year West claimed she introduced the dance to the New York stage in a Broadway revue, *Sometime*.

5. West, *Goodness*, 123-24; Eells and Musgrove, *Mae West*, 323; Ward, *Mae West*, 17-20, 190. West was director as well as author of *Pleasure Man*, a backstage drama that involved a drag ball and a castration scene. West was still appearing in *Diamond Lil* in another Broadway theater, and did not perform in *Pleasure Man*. When the case came to trial after eighteen months, the production was exonerated of charges that it corrupted morals, but West did not reopen the play.

6. See Bernard Sobel, *A Pictorial History of Vaudeville* (New York: Bonanza, 1961), 204, for a photograph of West in vaudeville. The daily *Los Angeles Examiner* printed a vaudeville photo of West in conjunction with new revelations about her 1911 marriage (which she had theretofore denied) under the heading: "At Last 'Mr. Mae' Gets Recognition!" 8 July 1937, A1. A photo of West in her *Diamond Lil* role appeared in the *American Weekly* supplement of the *Los Angeles Examiner*, 6 September 1942, 7. Stage photographs of West appeared also with the following articles: Kevin Thomas, "Mae Keeps Up with the Kids," *New York World Journal Tribune*, 25 December 1966; Richard Meryman, "Mae West: Going Strong at 75," *Life*, 28 April 1969, 46, 48.

7. On this point, see John Berger, *Ways of Seeing* (New York: Penguin, 1977), 83-127.

8. See Marjorie Rosen, *Popcorn Venus: Women, Movies and the American Dream* (New York: Coward, McCann & Geoghegan, 1973), 64-66; and Kathryn Weibel, *Mirror Mirror: Images of Women Reflected in Popular Culture* (Garden City, N.Y.: Doubleday/Anchor, 1977), 100.

9. See, for example, "Mae West Gives *Life* Scoop View of Her Many-Mirrored Apartment," *Life*, 19 February 1940, 64-65. Photo archives in the Margaret Herrick Library of the Academy of Motion Picture Arts and Sciences contain a series of photos of West in her apartment, all given a stamp of PCA approval dated 26 June 1934. Released in conjunction with publicity for the film *Belle of the Nineties*, the photos bear suggested captions that refer to the Louis XV style of West's apartment, its duplication in her forthcoming film, and the predominance of white and gold, satin, and luxurious animal-skin rugs in her apartment's decor. The captions also comment on individual features depicted, such as "the world's softest couch" and West's satin-upholstered bed and its positioning below a ceiling mirror. Some of these photographs appeared in the Sunday edition of the *Los Angeles Times*, 22 December 1935.

10. Colette, *Colette at the Movies: Criticism and Screenplays*, ed. Alain Virmaux and Odette Virmaux (New York: Frederick Ungar, 1980), 63.

11. For a discussion of behavioral strictures associated with bourgeois class status, see Pierre Bourdieu, *Distinction: A Social Critique of the Judgement of Taste*, trans. Richard Nice (Cambridge: Harvard University Press, 1984), esp. 183, 190-96, 256.

12. See, e.g., Elizabeth Yeaman, "Mae West's Purified Picture Scores Hit," *Citizen-News*, 18 August 1934. I discuss gender implications in West's liking for muscle-bound men in chapter 5.

13. See, e.g., Leonard, *Mae West*, 6-9.

14. This chorus number is patterned after the style of English burlesque performer Lydia Thompson and Her Blondes ensemble, who beginning in 1868 had appeared on stages in the United States. See Zeidman, *The American Burlesque Show*, 23-27.

15. See, for example, Marie Beynon Ray, "Curves Ahead," *Collier's*, 7 October 1933, 24, 40. Cecelia Ager, "Going Places," *Variety*, 17 October 1933, 57; "Diamond Lil," *Chicago Daily Tribune*, 7 December 1933; and Gertrude Hill, "Hollywood Leads the Fashion Parade," *Movie Classic*, May 1935, 40ff. Even discounting

the articles in the trade magazines, which helped disseminate studio publicity, one finds recurrent evidence that West represented a sexual ideal for some audiences into the 1950s; see, for example, Ira Berkow, "Mae West, Wilt and the King," interview with Charles Miron, *New York Times*, 2 December 1989, Y31.

16. Yeaman, "Mae West's Purified Picture."

17. Andre Sennwald, "Goin' to Town," *New York Times*, 11 May 1935, 21.

18. Elizabeth Yeaman, "Mae West to Abandon Corsets, Wear Modern Apparel in New Picture," *Citizen-News*, 22 August 1936.

19. Colette, *Colette at the Movies*, 62, 63-64.

20. "Mae West Gives *Life* Scoop," 64.

21. "Mae West Too 'Person'-al; CBS Junks Interview Tape," *Hollywood Reporter*, 16 October 1959; "Mae West a Little Bit Too Much of a 'Person' for CBS," *Variety*, 16 October 1959; "Mae and Myra," *Films and Filming*, February 1970, 69; Ted O. Thackrey and Kevin Thomas, "Mae West, Epitome of Witty Sexuality, Dies," *Los Angeles Times*, 23 November 1980, I22.

22. See Diane Arbus, "Emotion in Motion," *Show* (January 1965): 42-45; reprinted as "Mae West: Once upon Our Time," in *Diane Arbus, Magazine Work*, ed. Doon Arbus and Marvin Israel (Millerton, N.Y.: Aperture, 1984), 58-61.

23. Meryman, "Mae West," 46-56.

24. Phrases in quotations are taken from letters by Mrs. D. M. Callahan, Olga Strang, Robert Moore, and Rick Rado, respectively, published in *Life*, 9 May 1969.

25. My analysis of West's "dirty blues" performance style has been influenced by conversations with twentieth century historian Bruce Calder, film scholar and musician Deborah Tudor, and Chicago blues singer Angela Brown. See also Ward, *Mae West*, 42, 207 n. 178.

26. *Diamond Lil* included a "low-down" version of "Frankie and Johnnie," which was changed for the film *She Done Him Wrong*. See West, *Goodness*, 109-10. See also June Sochen, *Mae West: She Who Laughs, Lasts* (Arlington Heights, Ill.: Harlan Davidson, 1992), 18, 50.

27. The number "Troubled Waters" begins as a white-haired African American minister sings in bass, "Pray, children, and you be saved," and is answered by a choir that begins singing a spiritual. West's character, Ruby Carter, watching the scene from her balcony, looks pensive and begins to sing the following lyrics (camera shots and edits marked):

Oh, I'm gonna drown down   [West in medium long shot]
in those troubled waters that creep around my soul
they're way beyond control
I'm gonna wash my sins away before the morning.

They say that I'm one of the devil's daughters
They look at me with scorn
I'll never hear that horn
I'll be underneath the water judgment morning.

Oh, Lord, am I to blame   [cut to medium close-up]
Must I bow my head in shame
If people go round scandalizing my name.

[Repeat verse] Oh I'm gonna drown. . .

As West sings the last word, "morning," the shot of West dissolves to the African
Americans singing the spiritual; the camera then cuts back to West in medium
long shot as she repeats bridge,"Oh, Lord . . .," then cuts to medium close-up, as
West begins first verse again.

28. I discuss the comedic role of one male African American performer in *Goin'
to Town* and analyze the censorship of West's "dirty blues" lyrics in that film's production in my essay "*Goin' to Town* and Beyond: Mae West, Film Censorship, and
the Comedy of Unmarriage," in *Classical Film Comedy*, ed. Kristine Brunovska Karnick and Henry Jenkins (New York: Routledge, 1995), 211-37.

29. West claims in the 1970 addendum to her 1959 autobiography that she requested the presence of all the African American performers in her films (*Goodness*, 284-85). See also George Eells, letter, *Los Angeles Times*, 25 April 1982, Sunday Calendar, 95; and "Raquel Welch, Mae West Talk about Men, Morals and
'Myra Breckinridge,' " *Look*, 24 March 1970, 48.

30. It is a strong possibility that the reduction of the African American presence
in West's films after *Belle of the Nineties* relates to tightened censorship. Internal
film industry correspondence notes, for example, that censors eliminated the revival meeting scene in prints distributed in England (*Belle of the Nineties* PCA case
file). Producers may also have anticipated (or projected) resistance in the U.S.
South to what Donald Bogle has deemed West's comparatively egalitarian interactions with her black maids. See Donald Bogle, *Toms, Coons, Mulattoes, Mammies,
and Bucks: An Interpretive History of Blacks in American Films*, 2d ed. (New York:
Viking, 1989 [1973]), 45-46. Although geographic shifts in the story settings of
West's films after 1934 can also explain the reduced presence of black actors, extracinematic considerations may well have influenced the choice of settings. On
this possibility, see Lea Jacobs, *Wages of Sin: Censorship and the Fallen Woman Film
1928-1942* (Madison: University of Wisconsin Press, 1991), 89, 177-78.

31. For a discussion of Hazel Scott's influence in *The Heat's On*, see James Pines,
Blacks in Film: A Survey of Racial Themes and Images in the American Film (London:
Studio Vista, 1975), 57; see also Bogle, *Toms, Coons*, 122-25.

32. With relatively few exceptions (e.g., *The Cheat*, 1915, starring Sessue Ha-
yakawa), until the 1950s, Hollywood studios usually assigned leading parts to Caucasian actors regardless of the character's race, and used makeup and accents to
suggest "difference." The practice applied particularly when the script called for
characters of color to be romantically paired with white actors or to touch them
physically. For further discussion of this point with reference to Asian characters in
Hollywood, see Gina Marchetti, *Romance and the "Yellow Peril": Race, Sex and Discursive Strategies in Hollywood Fiction* (Berkeley: University of California Press,
1993). I discuss the significance of West's interactions with the Chinese character
Chan Lo in chapter 3.

33. The conjoined representation of racial and sexual difference is, of course, a recurrent feature in Hollywood films, beginning at the latest with *The Cheat* (Cecil B. DeMille, 1915) and *Broken Blossoms* (D. W. Griffith, 1919). On these early films, see ibid., 14-45; Sumiko Higashi, "Ethnicity, Class, and Gender in Film: DeMille's *The Cheat*," in *Unspeakable Images: Ethnicity and the American Cinema*, ed. Lester D. Friedman (Urbana: University of Illinois Press, 1991), 112-39; Judith Mayne, "The Limits of Spectacle," *Wide Angle* 6, no. 3 (1984): 7-9; Julia Lesage, "Artful Racism, Artful Rape: Griffith's *Broken Blossoms*," in *Home Is Where the Heart Is: Studies in Melodrama and the Woman's Film*, ed. Christine Gledhill (London: British Film Institute, 1987), 235-54. In other classic Hollywood films, "exotic" locales function as site and symbol of forbidden sexualities, for example, the South Sea setting of *Sadie Thompson* (1928) with Gloria Swanson and the remake of the same Somerset Maugham story as *Rain* (1932) with Joan Crawford; and the Indochinese settings in *Red Dust* (1932) and *China Seas* (1935), both starring Jean Harlow and Clark Gable. It is significant that *Bitter Tea* and *King Kong* were both produced prior to the tightened enforcement in 1934 of the 1930 Production Code, which included strictures against depiction of "miscegenation."

34. West, quoted in Edwin Schallert, " 'Films Should Be Fit for Children to See,' " *Los Angeles Times*, 23 September 1934.

35. West, *Goodness*, 137; see also Ward, *Mae West*, 144.

36. West, *Goodness*, 136-38; Ward, *Mae West*, 143; Eells and Musgrove, *Mae West*, 325.

37. "Mae West's Driver Hunted," *Los Angeles Times*, 11 October 1936.

38. West, *Goodness*, 235-36; see also "Mae West's Open-Door Policy," *Confidential*, November 1955, 18-19, 46-47.

39. See, e.g., Eells and Musgrove, *Mae West*, 142-43; Leonard, *Mae West*, 181-82, 205, 209, 292-93.

40. See, for example, Gilbert Seldes, "Sugar and Spice and Not So Nice," *Esquire*, March 1934, 60. For an extended analysis of the controversies surrounding these two plays and their significance in American theater history, see Curtin, *"We Can Always Call Them Bulgarians,"* 68-139.

41. Ruth Biery, "The Private Life of Mae West," *Movie Classic*, January 1934, 20-21, 56-58 (reprinted in Ward, *Mae West*, 108). See also Ward, *Mae West*, 95; Laurie, *Vaudeville*, 6-9; Carol Bergman, *Mae West, Entertainer* (New York: Chelsea House, 1988), 33.

42. On Dietrich's and Garbo's status as lesbian icons, see Andrea Weiss, *Vampires and Violets: Lesbians in Film* (New York: Penguin, 1993), 30-39, 42-50. On Dietrich's status also as a gay male cult figure, see Gaylyn Studlar, *In the Realm of Pleasure: Von Sternberg, Dietrich and the Masochistic Aesthetic* (Urbana: University of Illinois Press, 1988), 48-49, 214 n. 98. See also the biography *Marlene Dietrich*, by her daughter, Maria Riva (New York: Alfred A. Knopf, 1993).

43. George Davis, "The Decline of the West," *Vanity Fair*, May 1934, 82. Laurie writes of Bert Savoy, "Savoy did a character somewhat like [Jimmy] Russell [an Irish servant girl act], only, instead of a biddy, he did an overdressed trollop. Savoy & [Jay] Brennan were the tops of all fem imp comedy acts. . . . Savoy was killed by lightning while walking with Jack Haley at Long Beach" (*Vaudeville*, 89-90). See

also Eells and Musgrove *Mae West*, 35-36, for a description of Savoy's style, and Roger Baker, *Drag: A History of Female Impersonation on the Stage* (London: Triton, 1968), fig. 79, for a photograph of Savoy with Brennan. Laurie (87-95) gives an overview of female and male impersonation acts in American vaudeville from the 1880s to the 1920s. For more on Savoy's possible influence on West, see Pamela Robertson, " 'The Kinda Comedy That Imitates Me': Mae West's identification with the Feminist Camp," *Cinema Journal* 32, no. 2 (1993): 60-61.

44. Eells and Musgrove, *Mae West*, 34-35; Ward, *Mae West*, 7. Laurie calls Julian Eltinge "the greatest of all female impersonators past, present—and even future!" (*Vaudeville*, 91). A Broadway theater was named after Eltinge in 1910, the culmination of his stellar career as a fashionable female impersonator in vaudeville, who was popular with women patrons for the elegance and style of his presentation. His act was quite distinct from Savoy's comedic performance, and, also unlike Savoy, who was widely known to be gay, Eltinge received publicity that cultivated his off-stage (and offscreen, for he also appeared in several films) image as masculine and heterosexual. (For example, Buster Keaton's 1927 film *Seven Chances*, which shows a poster of Eltinge outside a theater, comedically illustrates what happens to people who seriously take the impersonator as a woman: Keaton is handily thrown out, his hat crushed around his ears.) West's own performance combines characteristics of the two styles: Eltinge's illusion of glamour and Savoy's comedic gender parody. For more on Eltinge and West's relation to his style, see Curtin, *"We Can Always Call Them Bulgarians,"* 18; Marybeth Hamilton, " 'I'm the Queen of the Bitches': Female Impersonation and Mae West's *Pleasure Man*," in *Crossing the Stage: Controversies on Cross-Dressing*, ed. Lesley Ferris (London: Routledge, 1993), 107-19. For photographs of Eltinge and countersuggestions that he was also gay, see Avery Willard, *Female Impersonation* (New York: Regiment, 1971), 30-33; see Baker for another photograph and descriptions of Eltinge's style.

45. West, *Goodness*, 80, 83, 90, 92.

46. In West's play *The Drag*, male homosexual characters refer to themselves as "queens." See Curtin, *"We Can Always Call Them Bulgarians,"* 76. For the currency in pre-1930s gay slang of *queen* to denote an effeminate or cross-dressing gay man, see George Chauncey, *Gay New York: Gender, Urban Culture, and the Making of the Gay Male World 1890-1940* (New York: Basic Books, 1994), 16, 101.

47. "Mae West Guarded after Threat," *Los Angeles Examiner*, 8 October 1935, 1.

48. Breen to Paramount, 16 January 1935, *Goin' to Town* PCA case file. "Nance," a short form of "Nancy," was well established in the 1920s as a pejorative for an effeminate man. See Chauncey, *Gay New York*, 15, 182.

49. Breen to Cohen, 1 September 1938, *Every Day's a Holiday* PCA case file.

50. West played the role of Cleopatra in a 1922 Broadway revue titled *The Mimic World*, produced by the Schuberts. See Eells and Musgrove, *Mae West*, 320. See also Leo McCarey, "Mae West Can Play Anything," *Photoplay*, June 1935, 32.

51. "So Mae West's Slipping? Not So She Can Notice It!" *Los Angeles Times*, 20 May 1934; Schallert, " 'Films Should Be Fit' "; McCarey, "Mae West," 30.

52. See, for example, "Court Tilt Won by Mae West," *Los Angeles Times*, 16 April 1947, which reports initial court action by two authors against West and *Catherine Was Great* producer Michael Todd. Daily reports in the *Los Angeles Daily*

News, 25 August-3 October 1948, of the eventual plagiarism trial regularly conjoined the names and personas of Mae West and Catherine the Great; see Ward, *Mae West*, 37-38. See also Leonard, *Mae West*, 221, 247, 332.

53. West, *Goodness*, 183-85, 203-11.

54. "Mae West Stands 'em Up Despite Pans," *Variety*, 9 August 1944, 1, 38; " 'Catherine Was Great' but Mae West Makes Her Dull," *Life*, 21 August 1944, 71-72.

55. West, *Goodness*, 184.

56. See, for example, Alexander Walker, *The Celluloid Sacrifice* (New York: Hawthorne, 1966), 71-75; Linda Williams, "What Does Mae West Have That All the Men Want?" *Frontiers* 1, no. 1 (1975): 120; and Leonard Maltin, *The Great Movie Comedians: From Charlie Chaplin to Woody Allen* (New York: Bell, 1978), 155-56.

57. Colette, *Colette at the Movies*, 62-63.

58. Rosen, *Popcorn Venus*, 153; Maltin, *The Great Movie Comedians*, 156; Joan Mellen, *Women and Their Sexuality in the New Film* (New York: Horizon, 1973), 230, 235; Robert Sklar, *Movie-Made America: A Cultural History of American Movies* (New York: Random House, 1975), 185; Michael Bavar, *Mae West* (New York: Pyramid, 1975), 146; Jacqueline Levitin, "Any Good Roles for Women?" *Film Reader* 5 (1982): 104. British film author Alexander Walker adopts similar terms for West in *The Celluloid Sacrifice*, 74.

59. Rosen, *Popcorn Venus*, 152-53.

60. For discussion of how actor and character become mutually defining, see Richard Dyer, *Stars* (London: British Film Institute, 1979), 72-98, 142-49. Scriptwriters and studio publicists have traditionally contributed to the interweaving of stars' "private lives" and their personas in film roles. Hollywood lore and even practice further foster the illusion of singular identities. For example, a biography of Clara Bow claims that a gambling scene was written into the star's next film after newspapers reported, to Paramount studio's dismay, that she had lost huge sums of money at blackjack. See Joe Morella and Edward Z. Epstein, *The "It" Girl: The Incredible Story of Clara Bow* (New York: Delacorte, 1976), 214-15.

61. Alfred Hitchcock used a clip from this cartoon in *Sabotage*, produced in 1936 in Britain. After learning that her young brother has died in a bomb explosion her husband set up, the female protagonist (Sylvia Sidney) wanders blindly into a movie theater, where she briefly sees—and smiles at—the amply feathered and full-breasted animated chicken strutting and crooning like Mae West, then the shadow of a crow shooting an arrow that kills the cartoon's Cock Robin. Sidney's character immediately returns to her home behind the theater and at dinner half accidentally kills her husband with a carving knife, an act for which she is not punished in the film. Viewers of the film who recognize the cartoon parody may see the parodic reference to West as an enabling factor in the woman's seeking revenge. I am indebted to my colleague Dan Majdiak for this observation.

62. See, for example, "Mae West Has Hope on Gems," *Los Angeles Times*, 14 October 1932; and "New Indictment Lists Friedman, Mae West Case Suspect to Be Arraigned Today," *Los Angeles Times*, 7 December 1933.

63. McCarthy, "Belle of the Nineties," *Motion Picture Herald*, 25 August 1934,

31, 35; Sennwald, "Goin' to Town," 21; "Klondike Annie," *Time*, 9 March 1936, 44-46; Colette, *Colette at the Movies*, 63. See also Mellen, *Women and Their Sexuality*, 243; Dyer, *Stars*, 175; Ward, *Mae West*, 21-22, 25, 135-44.

64. "Mae West Changes Her Role in Court," *Los Angeles Times*, 1 September 1948, 1; "Deposition Introduced in Mae West Case," *Los Angeles Times*, 2 September 1948. See also Ward, *Mae West*, 182-84. West ultimately won all her court cases, whether she was plaintiff or defendant.

65. Eells and Musgrove, *Mae West*, 75-76, 81-82, 110-11; Ward, *Mae West*, 136-37.

66. See Maltin, *The Great Movie Comedians*, 154; Mordden, *Movie Star*, 117; Kenneth Anger, *Hollywood Babylon* (New York: Dell, 1975), 257; Mitch Tuchman, "Scenes: Going Steady," *Penthouse*, February 1980, 46; Thackrey and Thomas, "Mae West," 19. See also West, *Goodness*, 169, 175.

67. Eells and Musgrove, *Mae West*, 144-45; Richard Meryman, "The One and Only Mae West," *Los Angeles Herald-Examiner*, 30 November 1980, G6.

68. Anger, *Hollywood Babylon*, 259.

69. Gerald Gardner, *The Censorship Papers: Movie Censorship Letters from the Hays Office, 1934-1968* (New York: Dodd, Mead, 1987), 139.

70. Rosen, *Popcorn Venus*, 151.

71. See Gardner, *The Censorship Papers*, 140, 145-47; and Anger, *Hollywood Babylon*, 261, 264-67. See also Leonard J. Leff and Jerold L. Simmons, *The Dame in the Kimono: Hollywood, Censorship, and the Production Code from the 1920s to the 1960s* (New York: Grove Weidenfeld, 1990).

72. See, for example, Anger, *Hollywood Babylon*, 264-68; Gardner, *The Censorship Papers*, 143-47; Rosen, *Popcorn Venus*, 153.

73. For a discussion of the prevalence of the "great man" theory in American film histories, see Robert C. Allen and Douglas Gomery, *Film History: Theory and Practice* (New York: Alfred A. Knopf, 1985), 110-13, 155.

74. "The Hays Office," *Fortune*, December 1938, 140.

75. Dyer, *Stars*, 48.

2. The Prostitute, the Production Code, and the Depression

1. Text in Vitaphone advertisement in *Variety*, 6 November 1929, 14-15. For discussion of Hollywood's recruitment of Broadway stars, see Henry Jenkins, " 'Shall We Make It for New York or for Distribution?': Eddie Cantor, *Whoopee*, and Regional Resistance to the Talkies," *Cinema Journal* 29, no. 3 (1990): 35-37. On Paramount's policy in developing West as a star, see reviews by "Bige" of *Night after Night* in *Variety*, 1 November 1932, 12, and of *She Done Him Wrong* in *Variety*, 14 February 1933, 12, 21; see also "Paramount Abandons Idea of Producing 'Sex,' " *Variety*, 28 February 1933, 2. See also Douglas Gomery, *The Hollywood Studio System* (New York: St. Martin's, 1986), 40-41.

2. See Ruth A. Inglis, *Freedom of the Movies: A Report on Self-Regulation from the Commission on Freedom of the Press* (Chicago: University of Chicago Press, 1947), 112-13.

3. Maurice McKenzie memo to Jason Joy, 11 January 1930, *She Done Him*

Wrong PCA case file. Unless otherwise noted, all correspondence cited in this chapter comes from this source.

4. Will Hays to Joy, 22 April 1930.

5. *Variety*, 1 November 1932, 12; 29 November 1932, 29.

6. Samples of studio publicity and exhibitor press kits for *Night after Night* are housed in the Margaret Herrick Library. See also the advertisement for the film in *Variety*, 25 October 1932, 24, and the review of *Night after Night* in *Variety*, 1 November 1932, 12. Paramount head Adolph Zukor suggests that *Night after Night* was West's screen test with movie audiences; see Adolph Zukor with Dale Kramer, *The Public Is Never Wrong* (New York: G. P. Putnam's Sons, 1953), 267-69. For examples of publicity and promotion of West as a star in *She Done Him Wrong*, released within four months of *Night after Night*, see Cecelia Ager, "No Good Women in History, Mae West Says, During Hot Sex Selling Talk," *Variety*, 31 January 1933, 1, 42; and *Variety*, 14 February 1933, 12, 21, 26.

7. Hays to Zukor, 18 October 1932; Hays to Warner, 19 October 1932. Hays's letter to Zukor emphasized that the titles *Diamond Lady* and *Diamonds* might not be registered as substitutes for *Diamond Lil*, and referred to a board resolution passed on 31 October 1930 that ruled out a member studio's retitling plays or books as a way to circumvent previous MPPDA bans.

8. John Hertz, founder of the car rental company that bears his name and a partner in Wall Street's Lehman Bros., was a key member of Paramount's board of directors from November 1931 to January 1933. See "Paramount," *Fortune*, March 1937, 96, 194. References to Hertz in interoffice MPPDA correspondence make clear that he, rather than Paramount board chairman Adolph Zukor, was Paramount's primary power in negotiations leading to the production of West's first starring vehicle. The MPPDA memos propose meeting with Hertz, without Zukor present, but caution against giving Zukor any impression that they might be going above his head; e.g., James Wingate to McKenzie, 11 November 1932; Wingate to Hays, 11 November 1932. See also "Hertz Talks on Para Coin," *Variety*, 14 November 1933, 9, 27.

9. Hays to Zukor, 28 November 1932; McKenzie interoffice memo, 28 November 1932. McKenzie's memo lists the MPPDA directors attending the special board meeting as M. H. Aylesworth, R. H. Cochran, E. W. Hammons, S. R. Kent, N. M. Schenck, Will Hays, H. M. Warner, Adolph Zukor, and John Hertz "also present for Paramount." But the change in title did not obscure the material's origins for critics, who in print frequently linked *She Done Him Wrong* to *Diamond Lil*. See *Variety*, 7 February 1933, 31, and 14 February 1933, 12; Sidney Skolsky, "Putting Them on the Spot," *Los Angeles Daily News*, 11 February 1933; Aaronson, "She Done Him Wrong," *Motion Picture Herald*, 18 February 1933, 31.

10. On these points, see Inglis, *Freedom of the Movies*, 70-72, 116; as well as "The Hays Office," *Fortune*, December 1938, 71-72; Will H. Hays, *The Memoirs of Will H. Hays* (Garden City, N.Y.: Doubleday, 1955), 446; Garth Jowett, *Film: The Democratic Art* (Boston: Little, Brown, 1976), 113-19, 237; Richard Maltby, " 'Baby Face' or How Joe Breen Made Barbara Stanwyck Atone for Causing the Wall Street Crash," *Screen* 27, no. 2 (1986): 29; Lea Jacobs, *The Wages of Sin: Censorship and the Fallen Woman Film 1928-1942* (Madison: University of Wisconsin

Press, 1991), 27-35; Ira H. Carmen, *Movies, Censorship, and the Law* (Ann Arbor: University of Michigan Press, 1966), 125-29, 141-212.

11. Wingate to Harold Hurley, 29 November 1932. MPPDA recruitment of Wingate from his post at the New York State censor board, to succeed Joy, who left to work for Fox Corporation, appears to have been a public relations strategy and a move to incorporate state censors' perspectives into the SRC. See Hays, *Memoirs,* 446. Harold Hurley worked in Paramount's public relations department; he later became supervising producer of the studio's "B" films.

12. Wingate probably meant the Motion Picture Production Code of 1930 when he referred in his letter to "the Formula" (the general name for explicit internal industry guidelines prior to 1930). See Gregory D. Black, *Hollywood Censored: Morality Codes, Catholics, and the Movies* (Cambridge: Cambridge University Press, 1994), 33. After 1930, "the Production Code" had become a basis for SRC arguments about films both with the state censors and the member film producers. See Jacobs, *The Wages of Sin,* 34-35, 82-83.

13. Maltby, " 'Baby Face,' " 29.

14. West sings an extended version of "Frankie and Johnnie" (probably similar to that she sang onstage in *Diamond Lil*) in the audio recording *Mae West: Sixteen Sultry Songs,* vol. 7, Women's Heritage series, (New York: Rosetta Cassettes, 1987).

15. Censor boards in the following export markets required deletions prior to the film's release: Quebec, Alberta, British Columbia, Britain, Australia, New Zealand, and Sweden. Australian censors withdrew the film a year after its initial acceptance in April 1934; a novelized version of *Diamond Lil* was also banned in Australia in 1935. State censors in Finland, Latvia, Java, and Germany banned *She Done Him Wrong* outright. The *Los Angeles Examiner* reported on 10 March 1934 that the semiofficial German state newspaper *Die Reichspost* had condemned the film shortly before its banning by the Nazi government as "nothing but uncouth and clumsy eroticism, appealing to basest instincts."

16. Even the subsequently much-quoted "come up and see me" line was cut by censor boards in Pennsylvania, Alberta, and Britain. Overall, the board in Pennsylvania, which in 1911 was the first U.S. state to adopt censorship, was most rigorous. See Jowett, *Film,* 119.

17. Versions of these two songs and several from West's other films are available on the audio recording *Mae West: Sixteen Sultry Songs.*

18. For example, a column in the *Chicago Tribune,* 7 December 1933, titled "Diamond Lil" makes evident that critics of the period read West's characterization in *She Done Him Wrong* as that of a lusty prostitute.

19. Besides the cuts of "lots of times," "hands ain't everything," and close-up views of West singing, the Kansas censor board required the following deletions: Gus's line to Flynn, "I must be pretty good" (to have a woman all the men are crazy for); Chick's dialogue in prison to Lou, from the line "If I can wait a year, so can you," to "I can be pretty mean"; and the prison guard's line "what for?" delivered in feigned innocence when Chick and Lou's friend Spider asks for Lou and Chick to be able to have more time together. While occasionally some board members may have missed potentially risqué implications of a given scene, censors were generally alert to violations of local standards, which differed in the degree of latitude al-

lowed. In the early 1930s, the Kansas board tended to be more tolerant of West's sexual innuendo than were the Ohio, Pennsylvania, and Massachusetts boards.

20. Responding to a letter to W. C. Fields objecting to the censorship of *My Little Chickadee*, Joseph Breen wrote, "You must remember that most reviewers on censor boards are women." Breen to Fields, 3 November 1939, *My Little Chickadee* PCA case file. See Black, *Hollywood Censored*, 13, 29-30, 33-34, 56-57, 61-62, on the involvement of the Women's Christian Temperance Union and local and national women's leagues in evaluating "movie morality." On the MPPDA policy of seeking cooperation of the women's club movement in working against existing or threatened government censorship, see "The Hays Office," 139; Hays, *Memoirs*, 409-12. On state censor boards' class and professional composition, see Carmen, *Movies, Censorship*, 126, 154, 167, 176; Jowett, *Films*, 119.

21. "She Done Him Wrong," *Film Daily*, 10 February 1933, 7. The critic's description of West as a "queen" and the film's locale as a "gay resort in the Bowery back in the 90s" may refer to West's prior transvestite associations as well as her own characterization as a prostitute. Historian George Chauncey documents that by the end of the 1890s the Bowery was well known to the New York public as a gathering place—called a "resort"—for male as well as female prostitutes (the original meaning of the slang term *gay*) and for effeminate gay men. See George Chauncey, *Gay New York: Gender, Urban Culture, and the Making of the Gay Male World 1890-1940* (New York: Basic Books, 1994), 33-45.

22. Aaronson, "She Done Him Wrong," *Motion Picture Herald*, 18 February 1933, 31.

23. The ad copy reads as follows: "NEW YORK—CHICAGO, NEW ORLEANS held over a second week—building daily—will equal boomtime grosses! LOS ANGELES without a stage show doubled average weekly gross with stage shows! HOUSTON, ROCHESTER normal week's business in three days! BOSTON—DETROIT, SPRINGFIELD in uproar. Doubling and tripling normal grosses! THE WHOLE COUNTRY IS GOING 'WEST'!" An identical ad appeared in *Variety*, 21 February 1933, 18.

24. *Motion Picture Herald*, 25 February 1933, back cover.

25. See, for example, "Par's Unusual 3d Week for Mae West," *Variety*, 28 February 1933, 4; "Mae West $28,000 as Brooklyn Feels Pinch" and "Even with Sub-Zero, Mpls. Proves Amusements Are Depresh-Proof," *Variety*, 14 March 1933, 8. See also McCarthy, "I'm No Angel," *Motion Picture Herald*, 7 October 1933, 38; "Mae West in 'I'm No Angel,' " *Film Daily*, 14 October 1933, 6; and Virginia Maxwell, "It's the Caveman within Us Calling for Mae," *Photoplay*, December 1933, 38.

26. Inglis, *Freedom of the Movies*, 62-73, 86-89, 116-25; Jowett, *Film*, 210-59; Maltby, " 'Baby Face,' " 28-31, 38-45.

27. Inglis, *Freedom of the Movies*, 62-125; Jowett, *Film*, 108-18; Black, *Hollywood Censored*, 7-72. See also Raymond Moley, *The Hays Office* (Indianapolis: Bobbs-Merrill, 1945), 52-88; and Mary Beth Haralovich, "Mandates of Good Taste: The Self-Regulation of Film Advertising in the Thirties," *Wide Angle* 6, no. 2 (1984): 50-57.

28. See Jacobs, *The Wages of Sin*, 20-24, 27-51, 106-31, on the gradual shift toward explicit enforcement of "the Code" by name.

29. See Haralovich, "Mandates of Good Taste"; Jacobs, *The Wages of Sin*; Maltby, " 'Baby Face' "; Black, *Hollywood Censored*; Peter Baxter, "The Birth of Venus," *Wide Angle* 10, no. 1 (1988): 4-15.

30. Jowett, *Film*, 170-71, 250-52, 399; Maltby, " 'Baby Face,' " 28-29; Black, *Hollywood Censored*, 9-14, 33-46. The industry strategy of gaining Catholic support was generally effective. Contrary to the arguments some historians have made, except for a brief period in mid-1934, Catholic leaders for the most part upheld their support of the industry against government regulation. See, for example, "Catholics Defend Pix, Legion of Decency Stands Up beside Hays in Support of Present Industry Practices," *Hollywood Reporter*, 2 March 1936, 1, 9.

31. Cobbett Steinberg, "The Production Code," in *Film Facts* (New York: Facts on File, 1980), 391. The Code is also reprinted in Moley, *The Hays Office*, 241-48; Jowett, *Film*, 468-72; Black, *Hollywood Censored*, 302-8.

32. On the persistent social dominance of white middle-class concepts of sexuality over the behaviors of African Americans and the working classes, even as middle-class views have gradually changed, see John D'Emilio and Estelle B. Freedman, *Intimate Matters* (New York: Harper & Row, 1988), xvi-xvii, 208-15.

33. See, for instance, an editorial by Karl Krug, *Pittsburgh Sun-Telegraph*, 22 February 1936; *New York World-Telegram*, quoted in *Hollywood Reporter*, 21 March 1936; Elizabeth Yeaman, "Big Crowds View Star's New Picture," *Citizen*, 28 February 1936; and "Controversy on Mae West Film Gathers Volume and Velocity," *Motion Picture Herald*, 14 March 1936, 34. See also Haralovich, "Mandates of Good Taste," 55.

34. See Pierre Bourdieu, *Distinction: A Social Critique of the Judgement of Taste*, trans. Richard Nice (Cambridge: Harvard University Press, 1984), 185, 190-96, 201-8, 218-19, 226-27, 244-47, 474-79.

35. Ibid., 7.

36. See Herbert Blumer, *Movies and Conduct* (Chicago: University of Chicago Press, 1933), 194-200; Martin Quigley, *Decency in Motion Pictures* (New York: Macmillan, 1937), 5-11; Moley, *The Hays Office*, 142-44; Inglis, *Freedom of the Movies*, 1-2; as well as Jowett, *Film*, 143-47; and Black, *Hollywood Censored*, 6-15, 40. The Motion Picture Production Code of 1930 repeatedly asserts movies' potentially damaging effects on "the immature, the young, or the criminal classes" in the "Reasons Supporting Preamble of Code," "Reasons Underlying the General Principles," and "Reasons Underlying Particular Applications" (printed in Steinberg, "The Production Code," 393-96).

37. See Miriam Hansen, "Early Cinema: Whose Public Sphere?" in *Early Cinema: Space, Frame, Narrative*, ed. Thomas Elsaesser (London: British Film Institute, 1990), 229, 243; and Miriam Hansen, *Babel and Babylon: Spectatorship in American Silent Film* (Cambridge: Harvard University Press, 1991), 62-70, 84-86. See also Margaret Farrand Thorp, *America at the Movies* (New Haven, Conn.: Yale University Press, 1939), 4-20. Thorp argues that, at the time of her writing, film producers targeted middle-class women living in cities with populations of more than fifty thousand as their primary audience.

38. On this point, see Robert S. Lynd and Helen Merrell Lynd's two works, *Middletown: A Study in Contemporary American Culture* (New York: Harcourt,

Brace & World, 1929), 263-69, and *Middletown in Transition: A Study in Cultural Conflicts* (New York: Harcourt, Brace & World, 1937), 260-63, 467. See also Jowett, *Film*, 87-91, 95-100, 129, 139-41.

39. For insightful discussion of the gradual development in American silent cinema of a generally "middle-class address," in movies' exhibition as well as production, see Hansen, *Babel and Babylon*, 76-89, 95. On film producers' consciously shaping films to attract middle-class women, their most reliable and profitable audience in the 1930s, see Thorp, *America at the Movies*, esp. 4-8, 15-16.

40. My thinking on this point has been stimulated by readings of Michel Foucault, *The History of Sexuality*, vol. 1, *An Introduction*, trans. Robert Hurley (New York: Random House, 1980), esp. 17-18, 24, 123-27. Annette Kuhn's *Cinema, Censorship and Sexuality 1909-1925* (London: Routledge, 1988) presents an extended case study of British film censorship that is informed by Foucauldian concepts of censorship as a shifting set of discursive practices and apparatuses; see esp. 4-8, 126-31.

41. For use of the term "sex pictures" in SRC correspondence, see Wingate to Halls, 30 October 1932. Adopting another term that occurs in SRC correspondence, Maltby, in " 'Baby Face,' " discusses films of this type produced beginning in mid-1931 as a "kept woman" cycle. Under Breen as PCA head, films that violated the Code primarily through their depiction of sex were often discussed under the more euphemistic but telling classification of "social problem" films.

42. Lea Jacobs, in *The Wages of Sin*, adopts the critical classification "fallen woman film" to discuss some of the films Maltby terms "kept woman" films. My discussion of Jacobs' work on PCA policies and practices around 1933-34 should not be taken to imply that West's films fit within Jacobs's "fallen woman" category. It is precisely in *not* being a "fallen woman" that the significance of West's characterizations lies: West's characters never experience a "fall," but rather at the outset of each film narrative are presumed to have practiced extramarital sex with judiciously chosen partners for some time, and to have benefited handsomely by it. However, West's films might be aptly described (and sometimes are in SRC correspondence) as a variation of the "kept woman" picture type.

43. Maltby, " 'Baby Face,' " 28.

44. Ibid., 30-31, 38-39.

45. Ibid., 29-31; Jacobs, *The Wages of Sin*, 49-51, 60-64.

46. Maltby, " 'Baby Face,' " 28.

47. Inglis, *Freedom of the Movies*, 119.

48. Hays was chairman of the Republican National Committee from 1918 to 1921 and postmaster general under President Warren Harding in 1921-22, before becoming the first director of the MPPDA in 1922. Maltby cites a report in the Richmond, Virginia, *Times-Dispatch* from 7 February 1933 as evidence of rumors about Hays's replacement (" 'Baby Face,' " 39).

49. Ibid., 39-40. See also Jacobs, *The Wages of Sin*, 108-10.

50. Synopses of the reports were serialized in the September, October, and November 1932 issues of *McCall's*; the reports themselves were not published until May 1933. On the genesis of the studies under the sponsorship of long-standing antimovie activist Reverend William H. Short and his Motion Picture Research

Council, and their impact, see Black, *Hollywood Censored*, 151-54; Jowett, *Film*, 220-32; and Jacobs, *The Wages of Sin*, 106-7.

51. See, for example, the following articles in *Variety* following the release of *I'm No Angel* in early October 1933: "Downtown Frisco Will Milk Next Mae West Opus; Nabes Can Squawk," 3 October 1933, 11; " 'Angel' Forces Open a 2d Dallas House for Day-and-Date Run," 10 October 1933, 7; "Strong Attractions Spur Loop B.O., 'Angel' a New Hit at Oriental, 51G," 10 October 1933, 8; " 'Angel' Starts Strong . . ." and " 'Angel' B'klyn's Big Noise, Rousing $50,000," 17 October 1933, 8; "B'way Grosses Read Like 1929, 'Angel' $80,000 . . ." and " 'Angel,' $36,000, St. L. Bonanza," 17 October 1933, 9; "West, 'Bowery' $44,000 in K.C." and " 'Bow- ery,' 'Angel' Has Cincy Talking Tuff Lingo, Helping Biz," 17 October 1933, 10; "Biz 30% Off in L.A., 'Angel' Clicks Again for $23,000 . . .," 24 October 1933, 8; "West's Wow 24G Won't Milk Pitt" and "Mae West Opera Wows Newark—Cops House Record, $28,000, and Held Over," 24 October 1933, 10; "Denver Goes to Town for West, a Zowie 16G" and "St. L. Back to Normal, West $53,000 in 2 Wks," 24 October 1933, 11; "West Bubbles Hub [Boston] for $47,000," 31 October 1933, 8; " 'Angel' on H.O. Still Leads N. Orleans" and "West $21,000, 2d Week after Record 37G," 31 October 1933, 10. The trade journal's review of *I'm No An- gel* begins, " 'I'm No Angel' is going to help redistribute a nice chunk of the na- tion's coin"; Land, "I'm No Angel," *Variety*, 17 October 1933, 19. *She Done Him Wrong* reportedly drew attendance of twelve million, and *I'm No Angel* thirty-five million, before mid-1934. See "So Mae West's Slipping? Not So She Can Notice It!" *Los Angeles Times*, 20 May 1934.

52. *Variety*, 31 January 1933, 5, and 14 November 1933, 9ff; "Paramount," 87, 194.

53. See "Paramount," 198; see also Gomery, *The Hollywood Studio System*, 32- 34, 40-41.

54. Land, "I'm No Angel," 19.

55. "Film Boycott: Churchmen's Crusade to 'Clean House' Brings Chill to Tor- rid Hollywood," *Newsweek*, 7 July 1934, 5.

56. PCA Case Files for *I'm No Angel*, *Belle of the Nineties*, and *Goin' to Town* provide plentiful evidence of this reading of West's character and censors' attempts to eliminate it. For example, deletions by state censors recorded in the PCA file on *I'm No Angel* include lines spoken by West's character Tira, that suggest that she has sex with men in exchange for material goods, for example "I don't like that word 'givin' '!" (spoken to a woman friend who has been admiring the many ex- pensive gifts Tira has received from men) and scenes of Tira's arranging to meet and seduce a man who flashes his diamond pinky ring to beguile her.

During the production of the film eventually released as *Belle of the Nineties* (ini- tially titled "It Ain't No Sin"), Joseph Breen criticized the script submitted to the PCA for "glorification of a prostitute" and called for the elimination of the follow- ing lines:

1ST LADY: That's the fifth man today that I've seen go in that Carter woman's [West's character's] cabin.

2ND LADY: I've seen them go in, but I've never seen them come out. What in the world does she do with them?

3RD LADY: Don't be indelicate, my dear.

The following lines spoken by West's character were also targeted: "Sensation House? Humm, what a home that must be!" and "A man in the house is worth three in the street." The latter line was left in the film (with "three" replaced by "two"), but was deleted by state censors.

In the December 1934 negotiations surrounding the script of *Goin' to Town* (working title "Now I'm a Lady"), Breen insisted that "there should be no indication of prostitution" and criticized the script as follows: "As we read it, it is the boasting of a woman of loose morals who has had any number of men in her time, and has climbed over them to the top of the ladder where she has finally married respectability" (16 January 1935). Breen was particularly alert to suggestions of prostitution in lyrics West proposed to sing in her films. For details on the censorship of this film, see my essay "*Goin' to Town* and Beyond: Mae West, Film Censorship and the Comedy of Unmarriage," in *Classical Film Comedy*, ed. Kristine Brunovska Karnick and Henry Jenkins (New York: Routledge, 1995), 211-37.

57. See, for example, Maltby, " 'Baby Face,' " 41-44; Baxter, "The Birth of Venus," 10-11; Jacobs, *The Wages of Sin*, 52-84, 115-31, 138-49.

58. Jacobs, *The Wages of Sin*, 68-70, 78-80, 111-15.

59. Charles Eckert, "The Anatomy of a Proletarian Film: Warner's *Marked Woman*," *Film Quarterly*, 27, no. 2 (1973-74): 11, 20-24.

60. Baxter, "The Birth of Venus," 9-14; Maltby, " 'Baby Face,' " 43-44. Maltby also makes this point in an unpublished essay, "From the Implausible to the Unspeakable: The Censorship of Sexuality from Mae West to Shirley Temple" (1986).

61. This observation applies not only to the characters in the working-class setting of *She Done Him Wrong* and the opening segments of *I'm No Angel* and *Goin' to Town* that establish the "rags to riches" scenario, but also aptly describes West's characters' intimate relationships even after these women have gained status and wealth, primarily through implicit sexual or explicit stage performances, for example, in *Belle of the Nineties* (in her relationship to the owner of the New Orleans Sensation House and another rich suitor) as well as in *I'm No Angel* and *Goin' to Town*. The primary economic basis of sexual relationships also appears between other male-female pairs in West's films, which sometimes show a wealthy older woman "buying" a younger, usually foreign-born, man (e.g., Rita and Sergei in *She Done Him Wrong* and, in *Goin' to Town*, the snobbish upper-class Mrs. Crane Brittany and Ivan, another Russian gigolo). See my essay "*Goin' to Town* and Beyond" for discussion of how West's early films represented sexual relationships and marriage across a range of classes as predominantly economic contracts.

62. Social historians have argued that impoverished women in nineteenth- and early twentieth-century United States and Britain often regarded occasional or full-time prostitution as a viable economic and familial option, despite the low social status of the profession and various attempts to control and eradicate it. For women from circumstances even more severely limited than those of middle-class

women, making a living by their wits and their bodies was a means of achieving comparative autonomy and some latitude in personal choices (both sexual and economic); for some, especially poor rural women, prostitution even bore a romantic aura associated with urbanity. See D'Emilio and Freedman, *Intimate Matters*, 133-38, 214; and Judith R. Walkowitz, "Male Vice and Female Virtue: Feminism and the Politics of Prostitution in Nineteenth Century Britain," in *Powers of Desire: The Politics of Sexuality*, ed. Ann Snitow, Christine Stansell, and Sharon Thompson (New York: Monthly Review Press, 1983), 419-38; as well as two books by Walkowitz, *Prostitution and Victorian Society: Women, Class and the State* (Cambridge: Cambridge University Press, 1980) and *City of Dreadful Delight: Narratives of Sexual Danger in Late-Victorian London* (Chicago: University of Chicago Press, 1992).

63. Richard Watts Jr., "She Done Him Wrong," *New York Herald-Tribune*, 10 February 1933.

64. Norr to Hays, MPAA files, Indianapolis; quoted in Maltby, " 'Baby Face,' " 44.

3. The Star Commodity from Asset to Liability

1. Film histories making these assertions include Kenneth Anger, *Hollywood Babylon* (New York: Dell, 1975), 257-68; Gerald Gardner, *The Censorship Papers: Movie Censorship Letters from the Hays Office, 1934-1968* (New York: Dodd, Mead, 1987), 139-47; Leonard Maltin, *The Great Movie Comedians: From Charlie Chaplin to Woody Allen* (New York: Bell, 1978), 154-55; Ethan Mordden, *Movie Star: A Look at the Women Who Made Hollywood* (New York: St. Martin's, 1983), 117-20; and Marjorie Rosen, *Popcorn Venus: Women, Movies and the American Dream* (New York: Coward, McCann & Geoghegan, 1973), 151-53.

2. See Douglas Gomery, "Hollywood, the National Recovery Administration and the Question of Monopoly Power," *Journal of the University Film Association* 31, no. 2 (1979): 47-52; and Mary Beth Haralovich, "Mandates of Good Taste: The Self-Regulation of Film Advertising in the Thirties," *Wide Angle* 6, no. 2 (1984): 50.

3. Berlin-born film director Lubitsch became managing director of Paramount studios in February 1935, sharing his executive power in the Hollywood facility with Henry Herzbrun as vice president and general manager. The team succeeded Emanuel Cohen, who had been chief of Paramount studios for two and one-half years, reportedly due to his reputation as a "star pamperer." Lubitsch was succeeded in early February 1936 by William LeBaron as general manager of production. See "Paramount," *Fortune*, March 1937, 87-96, 194-212, esp. 196ff.

4. In the first script Paramount submitted for PCA review, a scene depicts Doll stabbing Chan Lo with an ornate Malay knife. In the film released, only dialogue suggests that Doll killed her captor and that she did so in self-defense.

5. *Klondike Annie* PCA case file. See also the advertisement announcing the release of "Klondike Lou" in *Film Daily*, 13 January 1936, 6. Others of West's movie character's names that connote jewelry are Tira, recalling "tiara," in *I'm No Angel*, and Ruby Carter in *Belle of the Nineties*. Correspondence from November 1932 in

the *She Done Him Wrong* PCA case file indicates that the lead character and the project itself bore for a brief time the name "Ruby Red."

6. McLaglen won the 1935 Academy Award for Best Actor for his role in *The Informer*, directed by John Ford (this award was not made until March 1936, however, after *Klondike Annie* had been released). Lubitsch and West reportedly had conflicts during the production of *Klondike Annie* over her refusal to write a substantial role for McLaglen or to play to him as leading man, rather than in a distinctly supporting role. Lubitsch was quoted as saying that West had treated McLaglen "as a mere stooge" and "an extra." See "Lubitsch Waxes Caustic in Mae West Tiff," *Los Angeles Citizen-News*, 25 February 1936; and "Lubitsch Tells Cause of Row with Mae West," *Los Angeles Times*, 26 February 1936. Paramount publicity for the film featured McLaglen more prominently than does the film narrative. See, for example, the five-page spread advertising the film in *Motion Picture Herald*, 15 February 1936, 36-40.

7. A reviewer commented on West's costuming in *Klondike Annie*: "Miss West is handicapped by having to wear rather dowdy dresses in about half the footage. In other portions she struts fine feathers and wears a set of furs that will make the women gasp" (*Variety*, 18 March 1936, 17).

8. John Hammel to Will Hays, 19 June 1935; Hays to Hammel, 2 July 1935; Joseph Breen to Hammel, 3 September 1935, *Klondike Annie* PCA case file. Unless otherwise indicated, all subsequent citations of letters refer to this PCA case file.

9. Breen to Hammel, 3 September 1935; Breen to Hammel, 4 September 1935; Breen to Hammel, 19 October 1935.

10. For a detailed analysis of negotiations about the song lyrics in the 1935 film, see my essay "*Goin' to Town* and Beyond: Mae West, Film Censorship, and the Comedy of Unmarriage," in *Classical Film Comedy*, ed. Kristine Brunovska Karnick and Henry Jenkins (New York: Routledge, 1995), 211-37.

11. Breen to Hammel, 3 September 1935.

12. Undated excerpt quoted in the *Hollywood Reporter*, 21 March 1936.

13. The file notes action taken by censor boards in Ohio, Pennsylvania, Virginia, Maryland, British Columbia, Alberta, Ontario, Chicago, and England.

14. *Hollywood Reporter*, 5 February 1936; Breen to Paramount, 10 February 1936.

15. Based on the usually strict chronological ordering of materials in the Production Code files, this memo was probably dictated on 19 or 20 February 1936.

16. See, for example, "Is Politics Influencing Censorship?" *Pittsburgh Post-Gazette*, 20 February 1936, 1; and the editorial by Karl Krug in the *Pittsburgh Sun-Telegram*, 22 February 1936.

17. Two personal reasons given are that West had made a disparaging remark about Hearst's mistress, actress Marion Davies, and that Hearst was motivated by "the miscegenation theme." See, e.g., Elizabeth Yeaman, "Big Crowds View Star's New Picture," *Citizen*, 28 February 1936; and Eleanor Barnes, "Mae and 'Quints,' " *Los Angeles Daily News*, 28 February 1936. *Variety* attributed "Hearstian antipathy to 'Annie' " to "a peeve against the Joe Breen branch of the Hays office, rather than a direct objection to the Paramount picture"; see " 'Annie' Grosses Doubled by Hearst?" *Variety*, 18 March 1936, 1. The Los Angeles-based columnists either

did not know or did not consider it relevant that Hearst had previously criticized West's work (her plays *The Drag, Sex, Pleasure Man*) in the political drive to censor New York theater that Hearst had engaged in a decade earlier; see Kaier Curtin, *"We Can Always Call Them Bulgarians": The Emergence of Lesbians and Gay Men on the American Stage* (Boston: Alyson, 1987), 60-62, 70, 87, 155.

18. "Hearst-Block Papers Attack New Mae West Film; 'Klondike' Biz Good," *Variety*, 26 February 1936, 5, 66; Yeaman, "Big Crowds"; " 'Annie' N.Y. Opening Advanced by Paramount," *Film Daily*, 2 March 1936, 1; "Laurels for Hearst," *Hollywood Reporter*, 4 March 1936, 1; "Klondike Annie," *Motion Picture Herald*, 7 March 1936, 19; " 'Annie' Overcomes Hearst Taboo to Top Mild L.A. Biz," *Variety*, 4 March 1936, 8; "Boston Didn't Know 'Annie' Was Dirty till Hearst Told 'Em; $32,000 Socko," *Variety*, 4 March 1936, 9; and " 'Annie' Grosses." See also the advertisement for *Klondike Annie* in the *Hollywood Reporter*, 3 March 1936, which reports the film's record-breaking opening week under the caption "The Gold Rush Is On." The ad features a picture of Mae West saying, "Thanks, Boys . . . ." Exhibitors got around the Hearst-owned publications' refusal to advertise *Klondike Annie* by placing ads "for an important feature" or "that certain film," with their theaters' telephone numbers. See " 'Annie' Grosses," 66; and "Hearst Strike-Out," *Time*, 9 March 1936, 61.

19. Breen to Hammel, 26 February 1936; Breen to Hays, 27 February 1936; Hays to Breen, 29 February 1936.

20. Louella O. Parsons, "Mae-Studio Clash: Blonde Star Signs Contract with Cohen," *Los Angeles Examiner*, 22 February 1936.

21. West's autobiography asserts that she left Paramount because "Lubitsch had control over all the studio's productions and Paramount didn't seem like home to me any longer." Without specifying the basis of their differences, West writes, "We didn't see eye to eye about many things. Possibly that large black cigar he always had in his mouth helped to obscure our vision." Mae West, *Goodness Had Nothing to Do with It*, 2d ed. (New York: Macfadden-Bartell, 1970 [1959]), 178. Carol Ward perpetuates the view that West left because she didn't get along with Lubitsch in her *Mae West: A Bio-bibliography* (Westport, Conn.: Greenwood, 1989), 31.

22. The Hearst organization functioned as an integral aspect of the industry, due both to its control over newspaper publicity across the nation and to the direct financial and personal influence that Hearst himself exercised in Hollywood.

23. "Paramount," 198. See also Douglas Gomery, *The Hollywood Studio System* (New York: St. Martin's, 1986), 32-33, 39.

24. "Paramount," 198. See also George Eells and Stanley Musgrove, *Mae West: A Biography* (New York: William Morrow, 1982), 153. Eells and Musgrove point out that despite Paramount's initial denial, the studio had failed to renew West's option for further films after *Klondike Annie*. These authors suggest that the studio's failure to exercise its option derived from an oversight during the transition between Lubitsch and LeBaron as heads of production.

25. "Paramount," 198. See also Gomery, *The Hollywood Studio System*, 32-33, 41.

26. For example, the following authors make this argument: Anger, *Hollywood Babylon*, 268; Maltin, *The Great Movie Comedians*, 159; and Rosen, *Popcorn Venus*,

153. The made-for-TV movie *Mae West,* discussed in chapter 5, also suggests this motivation for West's departure from Paramount.

27. "Top Pix and Stars of 1937," *Variety,* 5 January 1938, 13.

28. My thanks to Richard Maltby for suggesting this point to me; certainly there is evidence that the PCA was not averse to using tactics of delay and even personal harassment, through the stationing of a PCA representative on the set, as a means of bringing West to heel in her 1934 production *Belle of the Nineties.*

29. See Lea Jacobs, *The Wages of Sin: Censorship and the Fallen Woman Film, 1928-1942* (Madison: University of Wisconsin Press, 1991), 32-33, for a discussion of short-term and long-term industry goals in relation to self-regulation policies.

30. On trade practices of block booking and blind buying, see Mae D. Huettig, *Economic Control of the Motion Picture Industry* (Philadelphia: University of Pennsylvania Press, 1944), 32, 36, 116-24, and passim, for an account of film distribution and exhibition practices of the major studios and their relation to the independents in the 1930s. For a succinct history and discussion of block booking and blind buying, see John Izod, *Hollywood and the Box Office: 1895-1986* (New York: Columbia University Press, 1988), 47-48.

31. Garth Jowett, *Film: The Democratic Art* (Boston: Little, Brown, 1976), 4-9, 123-25, 199-203. Federal bills opposing movie oligopolies had been introduced nearly yearly from 1915 on, but the coalition of reform elements with unaffiliated exhibitors to pressure bill passage on the grounds of local rights represented a new and more powerful threat.

32. U.S. Senate, 74/2, Subcommittee of the Committee on Interstate Commerce, *Compulsory Block-Booking and Blind Selling in the Motion-Picture Industry,* transcript of hearings on proposed Senate Bill S. 3012, 27-28 February 1936, (Washington, D.C.: U.S. Government Printing Office, 1938), 93, 95, 128, 130, 149, 152, 193-95, 200; U.S. House of Representatives, 74/2, Subcommittee of the Committee on Interstate and Foreign Commerce, *Motion Picture Films,* transcript of hearings on proposed House Bill H.R. 6472, 9-26 March 1936 (Washington, D.C.: U.S. Government Printing Office, 1936), 36, 39, 245, 253-54, 335, 471. See also Arthur W. Eddy, "Anti-Block Booking Bill Vigorously Attacked by Film Heads," *Film Daily,* 29 February 1936, 1, 6; and "Mae West Cops Spotlight at Block Booking Hearing," *Film Daily,* 29 February 1936, 6. It is worth noting that representatives of Catholic groups testified on behalf of the industry, as the film trade papers were quick to report. See, for example, "Catholics Defend Pix, Legion of Decency Stands Up beside Hays in Support of Present Industry Practices," *Hollywood Reporter,* 2 March 1936, 1, 9.

33. *Motion Picture Herald,* 7 March 1936, 19. See also "Pettijohn Assails Motives behind Block Booking Bill," *Hollywood Reporter,* 29 February 1936, 3.

34. Industry spokesmen otherwise dismissed the linking of the issue of morality to the industry's business practices in the hearings as "a red herring" and an "issue of rank hypocrisy"; see "Pettijohn Assails Motives," 3. By the time the Neely-Pettingill bill approached passage in 1940, MPPDA representatives had managed to convince congressmen that the morality issue was irrelevant. See Andrew R. Kelley, " 'Plenty Wrong with Pix,' " *Variety,* 25 September 1940, 3, 20. See also Jowett, *Film,* 278-89.

35. See Gomery, *The Hollywood Studio System*, 33-35, and, especially, Huettig, *Economic Control*, 134-35, for an overview of Paramount's theater holdings at this period. Huettig cites 1940 *United States v. Paramount Pictures, Inc., et al.* court records to show Paramount's dominance in theater ownership in a number of states, including Maine, Massachusetts, Illinois, Alabama, Texas, and Florida, where Paramount was the sole major movie company that owned theaters. (Huettig notes that some of the majors had a joint interest in at least two hundred theaters across the nation.) Paramount's releases also of course played in theaters owned by other majors in areas where their theaters dominated, such as western Pennsylvania (Warners) and Kansas and the Pacific Coast states (Twentieth Century Fox). (In 1940, Paramount owned only four theaters in California and none in Oregon or Washington, whereas Fox owned a total of 538 in the Pacific states.) I have not been able to obtain a precise accounting of Paramount's income for *Klondike Annie* or any other film, either by location or in total.

36. "Wake Up! Hollywood Producers," advertisement paid for by the Independent Theatre Owners Association, *Hollywood Reporter*, 3 May 1938, 5.

37. "Mae West Script Angers Listeners," *Hollywood Reporter*, 15 December 1937; "Religious Leader Warns U.S. Bd. on 'Risque' Radio Plays," *Los Angeles Herald*, 16 December 1937; "Legion of Decency Drive Impends on Radio 'Sacrilege,'" *Hollywood Reporter*, 17 December 1937, 1, 4; "Mae West Scene 'Mistake,' 'Won't Happen Again,' Says Air Sponsor," *Los Angeles Examiner*, 17 December 1937; "Furor Starts over Mae West Program: Radio Skit Declared Offensive," *Los Angeles Evening News*, 17 December 1937; "Mae West Radio Skit Stirs Row," *Los Angeles Times*, 17 December 1937, 1, 15; "Mae West Burlesques the Bible on the Air for Coffee Merchants," *Motion Picture Herald*, 18 December 1937, 27; "Mae West's Eve Brings Eden's Curse on Radio—Apology, Alibi, Indignation and Investigation," *Motion Picture Herald*, 25 December 1937, 12-13, 16; "Capital Takes Up New Film Loans, Taxes, Theatre 'Divorce,' Mae West," *Motion Picture Herald*, 25 December 1937, 17; "Mae West Case Big Dilemma in Washington," *Variety*, 29 December 1937; "Mae West Script Brings Sharp Rebuke from FCC," *New York Times*, 15 January 1938, 1, 18.

38. Martin Quigley, "Radio Begs Trouble," *Motion Picture Daily*, 14 December 1937, 10.

39. William R. Weaver, "Every Day's a Holiday," *Motion Picture Herald*, 25 December 1937, 36 (interestingly enough, Quigley also was publisher of the *Motion Picture Herald*); "Every Day's a Holiday," *Film Daily*, 27 December 1937, 8.

40. See, for example, "Frisco Drooping, 'Holiday' $17,000," *Variety*, 26 January 1938, 10, which notes that West's film was the only film doing well in San Francisco that week; "Benny Goodman-West Boffo B'way for $57,000," *Variety*, 2 February 1938, 9; "Mae West P.A. [personal appearance] Helps 'Holiday' to $35,000, L.A. Record," *Variety*, 2 February 1938, 2; and Frank S. Nugent, "Every Day's a Holiday," *New York Times*, 27 January 1938, 17. Although Nugent panned the film, he remarked on the strong attendance (though he attributed it to the appearance on the same program of Benny Goodman and His Orchestra).

41. "Paramount Rushing Mae West Release Rather Than Wait for Cool-Off," *Variety*, 29 December 1937, 7; "Paramount-Mae West Most Likely All Washed

Up," *Variety*, 5 January 1938, 1. The latter article reported that Paramount Theatre in New York had monitored audience reaction to trailers for the film, which was reported as "considerable applause for West, but also some hisses."

42. Quigley himself had testified before the House subcommittee at the behest of the MPPDA counsel to oppose block booking, which he argued would not "reach the objective of a wholesome screen." See U.S. House of Representatives, *Motion Picture Films*, 235-36. Quigley's criticism of West's radio broadcast jibed with the outrage other Catholic leaders were experssing at her performance of Eve.

43. "They Sent for Her," *Motion Picture Herald*, 25 December 1937, 7.

44. On the antitrust suit initiated in 1938 that resulted in the major studios' divesting themselves of exhibition outlets, see Tino Balio, ed., *The American Film Industry* (Madison: University of Wisconsin Press, 1976), 315-31; and Ernest Borneman's chapter in the Balio volume, "United States versus Hollywood: The Case Study of an Antitrust Suit," 332-70. See also Huettig, *Economic Control*, 139-42; and Jowett, *Film*, 275-80.

45. " 'Film Morals—or Else' NRA Commission to Curb Lapses," *Variety*, 21 November 1933, 5.

46. Arthur W. Eddy, "A Summary of Events Leading Up to the Motion Picture Code," in *The 1934 Daily Film Year Book of Motion Pictures*, ed. Jack Alicoate (New York: Film Daily, 1934), 596-97; see *Variety* and other trade journals from June-December 1933 for reports and editorials on the negotiations around the film industry's adoption of the NRA Code. For a summary of publicly enunciated industry attitudes toward this code, see Jack Alicoate, ed., *The 1934 Daily Film Year Book of Motion Pictures* (New York: Film Daily, 1934), 3, and also testimonials by Adolph Zukor and other industry leaders in that volume, 89ff. See also Jack Alicoate, "Introduction," in *The 1935 Daily Film Year Book of Motion Pictures*, ed. Jack Alicoate (New York: Film Daily, 1935), 3.

47. Gomery, "Hollywood, National Recovery," 47-52; Haralovich, "Mandates of Good Taste," 53-56.

48. See Richard Maltby, " 'Baby Face' or How Joe Breen Made Barbara Stanwyck Atone for Causing the Wall Street Crash," *Screen* 27, no. 2 (1986): 41; and Jacobs, *The Wages of Sin*, 20-21.

49. Andrew Bergman, *We're in the Money: Depression America and Its Films* (New York: Harper & Row, 1971), 49-51.

4. Comedic Performance from Social Satire to Self-Parody

1. I discuss this issue at length in my essay "*Goin' to Town* and Beyond: Mae West, Film Censorship, and the Comedy of Unmarriage," in *Classical Film Comedy*, ed. Kristine Brunovska Karnick and Henry Jenkins (New York: Routledge, 1995), 211-37. See also Steve Neale and Frank Krutnik, *Popular Film and Television Comedy* (London: Routledge, 1990), 4, 86-94, 151-52; and Jerry Palmer, *The Logic of the Absurd: On Film and Television Comedy* (London: British Film Institute, 1987), 9-18, 212-24.

2. James Wingate to Harold Hurley (Paramount's liaison to the Studio Relations Committee), 29 November 1932, *She Done Him Wrong* PCA case file.

3. Mae West, *Goodness Had Nothing to Do with It* (New York: Macfadden-Bartell, 1970 [1959]), 45-46, 107, 164. West made this claim also in interviews in the 1930s and 1940s. See Edwin Schallert, " 'Films Should Be Fit for Children to See,' " *Los Angeles Times*, 23 September 1934; and Philip K. Scheuer, "Town Called Hollywood: Mae West to Dance in Next," *Los Angeles Times*, 27 June 1943, 2, 5.

4. Breen PCA office memo, 20 February 1936, *Klondike Annie* PCA case file.

5. "Furor Starts over Mae West Program: Radio Skit Declared Offensive," *Los Angeles Evening News*, 17 December 1937.

6. The full program is available on an audiotape under the title *Mae West on the Chase and Sanborn Hour* (Radiola Records, CMR-1126, 1987). Both of West's numbers were scripted by Oboler, a writer with the William Morris Agency, which was managing some advance publicity for West's new film *Every Day's a Holiday*. See Land, "Mae West," *Variety*, 15 December 1937, 32; and "Mae West Burlesques the Bible on the Air for Coffee Merchants," *Motion Picture Herald*, 18 December 1937, 27.

7. "Mae West Case Big Dilemma in Washington," *Variety*, 29 December 1937, 28; "Mae West's Eve Brings Eden's Curse on Radio—Apology, Alibi, Indignation and Investigation," *Motion Picture Herald*, 25 December 1937, 12-13, 16.

8. Hal Humphrey, "Charlie and Mae Together Again," *Los Angeles Times*, 12 November 1964, IV13.

9. *Newsweek*, 16 January 1950, 46.

10. Both of West's *Chesterfield Supper Club* appearances are available on the audio recording *Mae West on the Air: Rare Recordings 1934-1960* (Sandy Hook Records CSH-2098, Radiola, 1987).

11. West's performance of the song appears on the audiocassettes *Mae West* (San Francisco: Mind's Eye, 1985) and also *Mae West: Sixteen Sultry Songs* (New York: Rosetta Records, 1987). The number, for which West herself probably wrote the lyrics, diverges entirely in words and music from a song of the same title composed in 1939 by Clyde Hager, Mack David, and Jerry Livingston. I thank Dennis Livingston and Rosetta Reitz for information about West's song.

12. West commented in interviews as well as song on the paradox of censorship's popularizing her work, declaring later in her life, "I believe in censorship. After all, I made a fortune out of it." See C. Robert Jennings, "Mae West: A Candid Conversation with the Indestructible Queen of Vamp and Camp," *Playboy*, January 1971, 82.

13. For a description of their act, see Carol Ward, *Mae West: A Bio-bibliography* (Westport, Conn.: Greenwood, 1989), 43; and Maurice Leonard, *Mae West: Empress of Sex* (New York: Carol, 1992), 314-17. A clip of the number was included in a self-referential nostalgia montage broadcast on the 1988 Academy Awards program.

14. "Mae West Too 'Person'-al; CBS Junks Interview Tape," *Hollywood Reporter*, 16 October 1959.

15. Cecil Smith, "Mae West Censored from New TV Show," *Los Angeles Times*, 15 October 1959; see also "Mae West a Little Bit Too Much of a 'Person' for CBS," *Daily Variety*, 16 October 1959.

16. Audio recordings of West's appearances on Dean Martin's and Red Skelton's shows are included on the tape *Mae West on the Air*.

17. Following Paramount's 1938 release of *Every Day's a Holiday*, West made *My Little Chickadee* (1940) with W. C. Fields at Universal and appeared in Gregory Ratoff's Columbia production *The Heat's On* (1943). This last film is only nominally a West star vehicle, for her character, Fay Lawrence, a stage actress, barely carries the story of New York theatrical intrigues and a zealous moral reform organization. Episodic, if visually and aurally striking, musical numbers featuring Hazel Scott, Lina Romay, and Xavier Cugat and His Orchestra come to dominate the film, along with a romantic subplot about an aspiring actress whose reformist aunt keeps her off the stage and the young woman's fiancé, an upstanding soldier played by Lloyd Bridges. See Figure 14 for a publicity still of West for *The Heat's On*; whatever film footage showed her in that particular costume ended up on the cutting room floor. The film received generally poor reviews and did disappointing business, and was West's last film until *Myra Breckinridge* (1970). In the intervening years, West wrote and toured in plays and had a nightclub act in Las Vegas, along with writing her autobiography and appearing occasionally on radio and television.

18. George Eells and Stanley Musgrove, *Mae West: A Biography* (New York: William Morrow, 1982), 160-61.

19. For an overview of comediennes in vaudeville and in silent and sound films, see Linda Martin and Kerry Segrave, *Women in Comedy* (Secaucus, N.J.: Citadel, 1986).

20. Henry Jenkins argues in *What Made Pistachio Nuts? Early Sound Comedy and the Vaudeville Aesthetic* (New York: Columbia University Press, 1992) that even though early sound film performers such as Charlotte Greenwood and Winnie Lightner often played humorous butts in their films, they also presented a physical vigor and unruly spectacle that suggested "possibilities for a resistance to the domestic containment of women" that was "totally absent from the male-centered comedies of the same vintage"; see 245-74, esp. 245-47, 274.

21. One study of West's comedic style utilized an audio frequency spectrum recorder to evaluate West's use of pauses and speech fillers (such as "ums" and "ahs"), compared with the style of other radio comedy performers. The author concludes as follows: "The comic effect achieved by Mae West centers around a wit that requires mental sharpness, intellectual abridgement and linguistic embodiment. . . . The key to her sultry speech style [is] a very fast speech rate interrupted by relatively long pauses. . . . Confidence in the voice is associated with a faster speech rate. . . . This confidence is shown in her speech and definitely enhanced the role she played." Mary Moore Landeros, "The Use of Temporal Aspects in Radio Comedy," unpublished manuscript, n.d., 11-12. My thanks to this author for making her research available.

22. On conventions of comedian comedy, see Neale and Krutnik, *Popular Film*, 103-7; and Jenkins, *What Made Pistachio Nuts?* passim.

23. A key text introducing the concept of "the male gaze" into film theory is, of course, Laura Mulvey's, "Visual Pleasure and Narrative Cinema," *Screen* 16, no. 3 (1975): 6-18. For a brief discussion of Mulvey's points in relation to the concept of "desire" in cinema, see Judith Mayne, *Cinema and Spectatorship* (London: Routledge, 1993), 22-23.

24. Mulvey, "Visual Pleasure"; Laura Mulvey, "Afterthoughts on 'Visual Pleasure and Narrative Cinema' Inspired by *Duel in the Sun*," *Framework* 6, nos. 15-17 (1981): 12-15 (both reprinted in Laura Mulvey, *Visual and Other Pleasures* [Bloomington: Indiana University Press, 1989]). See also Stephen Heath, *Questions of Cinema* (Bloomington: Indiana University Press, 1981). Of Barthes, see *The Pleasure of the Text*, trans. Richard Miller (New York: Hill & Wang, 1975) and *Image-Music-Text*, trans. Stephen Heath (New York: Hill & Wang, 1977). Mayne's *Cinema and Spectatorship* gives a nuanced overview of these developments in theories of narrative and cinema.

25. For the most widely discussed feminist argument on relations between voyeurism in the cinema and sadism, see Mulvey, "Visual Pleasure." For detailed arguments relating cinematic pleasure and masochism, see Gaylyn Studlar, *In the Realm of Pleasure: Von Sternberg, Dietrich and the Masochistic Aesthetic* (Urbana: University of Illinois Press, 1988), 9-49; and Kaja Silverman, *Male Subjectivity at the Margins* (London: Routledge, 1992). On the possible impact of West's voice in the psychodynamics of viewing cinema, see Kaja Silverman, *The Acoustic Mirror: The Female Voice in Psychoanalysis and Cinema* (Bloomington: Indiana University Press, 1988), 61.

26. Sigmund Freud, *Jokes and Their Relation to the Unconscious* (1905), in *Standard Edition of the Complete Psychological Works of Sigmund Freud*, trans. James Strachey (London: Hogarth Press and Institute of Psycho-analysis, 1960). For all subsequent references to this work, page numbers are included in parentheses in the text.

27. After beginning to explore how Freud's analysis might elucidate viewer reactions to film comedy, I discovered prior work on the approach, notably an essay by Steve Neale, "Psychoanalysis and Comedy," *Screen* 22, no. 2 (1981): 29-42, with commentary by Mick Eaton; and two essays by Patricia Mellencamp, "Jokes and Their Relation to the Marx Brothers," in *Cinema and Language*, ed. Stephen Heath and Patricia Mellencamp (Frederick, Maryland: American Film Institute, 1983), 63-78, esp. 67-69, and "Situation Comedy, Feminism and Freud: Discourses of Gracie and Lucy" in *Studies in Entertainment: Critical Approaches to Mass Culture*, ed. Tania Modleski (Bloomington: Indiana University Press, 1986), 80-89.

Consideration of West's comedic lines as jokes does not deny their original delivery as dialogue in a narrative and cinematic context delimited by genre conventions of film comedy. I concur with Neale's position that film comedy is not reducible to jokes, but rather must be seen as "a sequence, a *narration* of jokes and joke-like structures" (34). Neale and coauthor Krutnik develop the point in their book *Popular Film and Television Comedy*, 43-61, esp. 47-49.

28. Many of West's radio performances and interviews, which extensively reprise witticisms from her films, are often available at public libraries, such as the audiotape *Mae West: 1971 Interview and Christmas Songs* (San Francisco: Mind's Eye, 1985). Of the many published collections of Mae West quips and jokes drawn from her films, see, for example, Joseph Weintraub, ed., *The Wit and Wisdom of Mae West* (New York: G. P. Putnam, 1967), and *Quotable Women: A Collection of Shared Thoughts* (Philadelphia: Running Press, 1989).

29. Freud's presumption of gender difference is so fundamental that his usually clearly and methodically constructed sentences never specify through the use of appositive formulations or other direct reference that the object or "second per-

son" (in his triadic model) for smutty jokes is usually a woman. He moves immediately from defining smut (a means of expressing sexual excitement to its object) to the statement, "Smut is thus originally directed towards women and may be equated with attempts at seduction" (97). (In the original German: "Die Zote ist also ursprünglich an das Weib [the female] gerichtet." See Sigmund Freud, *Der Witz und seine Beziehung zum Unbewußten* (Leipzig: Franz Deuticke, 1905), 80.

30. The *She Done Him Wrong* PCA case file notes that state censors in Kansas and Virginia eliminated the "lots of times" quip, among others. Freud's argument relates the amount of pleasure a joke produces (for listeners whose particular inhibitions or personal sympathies do not preclude them from finding a joke funny) to the degree it violates social convention: the greater the infraction, the bigger the laugh.

31. See Robert C. Allen, *Horrible Prettiness: Burlesque and American Culture* (Chapel Hill: University of North Carolina Press, 1991), 272-74, for a discussion of the "red-hot mama" type in popular entertainment in the 1910s and 1920s; see Esther Newton, *Mother Camp: Female Impersonators in America* (Chicago: University of Chicago Press, 1968), 46, for a discussion of female impersonations of the type in the 1960s.

32. See Martin Grotjahn, *Beyond Laughter* (New York: McGraw-Hill, 1957), 103-6. Censors and women's groups that found West's image disrespectful to womanhood offered, to an extent, a lay version of this interpretation.

33. Ludwig Eidelberg, "A Contribution to the Study of Wit," *Psychoanalytic Review* 32 (1945): 33-61.

34. By essay's end, Eidelberg proposes reducing Freud's triadic model to a dual interaction between narrator and listener, both intent on gaining narcissistic, ego-gratifying pleasure from exhibiting their intellectual comprehension of the structure of a joke. He argues that both narrator and listener derive pleasure from the joke primarily from the occasion to feel ego superiority over the id-driven characters whom the joke describes. In so doing, he flattens any distinctions between smutty jokes, with their sexual and—for Freud—gender implications, and any other aggressive jokes, while yet implicitly accepting Freud's assertions about the narrator's and listeners' male identities. Eidelberg thus retains Freud's gender bias while discarding his predecessor's insights into the subconscious sexual workings (rather than intellectual and self-righteous impact) of jokes. I am obviously even less convinced by Eidelberg than by Freud.

35. The Tex Avery "Red Riding Hood" cartoon series has been released on videotape and laser disc. For a provocative analysis of its ideological uses in the wartime United States, see Jane Gaines, "The Showgirl and the Wolf," in *Cinema Examined*, ed. Richard Dyer MacCann and Jack C. Ellis (New York: E. P. Dutton, 1982), 282-97.

36. Neale and Krutnik, *Popular Film*, 19.

37. Linda Hutcheon, *A Theory of Parody: The Teachings of Twentieth-Century Art Forms* (New York: Methuen, 1985), 16-18, 25-26, 50-55, 58-63. Hutcheon argues that *Play It Again, Sam* also satirizes the social ideology of heroic sacrifice that occurs, cast in different terms, in both that film and in *Casablanca* (26).

38. Breen to Paramount, 16 January 1935, *Goin' to Town* PCA case file.

39. Censor boards in Ohio, Virginia, and the Canadian province of Quebec cut that particular word, whereas six other state or national censor boards cut other lines (Italian censors rejected the film outright). See *Goin' to Town* PCA case file. For further discussion of the censorship and reception of this film, see my essay "*Goin' to Town* and Beyond."

40. Breen to Universal, October 1939, *My Little Chickadee* PCA case file.

41. The *My Little Chickadee* PCA case file contains U.S. state censor reports from Ohio, Pennsylvania, and New York; Maryland, Massachusetts, and Kansas passed the film with no changes. Only the Ohio state censors eliminated any of West's dialogue or made extensive cuts. That board cut Fields's and West's dialogue equally throughout the film, including such Westian lines as "*Too bad I can't give out samples*" (spoken to Jeff Badger, the saloon keeper trying to seduce her) and her widely cited quip "I generally avoid temptation *unless I can't resist it*" (italics mark the phrases cut). Other boards cut Fields/Twillie's references to his failure to consummate the marriage to West/Flower Belle, generally in the scene in which he belatedly recognizes that she has substituted a goat in her bed for herself.

42. Walter Ames, "Who's Marilyn Monroe, Queen Mae West Asks," *Los Angeles Times*, 13 September 1953, 1, 4.

43. See reviews of *Go West, Young Man* in the London newspapers the *Sunday Referee* and the *Sunday Express*, both cited in *Hollywood Reporter*, 22 January 1937, and *Variety*, 25 November 1936, 14, which generally praises the changes West had made to the play *Personal Appearance*. On *The Heat's On*, see *Hollywood Citizen-News*, 17 January 1944.

44. See reviews of West's play *Catherine Was Great* in Earl Wilson, *Los Angeles Daily News*, 6 May 1944; *Life*, 21 August 1944, 71; and *Variety*, 9 August 1944. Virginia Wright's review of West in her play *Come on Up* in the *Los Angeles Daily News*, 11 February 1947, suggests, "Take along your lowest sense of humor, a strong constitution to digest the corn and . . . leave your critical faculties at home," and complains, "There has been no effort to change either the formula of her material or her standardized performance . . . even the unique West delivery grows monotonous after 20 minutes." But Wright also notes, "No Duse ever made an entrance to more thunderous applause . . . the audience remained just as loyal in its laughter as if the playwrights and the star hadn't exposed their entire bag of tricks."

45. During most of its original run, *Mister Ed* was scheduled in a traditionally desirable family prime-time slot from 6:30-7:00 p.m. on Sunday; it was preceded on CBS by *College Bowl* at 5:30 p.m. and *The 20th Century* at 6:00 and followed by *Lassie* at 7:00 p.m. and *Dennis the Menace* at 7:30. See Harry Castleman and Walter J. Podrazik, *The TV Schedule Book: Four Decades of Network Programming from Sign-On to Sign-Off* (New York: McGraw-Hill, 1984). A palomino gelding named Bamboo Harvester played Mister Ed; his voice was supplied by Allan "Rocky" Lane. Arthur Lubin produced and directed the series, which was written largely by Larry Rhine, Ben Starr, and Lou Derman, who later worked on *All in the Family*. See Joel Eisner and David Krinksy, *Television Comedy Series: An Episode Guide to 153 TV Sitcoms in Syndication* (London: McFarland, 1984), 557; and Cecil Adams, "The Straight Dope," *Chicago Reader*, 25 September 1987, 2. In recent years the

series has run repeatedly in syndication, both on cable (Nickelodeon) and on local independent stations.

46. The two entrance scenes are similar not only in the star's escort of three tall, dark-suited men, but also in the blocking that first conceals, then reveals West as she speaks before going through the opened door alone. The narrative buildup to West's entrance and its theatrical presentation is a convention for introducing a guest star on a situation comedy (and in its precursor, the variety skit); it is also in keeping with West's presentation in her starring vehicles, each of which employs a prologue to herald the star's arrival. The effect of this prologue, in which the other characters extol West's beauty, is to support the illusion of her beauty (and in this program, of her youthfulness).

The music that accompanies West's entrance on *Mister Ed* also recalls sound track motifs from her starring vehicles. When I first heard it, I thought the jazzy refrain resembled the entrance music sometimes played for burlesque queens, and I surmised that it had been adopted particularly to complement this aspect of West's image. However, I subsequently heard the same piece used over quite different scenes on other episodes of *Mister Ed* made *before* West's guest appearance. In any case, its associations with West in this scene accentuate the prior sexual implications that the jazzy music itself bears.

47. "Mister Ed Barges into a Boudoir," *TV Guide*, 29 February-6 March 1964, 20-21. The article also emphasizes director Lubin's associations with the star, asserting that he was "just a boy production assistant" at Paramount when West made her first starring feature there. Besides celebrating West's status as entertainment legend, this phrasing also underscores West's advanced age.

48. "Very Warm for Mae," *Hollywood Reporter*, 20 July 1964; "Return Engagement," *New York Times*, 16 August 1964. The episode, to be titled "Mae Goes West," was to feature the star as a saloon keeper, something like the character of Kitty on *Gunsmoke*. The unspoken implication, for those familiar with West's long-running stage hit or with her early movies, was that she would portray a version of her dance hall queen, Diamond Lil. As this was West's primary stage and movie persona, tantamount to her trademark, a further implication was that the episode would be designed as a conventional, if shortened, star vehicle for West. The episode was never broadcast; as far as I can ascertain, it was never filmed.

49. Susan Sontag, "Notes on 'Camp,' " in *Against Interpretation and Other Essays* (New York: Delta, 1967), 280-83; (reprinted from *Partisan Review* 31, no. 4 [1964]).

50. One early proponent of this position was Jack Babuscio. See his "Camp and the Gay Sensibility," in *Gays and Film*, ed. Richard Dyer, (New York: New York Zoetrope, 1977), 46. I discuss 1970s West's camp reception further in chapter 5.

51. See, for example, Merwyn Grote, "Girls, Boys! Use Your Gaydar! As Seen on TV!!" in the St. Louis weekly *News-Telegraph*, 10-23 December 1993, 20. Grote playfully identifies Wilbur as a gay TV figure.

52. An episode in which Ed suffers from a bad cold, which he caught from Wilbur, who had caught it from Carol, vividly illustrates this pattern of narrative displacement. In another episode, conflict arises when it appears that Wilbur will have to sell Mister Ed because Carol is allergic to him. These narratives and others that depict women as unwelcome interferences in Wilbur and Ed's close relation-

ship support a reading of the program as regularly having a strong homosocial focus and of Ed and Wilbur as gay male figures. I am indebted to Kate Kane and Alexander Doty for drawing these points to my attention.

53. Titles and descriptions of many of the 143 episodes in the series position Ed as an irrepressible, anarchic figure in relation to Wilbur: "Mr. Ed tells Wilbur he can drive and proves it in a milk truck"; "Mr. Ed volunteers to be the first horse in space"; "Wilbur goes on a cruise and Mr. Ed stows away in the bathroom." In many episodes Mister Ed wants and pursues something that Wilbur is reluctant to grant: usually more attention and more indulgent treatment. Examples: "Mr. Ed fears old age and wants Wilbur to buy him a pony" (alternately, his long-lost mother or a female companion); "Mr. Ed tries to hypnotize Wilbur into spending more time with him"; "Mr. Ed wants his stall redone in Hawaiian Modern." Ed is often jealous or upset about something Wilbur has done or will not do: "Mr. Ed is not eating and Wilbur's got a hard choice: stay and nurse Ed or go to the ballet with Carol"; "Mr. Ed is jealous when Wilbur puts a poodle in his barn"; "Mr. Ed is upset when a parrot takes over his stable." Eisner and Krinsky, Television Comedy Series, 557.

A clear pattern of narrative and character relations emerges. Mister Ed, depicted as emotionally expressive, initiates the action with the enunciation of a desire, the fulfillment of which would shift or redefine the relations among the characters. Ed's persistent desire for male attention fits within a reading of Mister Ed as a gay figure; from this perspective Ed's interest in matters such as interior decoration appears to be a convention of stereotyping. But Wilbur generally frustrates or denies Mister Ed's wishes and works to enforce the given order. The resolution to each episode is, in keeping with the conventions of situation comedy, the restoration and affirmation of the status quo.

54. See Mellencamp, "Situation Comedy," 92, for a discussion of this point.

55. Patricia Mellencamp's argument that whereas Lucy Ricardo always failed narratively on I Love Lucy, Lucille Ball always succeeded performatively (her emphasis) is well taken here. See her "Situation Comedy," 88.

56. For an account of these directors' attempts to recruit West, see Leonard, Mae West, 274-77, 331.

5. The Female Impersonator in Gender Politics

1. See, for example, Marjorie Rosen, Popcorn Venus: Women, Movies and the American Dream (New York: Coward, McCann & Geoghegan, 1973), 150-55; Joan Mellen, Women and Their Sexuality in the New Film (New York: Horizon, 1973), 229-43; and Claire Johnston, "Women's Cinema as Counter-Cinema," in Movies and Methods, vol. 1, ed. Bill Nichols (Berkeley: University of California Press, 1976), 208-17.

2. Parker Tyler, Screening the Sexes: Homosexuality in the Movies (Garden City, N.Y.: Doubleday, 1972), 2.

3. Parker Tyler, Sex Psyche Etcetera in the Film (New York: Horizon, 1969), 20. Tyler made his initial reference to West as a female impersonator in The Hollywood Hallucination (New York: Simon & Schuster, 1944), 96-98.

4. Susan Sontag, "Notes on 'Camp,' " in *Against Interpretation and Other Essays* (New York: Delta, 1967), 280.

5. Esther Newton, *Mother Camp: Female Impersonators in America* (Chicago: University of Chicago Press, 1968), 106. Newton undertook the study in the mid-1960s as a University of Chicago doctoral dissertation in anthropology.

6. Ibid., 107.

7. Ibid., 93-94, 46, 48.

8. Ibid., 49.

9. C. Robert Jennings, "A Candid Conversation with the Indestructible Queen of Vamp and Camp," *Playboy*, January 1971, 74; Mitch Tuchman, "Scenes: Going Steady," *Penthouse*, February 1980, 45.

10. See Marybeth Hamilton, " 'I'm the Queen of the Bitches': Female Impersonation and Mae West's *Pleasure Man*," in *Crossing the Stage: Controversies on Cross-Dressing*, ed. Lesley Ferris (London: Routledge, 1993), 107-19; and Kaier Curtin, *"We Can Always Call Them Bulgarians": The Emergence of Lesbians and Gay Men on the American Stage* (Boston: Alyson, 1987), 68-104, esp. 96-98.

11. George Chauncey, *Gay New York: Gender, Urban Culture, and the Making of the Gay Male World 1890-1940* (New York: Basic Books, 1994), 51, 61, 263. Chauncey notes that "Mae West" was a name and act favored by black as well as white drag queens.

12. Quoted in David MacLean, "Resurrecting Russell," *Epicene*, October 1987, 5.

13. In a show I observed at a French Quarter club in New Orleans in February 1993, a physically thick-set performer with broad shoulders impersonated both West and Bette Midler (in an act in which his impersonation of Midler impersonated Sophie Tucker). A performer who was tall and very slender impersonated Patsy Cline, Marilyn Monroe, and Cher.

14. Tyler, who was a published poet as well as a cultural critic, had, in 1933, written with Charles Henry Ford a novel about the experiences of two feminine gay men, *The Young and Evil* (New York: Arno, 1975 [1933]). That novel represented the authors' "coming out" in print, but due to the novel's original European publication (occasioned by U.S. censorship) and its limited stateside circulation, many who later admired Tyler's criticism and attended his public lectures did not know of his gay identity. On this point, see the preface by contemporary New York film critic Andrew Sarris to the new edition of Tyler's *Screening the Sexes* (New York: Da Capo, 1993), ix.

15. This event occurred on 29 June 1969, the evening of Judy Garland's funeral, sparked when gay patrons at the Stonewall club, many of them in drag, fought back against police who were attempting to arrest them. For a brief historical overview of the event, see John D'Emilio, *Sexual Politics, Sexual Communities: The Making of a Homosexual Minority in the United States, 1940-1970* (Chicago: University of Chicago Press, 1983), 231-33, as well as the extensive coverage in the *New York Times* and in gay weeklies in late June 1994, commemorating the event's twenty-fifth anniversary.

16. Gore Vidal, *Myra Breckinridge* (Boston: Little, Brown, 1968). Vidal collaborated on the initial script, which director Michael Sarne rewrote. The position of West's name in the credits reveals her extended capacity to command top billing,

West's contractual condition on all the films following her Hollywood debut in *Night after Night*. The billing also suggests that the studio invested substantially in West's appearance (reportedly paying West $350,000) for her potential audience draw. See "Raquel Welch, Mae West Talk about Men, Morals and 'Myra Breckinridge,'" *Look*, 24 March 1970, 45; and "Mae and Myra," *Films and Filming* (February 1970): 69.

17. Tyler, *Screening the Sexes*, 14-15.

18. Eric Braun, "Doing What Comes Naturally," *Films and Filming* (October 1970): 27-32; and "One for the Boys," *Films and Filming* (November 1970): 38-42. Although this publication was not openly gay in 1970, several factors marked it as such: its emphasis on Hollywood films and stars popular in the emerging gay community, such as James Dean; its extensive use of illustrations showing young male stars in pinup poses; and its encoded language—for example, "One for the *Boys*" (my emphasis), referring to *Myra Breckinridge*.

19. "Raquel Welch, Mae West," 45, 48.

20. "Raquel Welch, Mae West," 45; James Robert Parish, Michael R. Pitts, and Gregory W. Mank, "*Myra Breckinridge*," in *Hollywood on Hollywood* (Methuchen, N.J.: Scarecrow, 1978) 263-65.

21. On the MPAA film rating system, which in 1968 supplanted the 1930 Motion Picture Production Code as a guideline for film industry self-regulation, see David A. Cook, *A History of Narrative Film*, 2d ed. (New York: W. W. Norton, 1990), 536.

22. See, for example, Tyler, *Screening the Sexes*, 12-13. For a general overview of the force of gay subcultures in the move for sexual and other political liberation, see D'Emilio, *Sexual Politics*, 223-49.

23. Tyler hints at this as "underground gossip" in *Screening the Sexes*, 1. For explicit mention of this claim, see Christopher Stone, "Mae West," in *Advocate*, 8 October 1975, 34; Michael Bronski, "Judy Garland and Others: Notes on Idolization and Derision," in *Lavender Culture*, ed. Karla Jay and Allen Young, (New York: Harcourt Brace Jovanovich, 1978), 206; and George Eells and Stanley Musgrove, *Mae West: A Biography* (New York: William Morrow, 1982), 12.

24. Vito Russo, *The Celluloid Closet: Homosexuality in the Movies* (New York: Harper & Row, 1981), 54-55.

25. Edith Becker, Michelle Citron, Julia Lesage, and B. Ruby Rich make this argument for lesbian media consumers in their joint essay, "Lesbians and Film," in *Jump Cut: Hollywood, Politics and Counter Cinema*, ed. Peter Steven (New York: Praeger, 1985), 301-2.

26. See Russo, *The Celluloid Closet*, 47; and Gerald Mast, *Howard Hawks, Storyteller* (New York: Oxford University Press, 1982), 152; see also Gerald Mast, "Commentaries: *Bringing Up Baby*," in *Bringing Up Baby*, ed. Gerald Mast (New Brunswick, N.J.: Rutgers University Press, 1988), 306. For an argument about the currency of gay as a term referring to feminine homosexual men in the 1930s, see Chauncey, *Gay New York*, 14-21, 24-25, 358.

27. Charles Higham and Roy Moseley's book *Cary Grant: The Lonely Heart*

(New York: Avon, 1989) and reviews of it (including one in the *New York Times*) introduced bisexuality as an element of Grant's star image to a broad public. See the mention on the book's opening page (as the uppermost blurb about the book's contents) of Grant's apparent love affairs with Randolph Scott and Howard Hughes, as well as 58-68, 74-77, 94-95, 98, 202.

28. I am indebted to Craig Kois for this observation.

29. Some of West's other films encode characters as gay through character stereotyping, glances, and phrases. Russo notes the appearance of two male cellmates who have their arms around each other in the jail scene in *She Done Him Wrong*: "[West] refers to them nonchalantly as 'the Cherry sisters'" (*Celluloid Closet*, 55). A more recent work, Paul Roen's *High Camp: A Gay Guide to Camp and Cult Films*, vol. 1 (San Francisco: Leyland, 1994), describes that moment as "a fugitive scene of explicit gayness" (185).

The character Winslow (Gilbert Emery) in *Goin' to Town*, like Pinkowitz in *I'm No Angel*, plays a sympathetic and evidently asexual male sidekick to West. Like West's maids, these characters function as "straight men" to the star's comedic routines and help further the plot. Probably many heterosexual audiences did not discern these as gay characters on the films' first release, nor might they do so on watching the films now. But for viewers alert to alternative representations, these characters' visual stereotyping and dialogue encourage such interpretations.

The most evident homosexual scene in all of West's 1932-43 films comes in the one not even nominally a West vehicle: in *Night after Night* (1932), a montage sequence depicting an evening at a New York speakeasy culminates in a shot of two attractive women sharing a cigarette as they gaze into each other's eyes. The scene dissolves to a shot of the unexpectedly tipsy "old-maid teacher" (Alison Skipworth), who has been a manners coach for George Raft's gangster character, at a table in the club, as she is drinking champagne and laughing and talking with West/Maudie Triplett. The women sharing the cigarette are clearly coded as lesbian; the perception of any parallel homoeroticism in the Skipworth and West exchange is more an effect of retroactive queer readings. On this issue, see Alexander Doty, *Making Things Perfectly Queer: Interpreting Mass Culture* (Minneapolis: University of Minnesota Press, 1993).

30. Breen to Cohen, 1 September 1937, *Every Day's a Holiday* PCA case file.

31. For a contemporaneous account of West's act, see "Odds Are Sex-to-1 Mae West Makes Her Point in Las Vegas," *Variety*, 28 July 1954, 3; and "$25,000 per Week Worth of Sex-Appeal," in *Night O'Day*, December 1954. For additional pictures of West with her act's muscled members, see Bernard Sobel, *A Pictorial History of Vaudeville* (New York: Bonanza, 1961), 146; and Richard Meryman, "Mae West: Going Strong at 75," *Life*, 28 April 1969, 52. Among the men were Mr. America and Mr. Universe titleholders such as Mickey Hargitay, who married actress Jayne Mansfield. In 1956, general publicity about West's act flourished through reports of a "scandal" involving Hargitay, as he supposedly transferred his affections from West to Mansfield, and Chuck Krauser, who assaulted Hargitay publicly in apparent defense of West. (Krauser, who changed his name to Paul Novak after the scan-

dal, became West's long-term companion until her death.) On this point, see Carol Ward, *Mae West: A Bio-bibliography* (Westport, Conn.: Greenwood, 1989), 41-42, 49.

32. Mae West, *Goodness Had Nothing to Do with It* (New York: MacFadden-Bartell, 1970 [1959]), 230.

33. See Ira Berkow, "Mae West, Wilt and the King," *New York Times*, 2 December 1989, Y31. A male acquaintance who was stationed at an air force base near Las Vegas in the 1950s recalls that servicemen were sent postcards "signed by Mae West herself," inviting them to come to her show. Although he did not see her perform, he tells the story with evident appreciation for the "invitation" and suggests that she was regarded, if not as a woman the men themselves would have wished to pursue, still as a figure who was thought sexually "hot"—and not necessarily parodically.

34. Newton, *Mother Camp*, xiii.

35. *Time*, 2 July 1977; *Variety*, 8 March 1978; *People*, 4 December 1978; *Village Voice*, 1 October 1979. For an image of West surrounded by the skimpily clad athletes working out in *Sextette*, see R. L. Pela, "Way Out West," *Advocate*, 22 September 1992, 57.

36. Dean Billanti, "Sextette," *Films in Review*, August-September 1979, 434.

37. Sontag, "Notes on 'Camp,' " 277; Newton, *Mother Camp*, 111 n. 21, 109 n. 18. Newton makes this argument in a chapter entitled "Role Models," which is reprinted in *Camp Grounds: Style and Homosexuality*, ed. David Bergman (Amherst: University of Massachusetts Press, 1993), 39-53, retaining the 1979 note. But in her book *Cherry Grove, Fire Island: Sixty Years in America's First Gay and Lesbian Town* (Boston: Beacon, 1993) Newton seems to affirm the potential of "camping" to have political impact (see, e.g., 281-84).

38. Richard Dyer, "It's Being So Camp as Keeps Us Going," in *Only Entertainment* (London: Routledge, 1992), 135-47. The essay was first published in 1976 in the British gay journal *Playguy*, and was reprinted in the Toronto publication *The Body Politic* 36 (September 1977).

39. Ibid., 135.

40. Ibid., 146. GLF, which stands for Gay Liberation Front, signified the gay rights movement.

41. Jack Babuscio, "Camp and the Gay Sensibility," in *Gays and Film*, ed. Richard Dyer (British Film Institute, 1977), 46.

42. Richard Dyer briefly addresses this phenomenon from a feminist-sympathetic gay male perspective in his essay "It's Being So Camp as Keeps Us Going." Certainly, some women, especially lesbians, have been participants in camp culture, especially that of gay male drag queens. Homosocial (and possibly lesbian) groups of women have also long held their own drag balls. See Lillian Faderman, *Odd Girls and Twilight Lovers: A History of Lesbian Life in Twentieth Century America* (New York: Columbia University Press, 1991). Male female impersonators—gay or presumably straight—who have performed in gender-mixed clubs or large halls have often had appreciative female audiences, as some books on drag aimed at a

broad audience are quick to point out. See, for example, Peter Underwood, *Life's a Drag! Danny La Rue and the Drag Scene* (London: Leslie Frewin, 1974), for a description of the reception of female impersonators in Great Britain in the 1960s and 1970s. The descriptions generally imply that these female audiences were made up of straight women, probably out with their male partners for a risqué evening.

Still, not all female drag is camp, as I discuss in chapter 6. But whether entrenched in heterosexual relationships or as participants in a homosexual subculture, women traditionally have not themselves created what is regarded as a "camp aesthetic." An exploration of possible reasons for that lies beyond the scope of this book; for some insightful brief discussion of the issue, see Christine Riddiough, "Culture and Politics," in *Pink Triangles: Radical Perspectives on Gay Liberation*, ed. Pam Mitchell (New York: Alyson, 1980), 14-33, esp. 20-24. See also Sharon McDonald's "Lesbian Feminist Comedy: Dyke Humor Out of the Closet" (295-98) and Julia Penelope Stanley and Susan W. Robbins's "Mother Wit: Tongue in Cheek" (299-307), both in *Lavender Culture*, ed. Karla Jay and Allen Young (New York: Harcourt Brace Jovanovich, 1978).

43. Mellen, *Women and Their Sexuality*, 243.

44. See Newton, *Mother Camp*, 98-105, or "Role Models," 40-45; Bronski, "Judy Garland," 201-12; Andrew Hodges and David Hutter, *With Downcast Gays: Aspects of Homosexual Self-Oppression*, 2d ed. (Toronto: Pink Triangle Press, 1979 [1974]) 3-8.

45. Two anthologies provide a sampling of recent arguments about camp's value as a subcultural identity and survival strategy: Diana Fuss, ed., *Inside/Out: Lesbian Theories, Gay Theories* (New York: Routledge, 1991); and David Bergman, ed., *Camp Grounds: Style and Homosexuality* (Amherst: University of Massachusetts Press, 1993). In the volume edited by Fuss, see especially Judith Butler's "Imitation and Gender Insubordination" (13-31) and Carole-Anne Tyler's "Boys Will Be Girls: The Politics of Gay Drag" (32-70). In the anthology edited by Bergman, besides Esther Newton's essay "Role Models," see Andrew Ross's "Uses of Camp" (54-77) and David Román's " 'It's My Party and I'll Die If I Want To!': Gay Men, AIDS and the Circulation of Camp in U.S. Theater" (206-33). I further consider this issue in relation to West's image in chapter 6.

46. Mellen, *Women and Their Sexuality*, 241.

47. See, for example, Rosen's discussion of West "boned and corseted and looking like a turn-of-the-century sausage" in *Popcorn Venus*, 152. Rosen does not herself use the word *phallic*, however.

48. Ibid., 154.

49. Ibid.

50. Alice Echols, "The New Feminism of Yin and Yang," in *Powers of Desire: The Politics of Sexuality*, ed. Ann Snitow, Christine Stansell, and Sharon Thompson (New York: Monthly Review Press, 1983), 444.

51. Molly Haskell, *From Reverence to Rape: The Treatment of Women in the Movies* (New York: Holt, Rinehart & Winston, 1974), 115-16.

52. Johnston, "Women's Cinema," 211-12.

53. Linda Williams, "What Does Mae West Have That All the Men Want?" *Frontiers* 1, no. 1 (1975): 118-21. Three years later, British author Angela Carter also wrote admiringly of West in her *The Sadeian Woman and the Ideology of Pornography* (New York: Pantheon, 1978), 60-62.

54. See, for example, Arthur Knight, "Knight at the Movies," *Hollywood Reporter* 19 February 1982.

55. Charlotte Chandler, "The Outrageous Mae West," *Ms.*, February 1984, 51-56, 92.

56. Ward, *Mae West*, 153.

57. *Mae West* was produced by Hill-Mandelker Productions (Leonard Hill and Philip Mandelker), written by E. Arthur Kean, and directed by Lee Philips. It was first broadcast on The ABC television network on 2 May 1982, and has subsequently run on the Showtime channel on U.S. cable television.

58. Richard Dyer demonstrates in his book *Stars* (London: British Film Institute, 1979), 38-53, that movie stardom has historically been an amalgam of the following key concepts: conspicuous consumption, the American success myth, human "ordinariness," and the trials of heterosexual romance. He argues that some stars represent variants of those ideologies and may work to resolve contradictions in and among those values. He notes particularly that biopics about movie stars work to resolve contradictory elements, particularly in the success myth, by suggesting that an ordinary person can become a star (i.e., rich, famous, remarkably successful), but only when his or her special talent is supplemented by a combination of luck and hard work.

59. See "Mae West Scouts Talk of Rift," *Los Angeles Times*, 3 May 1934; and Mae West, *Goodness*, 112, 126, 214, 225. The *Los Angeles Times* article cites West as denying a rift between herself and Timony and insisting that he was not her sweetheart but rather her business manager. In her autobiography, West suggests that she had a romance with Timony, but "[by 1929] we had settled like many a domestic couple for a friendly business partnership" (126). See also Eells and Musgrove, *Mae West*, 55-57, 142-46. George Baxt's recent mystery novel *The Mae West Murder Case* (New York: St. Martin's, 1993), in which West impersonators are murdered, depicts Timony at the time the book is set, 1937, as a rather pathetic figure who yearns after a former intimate relationship with West, who tolerates his presence only as a dependable old friend and errand runner. See Chandler, "The Outrageous Mae West," for a record of the disdain West expressed about "falling in love," even in the last year of her life.

60. As Dyer argues in *Stars*, "Consumption and success, with their intimations of attendant values such as democracy, the open society, the value of the common/ ordinary person, are the key notes of the image of stardom, but it would be wrong I think to ignore elements that run counter to this. . . . Consumption can be characterized as wastefulness and decadence, while success may be short-lived or a psychological burden" (50).

61. The 1994 documentary *Mae West and the Men Who Knew Her*, which aired on the Arts & Entertainment (A&E) cable channel's *Biography* series, contributes to this ongoing recuperative effort. Introduced on A&E by actor Peter Graves, the

documentary intercuts movie clips and stills of Mae West with "talking head" interviews of more than a dozen men, including critic and actor Rex Reed and impersonator Charles Pierce. The male voices, along with occasional voice-over by Dom DeLuise, constitute the film's entire narration; presumably, no women West knew are still alive, or willing to be interviewed? But as the documentary's title suggests, it does not at all address West's reception among women. Surprisingly, it also makes no mention whatsoever of West's substantial reception among gay men. Yet well over half of the men interviewed come across, in contemporary American gender coding, as gay. In a private communication, Charles Pierce confirmed and underscored my impression, noting that indeed most of the interviewees in the A&E version of the film are gay. (The director, Gene Feldman, reportedly has a longer cut of the film, which may address other facets of West's following or career; however, that version has not been shown on television or received wide distribution). I thank my colleague James Hurt for drawing my attention to this documentary.

6. Merging Interests

1. For a succinct discussion characterizing and distinguishing between these two directions in feminist media scholarship, see Linda Williams, "Feminist Film Theory: Mildred Pierce and the Second World War," in Female Spectators: Looking at Film and Television, ed. E. Deidre Pribham (London: Verso, 1988), 12-30. See also Christine Gledhill, "Developments in Feminist Film Criticism," in Re-vision, ed. Mary Ann Doane, Patricia Mellencamp, and Linda Williams (Frederick, Md.: University Publications/American Film Institute, 1984), 18-45.

2. I delivered conference papers on research presented in this book at meetings of the Midwest Popular Culture Association and the Society of Cinema Studies in 1987 and 1989, respectively. My dissertation, "Power and Allure: The Mediation of Sexual Difference in the Star Image of Mae West" (Northwestern University, 1990) became available from UMI Press on microfilm in 1991, and my first published essay based on the material, "Mae West as Censored Commodity: The Case of Klondike Annie," appeared in Cinema Journal 31, no. 1 (1991): 57-84. Other feminist reevaluations of West in the 1980s, in addition to the 1984 article in Ms. mentioned in chapter 5, that have appeared in the past decade include Linda Martin and Kerry Segrave, Women in Comedy (Secaucus, N.J.: Citadel, 1986), 173-91; Carol Bergman, Mae West, Entertainer (New York: Chelsea House, 1988); Rosetta Reitz, "Mae West, Queen of Sex," Hot Wire 4 (March 1988): 40-41; and two books by June Sochen, Enduring Values: Women in Popular Culture (New York: Praeger, 1987), 66-73, and Mae West: She Who Laughs, Lasts (Arlington Heights, Ill.: Harlan Davidson, 1992). Of these, the essay by Reitz, a jazz historian who researches and issues recordings of little-known and rarely distributed women's music, most clearly becomes associated with specifically lesbian address through its appearance in the Chicago-based lesbian-feminist journal of women's music and culture.

3. Molly Haskell, "Mae West's Bawdy Spirit Spans the Gay 90s," New York Times, 15 August 1993, 14.

4. Curry, "Power and Allure." I also suggest this argument in my article "Ma-

donna from Marilyn to Marlene: Pastiche and/or Parody?" *Journal of Film and Video* 42, no. 2 (1990): 15-30.

5. Pamela Robertson, " 'The Kinda Comedy That Imitates Me': Mae West's Identification with the Feminist Camp," *Cinema Journal* 32, no. 2 (1993): 58.

6. This is, of course, the argument that Mellen and Rosen, particularly, made in the 1970s; Johnston's analysis of West as a phallic substitute makes a similar claim, from a more abstract point of departure. For a recent discussion of how women may respond not to West or to spectacular female impersonation on stage, but rather to male-to-female transvestism—by heterosexual as well as homosexual men—as an alienating displacement of their own gender identities, see Annie Woodhouse, *Fantastic Women: Sex, Gender and Transvestism* (New Brunswick, N.J.: Rutgers University Press, 1989), xv, 97-133, 145.

7. On Mickey Rooney, see the photo feature "Go West, Young Man," *Premiere*, November 1990, 47, showing Rooney (then known as Mickey McGuire, although born as Joe Yule Jr.) costumed as West. In an unpublished paper, "From the Implausible to the Unspeakable: The Censorship of Sexuality from Mae West to Shirley Temple" (1986), 4, Richard Maltby analyzes Shirley Temple's West impersonation in a 1932 short film, *Glad Rags to Riches*. Temple appears as "La Belle Diaperina," a Gay Nineties chanteuse who sings "She's Only a Bird in a Gilded Cage." The film was part of a series called *Baby Burlesks* that the four-year-old Temple made with a company called Educational Pictures. In other shorts in the series, she spoofed Dolores Del Rio and Marlene Dietrich (in the persona of a character called Morelegs Sweettrick). I am grateful to the author for making his manuscript available to me.

8. West herself claimed to inspire women casually to imitate her. In an interview with Richard Meryman ("Mae West: Going Strong at 75," *Life*, 28 April 1969), she asserted: "I'm the woman's ego, see. When women'd be leaving the theater at intermission, you'd see them sort of walking like the Mae West character, you know, giving an attitude—and the talk, too" (51).

A friend of mine provided anecdotal evidence that even the recollection of West can have this brief impact. The friend asked her wheelchair-bound seventy-year-old mother what she remembered or thought of Mae West. She reported that her mother, crippled with polio, immediately sat up straight and lifted her chin with a little toss before answering that she didn't recall much about her except that she was naughty. My friend considered her mother's gesture an unconscious (and approving!) impersonation of West.

9. Claire Johnston, "Women's Cinema as Counter-Cinema," in *Movies and Methods*, vol. 1, ed. Bill Nichols (Berkeley: University of California Press, 1976), 211-12. See also Sigmund Freud, "Fetishism" (1927), in *Standard Edition of the Complete Psychological Works of Sigmund Freud*, vol. 21, trans. James Strachey (London: Hogarth Press and Institute of Psycho-analysis, 1961), 152-57. Freud asserts specifically that fur and velvet appear in fetish objects because of these textures' resemblance to the hair on female genitals, which he says become associated with the phallus at the moment of the child's discovery of its absence. For development

of this concept, via Jacques Lacan, in media theory, in addition to Johnston, see, for example, Laura Mulvey, "Visual Pleasure and Narrative Cinema," *Screen* 16, no. 3 (1975): 6-18; and also her 1973 essay "Fears, Fantasies and the Male Unconscious *or* 'You Don't Know What Is Happening, Do You, Mr. Jones?' " reprinted in her collection *Visual and Other Pleasures* (Bloomington: Indiana University Press, 1989). See also "Morocco," a collective textual analysis of that 1932 von Sternberg/Dietrich production by the editors of *Cahiers du Cinéma* (November-December 1970): 5-13 (reprinted in *Sternberg*, ed. Peter Baxter, trans. Diana Matias [London: British Film Institute, 1980], 81-94).

10. In societies where men have historically dominated economic, political, religious, and cultural institutions, as well as individual women, it is clear that a signifier of the male body should serve to represent power. But as psychoanalysts such as Chasseguet-Smirgel have argued (Janine Chasseguet-Smirgel et al., *Recherches Psychonanalytiques Nouvelles sur la Sexualité Feminine*, 1964), the phallus cannot be identified with the penis, but rather signifies "the ideas and values that the penile organ represents"; quoted in Michele Montrelay, "Inquiry into Femininity," *m/f* 1 (1978). There has been much debate on this issue, with much slippage and contradictory usage of the terms. For a recent overview of some of the complex issues in the debate, see "The Phallus Issue" of *Differences* 4, no. 1 (1992), especially essays by Parveen Adams, Kaja Silverman, Charles Bernheimer, and Judith Butler. My point, made briefly here, is that although West's image may be phallic, it is not necessarily fetishistic in Freud's or Lacan's male-centered terms.

11. On this point, see Hélène Cixous, "The Laugh of the Medusa," trans. Keith Cohen and Paula Cohen, in *New French Feminisms*, ed. Elaine Marks and Isabelle de Courtivron (Amherst: University of Massachusetts Press, 1980), 251-58, 261-64; and also Martin Grotjahn, *Beyond Laughter* (New York: McGraw-Hill, 1957), 113, 244-45.

12. Angela Carter writes of West in *The Sadeian Woman and the Ideology of Pornography* (New York: Pantheon, 1978) as embodying "the sterile phallic mother," having a wit that is "castratory, if tender," and inverting "the myth of female masochism" (61).

13. George Kent, "The Mammy and Daddy of Us All," *Photoplay*, May 1934, 32-33, 100-103. The "Daddy" to whom the *Photoplay* article refers is Will Rogers, whose appeal is noted to be asexual and comfortable. For many, West's appeal is still both vaguely sexual *and* comfortable. As Mark Booth remarks, West "divests sex of everything that is dark, dangerous and primeval: under her aegis, it becomes nothing more than a children's romp." *Camp* (London: Quartet, 1983), 134.

14. Gilbert Seldes's "Sugar and Spice and Not So Nice," *Esquire*, March 1934, 60, is accompanied by a humorous poem by Meyer Levin, "Esquire in Quest of His Youth: A Poem with Puppets," 61-62. Six color photographs of two puppets—one of West, one of "Esquire" (a.k.a. Esky), the magazine's caricatured, bug-eyed old gentleman who appeared on *Esquire* covers of the period—illustrate the poem, which ends:

His head sank in her lap
He heard her murmur, "You poor sap."
Then dreamily there came to him the moral of this fable:
If under the table one must be,
He is blest
Who's under the table with Mae West.

15. Esther Newton, *Mother Camp: Female Impersonators in America* (Chicago: University of Chicago Press, 1968), xx.

16. Ibid., 104-5.

17. Parker Tyler, *Screening the Sexes: Homosexuality in the Movies* (Garden City, N.Y.: Doubleday, 1972), 5.

18. As noted in chapter 5, both Newton (*Mother Camp*, 46-49, 91-94) and Tyler (*Screening the Sexes*, 1-15) discuss West's status as camp in the 1960s-early 1970s. For documentation and discussion of West's more recent camp reception, see Booth, *Camp*; Michael Bronski, *Culture Clash: The Making of Gay Sensibility* (Boston: South End, 1984); Philip Core, *Camp: The Lie That Tells the Truth* (New York: Delilah Communications, 1984); Wayne Koestenbaum, *The Queen's Throat: Opera, Homosexuality, and the Mystery of Desire* (New York: Poseidon, 1993); and Paul Roen, *High Camp: A Gay Guide to Camp and Cult Films*, vol. 1 (San Francisco: Leyland, 1994).

19. Among the recent articles from feminist (and often lesbian feminist perspectives) that analyze the ontological status, impact, or strategic use for women of the concept of "gay drag," see Judith Butler, "Imitation and Gender Insubordination" (13-31) and Carole-Anne Tyler, "Boys Will Be Girls: The Politics of Gay Drag" (32-70), both in *Inside/Out: Lesbian Theories, Gay Theories*, ed. Diana Fuss (New York: Routledge, 1991). See also Judith Butler, *Gender Trouble: Feminism and the Subversion of Identity* (New York: Routledge, 1990), esp. 134-49; and Carole-Anne Tyler, "The Supreme Sacrifice? Tv, 'TV,' and the Renee Richards Story," *Differences* 1, no. 3 (1989): 160-86. Further, see Mary Russo, "Female Grotesques: Carnival and Theory," in *Feminist Studies/Critical Studies*, ed. Teresa de Lauretis (Bloomington: Indiana University Press, 1986), 213-29; Marjorie Garber, *Vested Interests: Cross-Dressing and Cultural Anxiety* (New York: Routledge, 1992); and Robertson, " 'The Kinda Comedy That Imitates Me.' " For a sympathetic analysis of gay camp from a lesbian socialist perspective in 1980, see Christine Riddiough, "Culture and Politics," in *Pink Triangles: Radical Perspectives on Gay Liberation*, ed. Pam Mitchell (New York: Alyson, 1980), 14-33, esp. 22-24, 31-32.

20. A variant of the joke appears in George Eells and Stanley Musgrove, *Mae West: A Biography* (New York: William Morrow, 1982): "[West] and Marlene Dietrich did become friends after they were assigned side-by-side dressing rooms at Paramount in the 1930s. Mae was pleased to have Dietrich prepare good German food for her. 'But I had to pull back when she started wantin' to wash my hair,' Mae said. 'I was afraid it wasn't all on my head' "(14). In this version of the joke, which seems anti-lesbian, West explicitly rejects the prospect of sexual intimacy with Dietrich. The version that I have heard circulated and that I discuss is more ambiguous and, in my experience, much more pleasurable to lesbians. But both ver-

sions introduce the possibility of Dietrich's possibly desiring West, and West's consciously responding to that desire.

21. My thanks to Joyce Bolinger and Robert Dale Parker for these observations.

22. Mary Ann Doane, "Film and the Masquerade: Theorizing the Female Spectator," *Screen* 23, nos. 3-4 (1982): 82. Doane's essay draws on Riviere's essay,
"Womanliness as Masquerade," first published in the *International Journal of Psychoanalysis* 10 (1929). For a critique of Doane's positing female spectatorship as a
masquerade, considered in relation to lesbian femme masquerade and to camp, see
Sue-Ellen Case, "Toward a Butch-Femme Aesthetic," in *Making a Spectacle: Feminist Essays on Contemporary Women's Theater*, ed. Lynda Hart (Ann Arbor: University of Michigan Press, 1989), 282-99, esp. 290-93.

23. Doane, "Film and the Masquerade," 87.

24. A 1953 animated TV spot put a Westian head atop a Muriel cigar (the
smoke forming her halo of hair) and had "Muriel" murmur, "Come up and smoke
me some time." The image appears on the back cover and as a title-page logo in the
autobiography of the ad's creator, Shamus Culhane. See his *Talking Animals and
Other People* (New York: St. Martin's, 1986), esp. 309-10, 319. West (who always
said she hated cigars) reportedly threatened to sue. Says Culhane, "The publicity
would have been priceless. When Winston Churchill came to the United States he
was asked what he thought of American television. He replied that he didn't think
much of it except for the dancing cigar" (310).

Selected Bibliography

Aaronson. "She Done Him Wrong." *Motion Picture Herald*, 18 February 1933, 31.

Adams, Cecil [pseudonym]. "The Straight Dope." *Chicago Reader*, 25 September 1987, 2.

Ades, Dawn. *Dalí*. London: Thames & Hudson, 1982.

Ager, Cecelia. "Going Places." *Variety*, 17 October 1933, 57.

_____. "No Good Women in History, Mae West Says, During Hot Sex Selling Talk." *Variety*, 31 January 1933, 1, 42.

Alicoate, Jack, ed. *The 1934 Daily Film Year Book of Motion Pictures*. New York: Film Daily, 1934.

_____, ed. *The 1935 Daily Film Year Book of Motion Pictures*. New York: Film Daily, 1935.

_____, ed. *The 1936 Daily Film Year Book of Motion Pictures*. New York: Film Daily, 1936.

Allen, Robert C. *Horrible Prettiness: Burlesque and American Culture*. Chapel Hill: University of North Carolina Press, 1991.

Allen, Robert C., and Douglas Gomery. *Film History: Theory and Practice*. New York: Alfred A. Knopf, 1985.

Ames, Walter. "Who's Marilyn Monroe, Queen Mae Asks." *Los Angeles Times*, 13 September 1953, 1, 4.

Anger, Kenneth. *Hollywood Babylon*. New York: Dell, 1975.

" 'Annie' Grosses Doubled by Hearst?" *Variety*, 18 March 1936, 1, 66.

" 'Annie' N.Y. Opening Advanced by Paramount." *Film Daily*, 2 March 1936, 1.

" 'Annie' Overcomes Hearst Taboo to Top Mild L.A. Biz." *Variety*, 4 March 1936, 8.

Arbus, Diane. "Emotion in Motion." *Show* (January 1965): 42-45. (Reprinted as "Mae West: Once upon Our Time," in *Diane Arbus, Magazine Work*, ed. Doon Arbus and Marvin Israel, 58-61. Millerton, N.Y.: Aperture, 1984.)

"At Last 'Mr. Mae' Gets Recognition!" *Los Angeles Examiner*, 8 July 1937, A1.

"Author-Star of 'Sex' Taken to Workhouse." *Chicago Daily News*, 20 April 1927, 3.

Babuscio, Jack. "Camp and the Gay Sensibility." In *Gays and Film*, ed. Richard Dyer, 40-57. London: British Film Institute, 1977. (Reprinted in *Camp Grounds: Style and Homosexuality*, ed. David Bergman, 19-38. Amherst: University of Massachusetts Press, 1993.)

Baker, Roger. *Drag: A History of Female Impersonation on the Stage*. London: Triton, 1968.

Balio, Tino, ed. *The American Film Industry*. Madison: University of Wisconsin Press, 1976.

Barnes, Eleanor. "Mae and 'Quints.' " *Los Angeles Daily News*, 28 February 1936.
Barthes, Roland. *Image-Music-Text*. Trans. Stephen Heath. New York: Hill & Wang, 1977.
_____. *The Pleasure of the Text*. Trans. Richard Miller. New York: Hill & Wang, 1975.
Bavar, Michael. *Mae West*. New York: Pyramid, 1975.
Baxt, George. *The Mae West Murder Case*. New York: St. Martin's, 1993.
Baxter, Peter. "The Birth of Venus." *Wide Angle* 10, no. 1 (1988): 4-15.
Becker, Edith, Michelle Citron, Julia Lesage, and B. Ruby Rich. "Lesbians and Film." In *Jump Cut: Hollywood, Politics and Counter Cinema*, ed. Peter Steven, 296-314. New York: Praeger, 1985.
Berger, John. *Ways of Seeing*. New York: Penguin, 1977.
Bergman, Andrew. *We're in the Money: Depression America and Its Films*. New York: Harper & Row, 1971.
Bergman, Carol. *Mae West, Entertainer*. New York: Chelsea House, 1988.
Bergman, David, ed. *Camp Grounds: Style and Homosexuality*. Amherst: University of Massachusetts Press, 1993.
Berkow, Ira. "Mae West, Wilt and the King." *New York Times*, 2 December 1989, Y31.
Biery, Ruth. "The Private Life of Mae West." *Movie Classic*, January 1934, 20-21, 56-58. (Reprinted in Carol Ward, *Mae West: A Bio-Bibliography*, 103-9. Westport, Conn.: Greenwood, 1989.)
Bige. "Night after Night." *Variety*, 1 November 1932, 12.
_____. "She Done Him Wrong." *Variety*, 14 February 1933, 12, 21.
Billanti, Dean. "Sextette." *Films in Review*, August-September 1979, 434-35.
Black, Gregory D. *Hollywood Censored: Morality Codes, Catholics, and the Movies*. Cambridge: Cambridge University Press, 1994.
Blumer, Henry. *Movies and Conduct*. Chicago: University of Chicago Press, 1933.
Bogle, Donald. *Toms, Coons, Mulattoes, Mammies, and Bucks: An Interpretive History of Blacks in American Films*. New York: Viking, 1989 [1973].
Booth, Mark. *Camp*. London: Quartet, 1983.
Borneman, Ernest. "United States versus Hollywood: The Case Study of an Antitrust Suit." In *The American Film Industry*, ed. Tino Balio, 332-70. Madison: University of Wisconsin Press, 1976.
Bourdieu, Pierre. *Distinction: A Social Critique of the Judgement of Taste*. Trans. Richard Nice. Cambridge: Harvard University Press, 1984.
Braun, Eric. "Doing What Comes Naturally." *Films and Filming* (October 1970): 27-32.
_____. "One for the Boys." *Films and Filming* (November 1970): 38-42.
Bronski, Michael. *Culture Clash: The Making of Gay Sensibility*. Boston: South End, 1984.
_____. "Judy Garland and Others: Notes on Idolization and Derision." in *Lavender Culture*, ed. Karla Jay and Allen Young, 201-12. New York: Harcourt Brace Jovanovich, 1978.
Butler, Judith. *Gender Trouble: Feminism and the Subversion of Identity*. New York: Routledge, 1990.

_____. "Imitation and Gender Insubordination," in *Inside/Out: Lesbian Theories, Gay Theories*, ed. Diana Fuss, 13-31. New York: Routledge, 1991.

"Capital Takes Up New Film Loans, Taxes, Theatre 'Divorce,' Mae West." *Motion Picture Herald*, 25 December 1937, 17.

Carmen, Ira H. *Movies, Censorship, and the Law*. Ann Arbor: University of Michigan Press, 1966.

Carter, Angela. *The Sadeian Woman and the Ideology of Pornography*. New York: Pantheon, 1978.

Case, Sue-Ellen. "Toward a Butch-Femme Aesthetic." In *Making a Spectacle: Feminist Essays on Contemporary Women's Theater*, ed. Lynda Hart, 282-99. Ann Arbor: University of Michigan Press, 1989.

Castleman, Harry, and Walter J. Podrazik. *The TV Schedule Book: Four Decades of Network Programming from Sign-On to Sign-Off*. New York: McGraw-Hill, 1984.

" 'Catherine Was Great' but Mae West Makes Her Dull." *Life*, 21 August 1944, 71-72.

"Catholics Defend Pix, Legion of Decency Stands Up beside Hays in Support of Present Industry Practices." *Hollywood Reporter*, 2 March 1936, 1, 9.

Chandler, Charlotte. "The Outrageous Mae West." *Ms.*, February 1984, 51-56, 92.

Chauncey, George. *Gay New York: Gender, Urban Culture, and the Making of the Gay Male World 1890-1940*. New York: Basic Books, 1994.

Chic. "*Klondike Annie*." *Variety*, 18 March 1936, 17.

Cixous, Hélène. "The Laugh of the Medusa." Trans. Keith Cohen and Paula Cohen. In *New French Feminisms*, ed. Elaine Marks and Isabelle de Courtivron, 245-64. Amherst: University of Massachusetts Press, 1980.

Colette. *Colette at the Movies: Criticism and Screenplays*. Ed. Alain Virmaux and Odette Virmaux. New York: Frederick Ungar, 1980.

Cook, David A. *A History of Narrative Film*, 2d ed. New York: W. W. Norton, 1990.

Core, Philip. *Camp: The Lie That Tells the Truth*. New York: Delilah Communications, 1984.

"Court Tilt Won by Mae West." *Los Angeles Times*, 16 April 1947.

Culhane, Shamus. *Talking Animals and Other People*. New York: St. Martin's, 1986.

Curry, Ramona. "*Goin' to Town* and Beyond: Mae West, Film Censorship, and the Comedy of Unmarriage." In *Classical Film Comedy*, ed. Kristine Brunovska Karnick and Henry Jenkins, 211-37. New York: Routledge, 1995.

_____. "Madonna from Marilyn to Marlene: Pastiche and/or Parody?" *Journal of Film and Video* 42, no. 2 (1990): 15-30.

_____. "Mae West as Censored Commodity: The Case of *Klondike Annie*." *Cinema Journal* 31, no. 1 (1991): 57-84.

Curtin, Kaier. "*We Can Always Call Them Bulgarians*": *The Emergence of Lesbians and Gay Men on the American Stage*. Boston: Alyson, 1987.

Davis, George. "The Decline of the West." *Vanity Fair*, May 1934, 46, 82.

D'Emilio, John. *Sexual Politics, Sexual Communities: The Making of a Homosexual Minority in the United States, 1940-1970*. Chicago: University of Chicago Press, 1983.

D'Emilio, John, and Estelle B. Freedman. *Intimate Matters*. New York: Harper & Row, 1988.

de La Serna, Ramon Gomez. *Dalí*. New York: Park Lane, 1978.

de Lauretis, Teresa. "Oedipus Interruptus." *Wide Angle* 7, nos. 1-2 (1985): 34-40.

Doane, Mary Ann. "Film and the Masquerade: Theorizing the Female Spectator." *Screen* 23, nos. 3-4 (1982): 74-87. (Reprinted in Mary Ann Doane, *Femmes Fatales*, 17-32. New York: Routledge, 1991.)

Doane, Mary Ann, Patricia Mellencamp, and Linda Williams, eds. *Re-vision*. Frederick, Md.: University Publications/American Film Institute, 1984.

Doty, Alexander. *Making Things Perfectly Queer: Interpreting Mass Culture*. Minneapolis: University of Minnesota Press, 1993.

Dyer, Richard, ed. *Gays and Film*, rev. ed. New York: New York Zoetrope, 1984.

_____. *Heavenly Bodies: Film Stars and Society*. New York: St. Martin's, 1986.

_____. "Homosexuality and Film Noir." *Jump Cut* 16 (1977): 18-21.

_____. "It's Being So Camp as Keeps Us Going." In *Only Entertainment*, 135-47. London: Routledge, 1992. (First published in *Playguy*, 1976, and reprinted in *The Body Politic* 36 [September 1977]: 11ff.)

_____. *Only Entertainment*. London: Routledge, 1992.

_____. *Stars*. London: British Film Institute, 1979.

Echols, Alice. "The New Feminism of Yin and Yang." In *Powers of Desire: The Politics of Sexuality*, ed. Ann Snitow, Christine Stansell, and Sharon Thompson, 439-59. New York: Monthly Review Press, 1983.

Eckert, Charles. "The Anatomy of a Proletarian Film: Warner's *Marked Woman*." *Film Quarterly* 27, no. 2 (1973-74): 10-24. (Reprinted in *Movies and Methods*, vol. 2, ed. Bill Nichols, 407-28. Berkeley: University of California Press, 1985.)

Eddy, Arthur W. "Anti-Block Booking Bill Vigorously Attacked by Film Heads." *Film Daily*, 29 February 1936, 1, 6.

_____. "A Summary of Events Leading Up to the Motion Picture Code." In *The 1934 Daily Year Book of Motion Pictures*, ed. Jack Alicoate, 596-97. New York: Film Daily, 1934.

Eells, George. Letter. *Los Angeles Times*, 25 April 1982, Sunday Calendar, 95.

Eells, George, and Stanley Musgrove. *Mae West: A Biography*. New York: William Morrow, 1982.

Eidelberg, Ludwig. "A Contribution to the Study of Wit." *Psychoanalytic Review* 32 (1945): 33-61.

Eisner, Joel, and David Krinsky. *Television Comedy Series: An Episode Guide to 153 TV Sitcoms in Syndication*. London: McFarland, 1984.

"Every Day's a Holiday." *Film Daily*, 27 December 1937, 8.

Faderman, Lillian. *Odd Girls and Twilight Lovers: A History of Lesbian Life in Twentieth Century America*. New York: Columbia University Press, 1991.

"Film Boycott: Churchmen's Crusade to 'Clean House' Brings Chill to Torrid Hollywood." *Newsweek*, 7 July 1934, 5.

Foucault, Michel. *The History of Sexuality*, vol. 1, *An Introduction*. Trans. Robert Hurley. New York: Random House, 1980.

Frank, Lisa, and Paul Smith, eds. *Madonnarama: Essays on Sex and Popular Culture*. Pittsburgh: Cleiss, 1993.

Freedman, Estelle B. " 'Uncontrolled Desires': The Response to the Sexual Psychopath, 1920-1960." In *Passion and Power: Sexuality in History*, ed. Kathy Peiss and Christina Simmons, 199-225. Philadelphia: Temple University Press, 1989.

Freud, Sigmund. "Fetishism." In *Standard Edition of the Complete Psychological Works of Sigmund Freud*, vol. 21. Trans. James Strachey, 152-57. London: Hogarth Press and Institute of Psycho-analysis, 1961.

_____. *Jokes and Their Relation to the Unconscious* (1905). In *Standard Edition of the Complete Psychological Works of Sigmund Freud*, vol. 8. Trans. James Strachey. London: Hogarth Press and Institute of Psycho-analysis, 1960.

_____. *Der Witz und seine Beziehung zum Unbewußten*. Leipzig: Franz Deuticke, 1905.

"Furor Starts over Mae West Program: Radio Skit Declared Offensive." *Los Angeles Evening News*, 17 December 1937.

Fuss, Diana. *Inside/Out: Lesbian Theories, Gay Theories*. New York: Routledge, 1991.

Gaines, Jane. "The Showgirl and the Wolf." In *Cinema Examined*, ed. Richard Dyer MacCann and Jack C. Ellis, 282-97. New York: E. P. Dutton, 1982.

Garber, Marjorie. *Vested Interests: Cross-Dressing and Cultural Anxiety*. New York: Routledge, 1992.

Gardner, Gerald. *The Censorship Papers: Movie Censorship Letters from the Hays Office, 1934-1968*. New York: Dodd, Mead, 1987.

Gilbert, Douglas. *American Vaudeville—Its Life and Times*. New York: McGraw-Hill, 1940.

Gledhill, Christine. "Developments in Feminist Film Criticism." In *Re-vision*, ed. Mary Ann Doane, Patricia Mellencamp, and Linda Williams, 18-45. Frederick, Md.: University Publications/American Film Institute, 1984.

"*Goin' to Town*." *Hollywood Reporter*, 23 April 1935.

Gomery, Douglas. "Hollywood, the National Recovery Administration and the Question of Monopoly Power." *Journal of the University Film Association* 31, no. 2 (1979): 47-52.

_____. *The Hollywood Studio System*. New York: St. Martin's, 1986.

Grotjahn, Martin. *Beyond Laughter*. New York: McGraw-Hill, 1957.

Hamilton, Marybeth. " 'I'm the Queen of the Bitches': Female Impersonation and Mae West's *Pleasure Man*." In *Crossing the Stage: Controversies on Cross-Dressing*, ed. Lesley Ferris, 107-19. London: Routledge, 1993.

Hansen, Miriam. *Babel and Babylon: Spectatorship in American Silent Film*. Cambridge: Harvard University Press, 1991.

_____. "Early Cinema: Whose Public Sphere?" In *Early Cinema: Space, Frame, Narrative*, ed. Thomas Elsaesser, 228-46. London: British Film Institute, 1990.

_____. "Pleasure, Ambivalence, Identification: Valentino and Female Spectatorship." *Cinema Journal* 25, no. 4 (1986): 6-32.

Haralovich, Mary Beth. "Mandates of Good Taste: The Self-Regulation of Film Advertising in the Thirties." *Wide Angle* 6, no. 2 (1984): 50-57.

Haskell, Molly. *From Reverence to Rape: The Treatment of Women in the Movies*. New York: Holt, Rinehart & Winston, 1974.

_____. "Mae West's Bawdy Spirit Spans the Gay 90s." *New York Times*, 15 August 1993, 14.

Hays, Will H. *The Memoirs of Will H. Hays.* Garden City, N.Y.: Doubleday, 1955.

"The Hays Office." *Fortune,* December 1938, 69-72ff. (Reprinted in *The American Film Industry,* ed. Tino Balio, 295-314. Madison: University of Wisconsin Press, 1976).

"Hearst-Block Papers Attack New Mae West Film; 'Klondike' Biz Good." *Variety,* 26 February 1936, 5, 66.

"Hearst Strike-Out." *Time,* 9 March 1936, 61.

Heath, Stephen. *Questions of Cinema.* Bloomington: Indiana University Press, 1981.

Higashi, Sumiko. "Ethnicity, Class, and Gender in Film: DeMille's *The Cheat.*" In *Unspeakable Images: Ethnicity and the American Cinema,* ed. Lester D. Friedman, 112-39. Urbana: University of Illinois Press, 1991.

Higham, Charles, and Roy Moseley. *Cary Grant: The Lonely Heart.* New York: Avon, 1989.

Hill, Gertrude. "Hollywood Leads the Fashion Parade." *Movie Classic,* May 1935, 40-41.

Hodges, Andrew, and David Hutter. *With Downcast Gays: Aspects of Homosexual Self-Oppression.* 2d ed. Toronto: Pink Triangle, 1979 [1974].

Huettig, Mae D. *Economic Control of the Motion Picture Industry.* Philadelphia: University of Pennsylvania Press, 1944.

Hutcheon, Linda. *A Theory of Parody: The Teachings of Twentieth-Century Art Forms.* New York: Methuen, 1985.

Inglis, Ruth A. *Freedom of the Movies: A Report on Self-Regulation from the Commission on Freedom of the Press.* Chicago: University of Chicago Press, 1947.

"Is Politics Influencing Censorship?" *Pittsburgh Post-Gazette,* 20 February 1936, 1.

Izod, John. *Hollywood and the Box Office: 1895-1986.* New York: Columbia University Press, 1988.

Jacobs, Lea. "The Censorship of *Blonde Venus*: Textual Analysis and Historical Method." *Cinema Journal* 27, no. 3 (1988): 21-26.

_____. *The Wages of Sin: Censorship and the Fallen Woman Film 1928-1942.* Madison: University of Wisconsin Press, 1991.

Jay, Karla, and Allen Young, eds. *Lavender Culture.* New York: Harcourt Brace Jovanovich, 1978.

Jenkins, Henry. " 'Shall We Make It for New York or for Distribution?': Eddie Cantor, *Whoopee,* and Regional Resistance to the Talkies." *Cinema Journal* 29, no. 3 (1990): 32-52.

_____. *What Made Pistachio Nuts? Early Sound Comedy and the Vaudeville Aesthetic.* New York: Columbia University Press, 1992.

Jennings, C. Robert. "Mae West: A Candid Conversation with the Indestructible Queen of Vamp and Camp." *Playboy,* January 1971, 73-82.

Johnston, Claire. "Femininity and the Masquerade: *Anne of the Indies.*" In *Jacques Tourneur,* ed. Claire Johnston and Paul Willemen, 36-44. Edinburgh: Edinburgh Film Festival, 1975.

_____. "Women's Cinema as Counter-Cinema." In *Movies and Methods,* vol. 1, ed. Bill Nichols, 208-17. Berkeley: University of California Press, 1976.

Jowett, Garth. *Film: The Democratic Art.* Boston: Little, Brown, 1976.

Kaminsky, Stuart. *He Done Her Wrong*. New York: St. Martin's, 1983.

Kelley, Andrew R. " 'Plenty Wrong with Pix.' " *Variety*, 25 September 1940, 3, 20.

Kent, George. "The Mammy and Daddy of Us All." *Photoplay*, May 1934, 32-33, 100-103.

"Klondike Annie." *Motion Picture Herald*, 7 March 1936, 19.

"Klondike Annie." *Time*, 9 March 1936, 44-46.

Koestenbaum, Wayne. *The Queen's Throat: Opera, Homosexuality, and the Mystery of Desire*. New York: Poseidon, 1993.

Krug, Karl. Editorial. *Pittsburgh Sun-Telegram*, 22 February 1936.

Kuhn, Annette. *Cinema, Censorship and Sexuality 1909-1925*. London: Routledge, 1988.

Land. "I'm No Angel." *Variety*, 17 October 1933, 19.

"Laurels for Hearst." *Hollywood Reporter*, 4 March 1936, 1.

Laurie, Joe, Jr. *Vaudeville: From the Honky-Tonks to the Palace*. New York: Henry Holt, 1953.

Leff, Leonard J., and Jerold L. Simmons. *The Dame in the Kimono: Hollywood, Censorship, and the Production Code from the 1920s to the 1960s*. New York: Grove Weidenfeld, 1990.

"Legion of Decency Drive Impends on Radio 'Sacrilege.' " *Hollywood Reporter*, 17 December 1937, 1, 4.

Leonard, Maurice. *Mae West: Empress of Sex*. New York: Carol, 1992.

Lesage, Julia. "Artful Racism, Artful Rape: Griffith's *Broken Blossoms*." In *Home Is Where the Heart Is: Studies in Melodrama and the Woman's Film*, ed. Christine Gledhill, 235-54. London: British Film Institute, 1987. (Reprinted from *Jump Cut* 26 [1981]: 51-55.)

Levin, Meyer. "Esquire in Quest of His Youth: A Poem with Puppets." *Esquire*, March 1934, 61-62.

Levitin, Jacqueline. "Any Good Roles for Women?" *Film Reader* 5 (1982): 95-108.

"Lubitsch Tells Cause of Row with Mae West." *Los Angeles Times*, 26 February 1936.

"Lubitsch Waxes Caustic in Mae West Tiff." *Los Angeles Citizen-News*, 25 February 1936.

Lynd, Robert S., and Helen Merrell Lynd. *Middletown: A Study in Contemporary American Culture*. New York: Harcourt, Brace & World, 1929.

_____. *Middletown in Transition: A Study in Cultural Conflicts*. New York: Harcourt, Brace & World, 1937.

MacLean, David. "Resurrecting Russell." *Epicene*, October 1987, 4-7, 52.

Madame Sylvia. "Is Mae West Skidding on the Curves?" *Photoplay*, November 1936, 48-49, 86-88.

Maddox, Conroy. *Salvador Dalí, 1904-1989*. Cologne: Benedikt Taschen, 1990.

"Mae and Myra." *Films and Filming* (February 1970): 68-69.

"Mae West and 2 Men in Jail for Play 'Sex.' " *New York Herald Tribune*, 20 April 1927, 1.

"Mae West Burlesques the Bible on the Air for Coffee Merchants." *Motion Picture Herald*, 18 December 1937, 27.

"Mae West Case Big Dilemma in Washington." *Variety*, 29 December 1937, 28.

"Mae West Cops Spotlight at Block Booking Hearing." *Film Daily*, 29 February 1936, 6.

"Mae West Gives *Life* Scoop View of her Many-Mirrored Apartment." *Life*, 19 February 1940, 64-65.

"Mae West Guarded after Threat." *Los Angeles Examiner*, 8 October 1935, 1.

"Mae West in 'I'm No Angel.' " *Film Daily*, 14 October 1933, 6.

"Mae West Jailed with 2 Producers." *New York Times*, 20 April 1927, 1.

"Mae West Mum in Lubitsch, Timony Debate." *Citizen-News*, 26 February 1936.

"Mae West Radio Skit Stirs Row." *Los Angeles Times*, 17 December, 1937, 1, 15.

"Mae West Row Told, Lubitsch Held Loser in Tilt." *Los Angeles Times*, 25 February 1936.

"Mae West Scene 'Mistake,' 'Won't Happen Again,' Says Air Sponsor." *Los Angeles Examiner*, 17 December 1937.

"Mae West Scouts Talk of Rift." *Los Angeles Times*, 3 May 1934.

"Mae West Script Angers Listeners." *Hollywood Reporter*, 15 December 1937.

"Mae West Script Brings Sharp Rebuke from FCC." *New York Times*, 15 January 1938, 1, 18.

"Mae West's Driver Hunted." *Los Angeles Times*, 11 October 1936.

"Mae West's Eve Brings Eden's Curse on Radio—Apology, Alibi, Indignation and Investigation." *Motion Picture Herald*, 25 December 1937, 12-13, 16.

"Mae West Stands 'em Up Despite Pans." *Variety*, 9 August 1944, 1, 38.

Maltby, Richard. " 'Baby Face' or How Joe Breen Made Barbara Stanwyck Atone for Causing the Wall Street Crash." *Screen* 27, no. 2 (1986): 22-45.

———. "From the Implausible to the Unspeakable: The Censorship of Sexuality from Mae West to Shirley Temple." Unpublished essay, 1986.

———. *Harmless Entertainment: Hollywood and the Ideology of Consensus.* Metuchen, N.J.: Scarecrow, 1983.

Maltin, Leonard. *The Great Movie Comedians: From Charlie Chaplin to Woody Allen.* New York: Bell, 1978.

Marchetti, Gina. *Romance and the "Yellow Peril": Race, Sex and Discursive Strategies in Hollywood Fiction.* Berkeley: University of California Press, 1993.

Marlowe, Kenneth. *Mr. Madam: Confessions of a Male Madam.* Los Angeles: Sherbourne, 1964.

Martin, Linda, and Kerry Segrave. *Women in Comedy.* Secaucus, N.J.: Citadel, 1986.

"Masquerade Follies." *Windy City Times*, 19 January 1989, 19.

Mast, Gerald, "Commentaries: *Bringing Up Baby*." In *Bringing Up Baby*, ed. Gerald Mast. New Brunswick, N.J.: Rutgers University Press, 1988.

———. *Howard Hawks, Storyteller.* New York: Oxford University Press, 1982.

Maxwell, Virginia. "It's the Caveman within Us Calling for Mae." *Photoplay*, December 1933, 38-39, 102.

May, Lary. *Screening Out the Past: The Birth of Mass Culture and the Motion Picture Industry.* Chicago: University of Chicago Press, 1983.

Mayne, Judith. *Cinema and Spectatorship.* London: Routledge, 1993.

———. "The Limits of Spectacle." *Wide Angle* 6, no. 3 (1984): 4-15.

McCarey, Leo. "Mae West Can Play Anything." *Photoplay*, June 1935, 30-31, 126.

McCarthy. "Belle of the Nineties." *Motion Picture Herald*, 25 August 1934, 31, 35.

_____. "I'm No Angel." *Motion Picture Herald*, 7 October 1933, 38.

_____. "Klondike Annie." *Motion Picture Herald*, 15 February 1936, 44.

McDonald, Sharon. "Lesbian Feminist Comedy: Dyke Humor Out of the Closet." In *Lavender Culture*, ed. Karla Jay and Allen Young, 295-98. New York: Harcourt Brace Jovanovich, 1978.

Mellen, Joan, *Women and Their Sexuality in the New Film*. New York: Horizon, 1973.

Mellencamp, Patricia. "Jokes and Their Relation to the Marx Brothers." In *Cinema and Language*, ed. Stephen Heath and Patricia Mellencamp, 63-78. Frederick, Md.: American Film Institute, 1983.

_____. "Situation Comedy, Feminism and Freud: Discourses of Gracie and Lucy." In *Studies in Entertainment: Critical Approaches to Mass Culture*, ed. Tania Modleski, 80-89. Bloomington: Indiana University Press, 1986.

Meryman, Richard. "Mae West: Going Strong at 75." *Life*, 28 April 1969, 46-56.

_____. "The One and Only Mae West." *Los Angeles Herald-Examiner*, 30 November 1980, G6.

"Mister Ed Barges into a Boudoir." *TV Guide*, 29 February-6 March 1964, 20-21.

Moley, Raymond. *The Hays Office*. Indianapolis: Bobbs-Merrill, 1945.

Montrelay, Michele. "Inquiry into Femininity." *m/f* 1 (1978): 83-101.

Mordden, Ethan. *Movie Star: A Look at the Women Who Made Hollywood*. New York: St. Martin's, 1983.

Morella, Joe, and Edward Z. Epstein. *The "It" Girl: The Incredible Story of Clara Bow*. New York: Delacorte, 1976.

Morin, Edgar. *The Stars*. Trans. Richard Howard. New York: Grove, 1960.

"Morocco." *Cahiers du Cinéma* (November-December 1970): 5-13. (Reprinted in *Sternberg*, ed. Peter Baxter, trans. Diana Matias, 81-94. London: British Film Institute, 1980.)

Mulvey, Laura. "Afterthoughts on 'Visual Pleasure and Narrative Cinema' Inspired by *Duel in the Sun*." *Framework* 6, nos. 15-17 (1981): 12-15. (Reprinted in *Visual and Other Pleasures*, 29-38.)

_____. "Fears, Fantasies and the Male Unconscious or 'You Don't Know What Is Happening, Do You, Mr. Jones?'" *Spare Rib* (1973). (Reprinted in *Visual and Other Pleasures*, 6-13.)

_____. "Feminism, Film and the Avant-Garde." *Framework* 10 (1979): 3-10. (Reprinted in *Visual and Other Pleasures*, 21-26.)

_____. *Visual and Other Pleasures*. Bloomington: Indiana University Press, 1989.

_____. "Visual Pleasure and Narrative Cinema." *Screen* 16, no. 3 (1975): 6-18. (Reprinted in *Visual and Other Pleasures*, 14-26.)

Neale, Steve, and Frank Krutnik. *Popular Film and Television Comedy*. London: Routledge, 1990.

Neale, Steve. "Psychoanalysis and Comedy." *Screen* 22, no. 2 (1981): 29-42.

Newton, Esther. *Cherry Grove, Fire Island: Sixty Years in America's First Gay and Lesbian Town*. Boston: Beacon, 1993.

_____. *Mother Camp: Female Impersonators in America*. Chicago: University of Chicago Press, 1968.

_____. "Role Models." In *Camp Grounds: Style and Homosexuality*, ed. David Bergman, 39-53 (excerpted from *Mother Camp*). Amherst: University of Massachusetts Press, 1993.

Nugent, Frank S. "Every Day's a Holiday." *New York Times*, 27 January 1938, 17.

"Odds Are Sex-to-1 Mae West Makes Her Point in Las Vegas." *Variety*, 28 July 1954, 3.

Palmer, Jerry. *The Logic of the Absurd: On Film and Television Comedy*. London: British Film Institute, 1987.

"Paramount." *Fortune*, March 1937, 86-96, 194-212.

"Paramount Abandons Idea of Producing 'Sex.' " *Variety*, 28 February 1933, 2.

"Paramount-Mae West Most Likely All Washed Up." *Variety*, 5 January 1938, 1.

"Paramount Rushing Mae West Release Rather Than Wait for Cool-Off." *Variety*, 29 December 1937, 7.

Parish, James Robert, Michael R. Pitts, and Gregory W. Mank. "Myra Breckinridge." In *Hollywood on Hollywood*, 263-65. Metuchen, N.J.: Scarecrow, 1978.

Parsons, Louella. "Mae-Studio Clash: Blonde Star Signs Contract with Cohen." *Los Angeles Examiner*, 22 February 1936.

Pela, R. L. "Way Out West." *Advocate*, 22 September 1992, 57.

"Pettijohn Assails Motives behind Block Booking Bill." *Hollywood Reporter*, 29 February 1936, 3.

Pines, James. *Blacks in Film: A Survey of Racial Themes and Images in the American Film*. London: Studio Vista, 1975.

"Principals in Play 'Sex' Go to Jail in Cleanup." *Chicago Tribune*, 20 April 1927, 17.

Quigley, Martin. *Decency in Motion Pictures*. New York: Macmillan, 1937.

———. "Radio Begs Trouble." *Motion Picture Daily*, 14 December 1937, 1, 10.

Quotable Women: A Collection of Shared Thoughts. Philadelphia: Running Press, 1989.

"Raquel Welch, Mae West Talk about Men, Morals and 'Myra Breckinridge.' " *Look*, 24 March 1970, 45-51.

Ray, Marie Beynon. "Curves Ahead." *Collier's*, 7 October 1933, 24, 40.

Reitz, Rosetta. "Mae West, Queen of Sex." *Hot Wire* 4 (March 1988): 40-41.

"Religious Leader Warns U.S. Bd. on 'Risque' Radio Plays." *Los Angeles Herald*, 16 December 1937.

Riddiough, Christine. "Culture and Politics." In *Pink Triangles: Radical Perspectives on Gay Liberation*, ed. Pam Mitchell, 14-33. New York: Alyson, 1980.

Riva, Maria. *Marlene Dietrich*. New York: Alfred A. Knopf, 1993.

Robertson, Pamela. " 'The Kinda Comedy That Imitates Me': Mae West's Identification with the Feminist Camp." *Cinema Journal* 32, no. 2 (1993): 57-72. (Reprinted in *Camp Grounds: Style and Homosexuality*, ed. David Bergman, 156-72. Amherst: University of Massachusetts Press, 1993.)

Roen, Paul. *High Camp: A Gay Guide to Camp and Cult Films*, vol. 1. San Francisco: Leyland, 1994.

Román, David. " 'It's My Party and I'll Die If I Want To!': Gay Men, AIDS and the Circulation of Camp in U.S. Theater." In *Camp Grounds: Style and Homosexuality*, ed. David Bergman, 206-33. Amherst: University of Massachusetts Press, 1993. (Reprinted from *Theater Journal* 44, no. 3 [1992].)

Rosen, Marjorie. *Popcorn Venus: Women, Movies and the American Dream*. New York: Coward, McCann & Geoghegan, 1973.

Ross, Andrew. "Uses of Camp." In *Camp Grounds: Style and Homosexuality*, ed. David Bergman, 54-77. Amherst: University Massachusetts Press, 1993. (Reprinted from *Yale Journal of Criticism* 2, no. 2 [1988].)

Russo, Mary. "Female Grotesques: Carnival and Theory." In *Feminist Studies/ Critical Studies*, ed. Teresa de Lauretis, 213-29. Bloomington: Indiana University Press, 1986.

Russo, Vito. *The Celluloid Closet: Homosexuality in the Movies*. New York: Harper & Row, 1981.

Schallert, Edwin. " 'Films Should Be Fit for Children to See.' " *Los Angeles Times*, 23 September 1934.

Scheuer, Philip K. "Town Called Hollywood: Mae West to Dance in Next." *Los Angeles Times*, 27 June 1943, 2, 5.

Seldes, Gilbert. "Sugar and Spice and Not So Nice." *Esquire*, March 1934, 60, 120.

Sennwald, Andre. "Goin' to Town." *New York Times*, 11 May 1935, 21.

"She Done Him Wrong." *Film Daily*, 10 February 1933, 7.

Silverman, Kaja. *The Acoustic Mirror: The Female Voice in Psychoanalysis and Cinema*. Bloomington: Indiana University Press, 1988.

_____. *Male Subjectivity at the Margins*. London: Routledge, 1992.

Sklar, Robert. *Movie-Made America: A Cultural History of American Movies*. New York: Random House, 1975.

Skolsky, Sidney. "Putting Them on the Spot." *Los Angeles Daily News*, 11 February 1933.

Snitow, Ann, Christine Stansell, and Sharon Thompson, ed. *Powers of Desire: The Politics of Sexuality*. New York: Monthly Review Press, 1983.

"So Mae West's Slipping? Not So She Can Notice It!" *Los Angeles Times*, 20 May 1934.

Sobel, Bernard. *A Pictorial History of Vaudeville*. New York: Bonanza, 1961.

Sochen, June. *Enduring Values: Women in Popular Culture*. New York: Praeger, 1987.

_____. *Mae West: She Who Laughs, Lasts*. Arlington Heights, Ill.: Harlan Davidson, 1992.

Sontag, Susan. "Notes on 'Camp.' " In *Against Interpretation and Other Essays*, 280-83. New York: Delta, 1967. (Reprinted from *Partisan Review* 31, no. 4 [1964].)

Stanley, Julia Penelope, and Susan W. Robbins. "Mother Wit: Tongue in Cheek." In *Lavender Culture*, ed. Karla Jay and Allen Young, 299-307. New York: Harcourt Brace Jovanovich, 1978.

Steinberg, Cobbett. "The Production Code." In *Film Facts*, 389-98. New York: Facts on File, 1980.

Stone, Christopher. "Mae West." *Advocate*, 8 October 1975, 33-34.

Studlar, Gaylyn. "Gaylyn Studlar Responds to Miriam Hansen." *Cinema Journal* 26, no. 2 (1987): 51-53.

_____. *In the Realm of Pleasure: Von Sternberg, Dietrich and the Masochistic Aesthetic*. Urbana: University of Illinois Press, 1988.

Thackrey, Ted O., and Kevin Thomas. "Mae West, Epitome of Witty Sexuality, Dies." Los Angeles Times, 23 November 1980, I1, I22.
"They Sent for Her." Motion Picture Herald, 25 December 1937, 7-8.
Thomas, Kevin. "Mae Keeps Up with the Kids." New York World Journal Tribune, 25 December 1966.
———. "Mae West Returns to the Scene of Her Prime." Los Angeles Times, 2 March 1978.
Thorp, Margaret Farrand. America at the Movies, New Haven, Conn.: Yale University Press, 1939.
"Top Pix and Stars of 1937." Variety, 5 January 1938, 13.
Tuchman, Mitch. "Scenes: Going Steady." Penthouse, February 1980, 45-46.
Tyler, Carole-Anne. "Boys Will Be Girls: The Politics of Gay Drag." In Inside/Out: Lesbian Theories, Gay Theories, ed. Diana Fuss, 32-70. New York: Routledge, 1991.
———. "The Supreme Sacrifice? Tv, 'TV,' and the Renee Richards Story." Differences 1, no. 3 (1989): 160-86.
Tyler, Parker. The Hollywood Hallucination. New York: Simon & Schuster, 1944.
———. Screening the Sexes: Homosexuality in the Movies. New York: Da Capo, 1993 [1972].
———. Sex Psyche Etcetera in the Film. New York: Horizon, 1969.
Tyler, Parker, and Charles Henry Ford. The Young and Evil. New York: Arno, 1975 [Paris: Obelisk, 1933].
Underwood, Peter. Life's a Drag! Danny La Rue and the Drag Scene. London: Leslie Frewin, 1974.
U.S. House of Representatives, 74/2, Subcommittee of the Committee on Interstate and Foreign Commerce. Motion Picture Films. Transcript of hearings on proposed House Bill H.R. 6472, 9-26 March 1936. Washington, D.C.: U.S. Government Printing Office, 1936.
U.S. Senate, 74/2, Subcommittee of the Committee on Interstate Commerce. Compulsory Block-Booking and Blind Selling in the Motion-Picture Industry. Transcript of hearings on proposed Senate bill S. 3012, 27-28 February 1936. Washington, D.C.: U.S. Government Printing Office, 1938.
Vidal, Gore. Myra Breckinridge. Boston: Little, Brown, 1968.
"Wake Up! Hollywood Producers." Advertisement paid for by the Independent Theatre Owners Association, Hollywood Reporter, 3 May 1938, 5.
Walker, Alexander. The Celluloid Sacrifice. New York: Hawthorne, 1966.
Walkowitz, Judith R. City of Dreadful Delight: Narratives of Sexual Danger in Late-Victorian London. Chicago: University of Chicago Press, 1992.
———. "Male Vice and Female Virtue: Feminism and the Politics of Prostitution in Nineteenth Century Britain." In Powers of Desire: The Politics of Sexuality, ed. Ann Snitow, Christine Stansell, and Sharon Thompson, 419-38. New York: Monthly Review Press, 1983.
———. Prostitution and Victorian Society: Women, Class and the State. Cambridge: Cambridge University Press, 1980.
Ward, Carol. Mae West: A Bio-bibliography. Westport, Conn.: Greenwood, 1989.

Weaver, William R. "Every Day's a Holiday." *Motion Picture Herald*, 25 December 1937, 36.

Weibel, Kathryn. *Mirror Mirror: Images of Women Reflected in Popular Culture.* Garden City, N.Y.: Doubleday/Anchor, 1977.

Weintraub, Joseph, ed. *The Wit and Wisdom of Mae West.* New York: G. P. Putnam, 1967.

Weiss, Andrea. *Vampires and Violets: Lesbians in Film.* New York: Penguin, 1993.

West, Mae. *Goodness Had Nothing to Do with It.* 2d ed. New York: Macfadden-Bartell, 1970 [1959].

———. "Sex in the Theatre." *Parade*, September 1929, 12-13, 32.

Willard, Avery. *Female Impersonation.* New York: Regiment, 1971.

Williams, Linda. "Feminist Film Theory, *Mildred Pierce* and the Second World War." In *Female Spectators: Looking at Film and Television*, ed. E. Deidre Pribham, 12-30. London: Verso, 1988.

———. "What Does Mae West Have That All the Men Want?" *Frontiers* 1, no. 1 (1975): 118-21.

Woodhouse, Annie. *Fantastic Women: Sex, Gender and Transvestism.* New Brunswick, N.J.: Rutgers University Press, 1989.

Yeaman, Elizabeth. "Big Crowds View Star's New Picture." *Citizen*, 28 February 1936.

———. "Mae West's Purified Picture Scores Hit." *Citizen-News*, 18 August 1934.

———. "Mae West to Abandon Corsets, Wear Modern Apparel in New Picture." *Citizen-News*, 22 August 1936.

Zeidman, Irving. *The American Burlesque Show.* New York: Hawthorne, 1967.

Zukor, Adolph. "Faith in NRA." In *The 1934 Daily Film Year Book of Motion Pictures*, ed. Jack Alicoate, 89. New York: Film Daily, 1934.

Zukor, Adolph, with Dale Kramer. *The Public Is Never Wrong.* New York: G. P. Putnam's Sons, 1953.

Recorded Performances

Belle of the Nineties. Released September 1934. Paramount Pictures. Produced by William LeBaron. Directed by Leo McCarey. Written by Mae West. Starring Mae West, with Roger Pryor, John Mack Brown, John Miljan, Libby Taylor, and Duke Ellington and His Orchestra.

Every Day's a Holiday. January 1938. Paramount Pictures, with Major Pictures Productions. Produced by Emanuel Cohen. Directed by Edward Sutherland. Written by Mae West. Photography by Karl Struss. Starring Mae West, with Edmund Lowe, Charles Butterworth, and Charles Winninger; cameo by Louis Armstrong.

Go West, Young Man. November 1936. Paramount Pictures, with Major Pictures Productions. Produced by Emanuel Cohen. Directed by Henry Hathaway. Written by Mae West, based on play *Personal Appearance* by Lawrence Riley. Starring Mae West, with Warren William and Randolph Scott.

Goin' to Town. May 1935. Paramount Pictures. Produced by William LeBaron. Directed by Alexander Hall. Written by Mae West. Starring Mae West, with Paul Cavanagh, Gilbert Emery, Marjorie Gateson, Tito Coral, and Joe Frye.

The Heat's On. November 1943. Columbia Pictures. Produced and directed by Gregory Ratoff. Written by Fitzroy Davis, George S. George, and Fred Schiller. With Mae West, William Gaxton, and Victor Moore; also Lloyd Bridges, Hazel Scott, Lina Romay, Xavier Cugat and His Orchestra.

I'm No Angel. October 1933. Paramount Pictures. Produced by William LeBaron. Directed by Wesley Ruggles. Written by Mae West. Starring Mae West, with Cary Grant, Gregory Ratoff, and Edward Arnold; also Gertrude Howard, Libby Taylor, and Hattie McDaniel (uncredited).

Klondike Annie. February 1936. Paramount Pictures. Produced by William LeBaron. Directed by Raoul Walsh. Written by Mae West, based on a play by Mae West and story by Marion Morgan and George B. Dowell. Starring Mae West, with Victor McLaglen, Harold Huber, Philip Reed, Soo Young, Lucille Webster Gleason, and Helen Jerome Eddy.

Mae West. 1982. Produced by Hill-Mandelker Productions. Directed by Lee Philips. Starring Ann Jillian as Mae West and James Brolin as Jim Timony. First broadcast on ABC-TV on 2 May 1982.

Mae West: 1971 Interview and Christmas Songs. San Francisco: Mind's Eye, 1985.

Mae West and the Men Who Knew Her. 1994. Documentary produced by Gene Feldman and Suzette Winter. Directed by Gene Feldman. Narrated by Dom DeLuise.

Broadcast on the Arts & Entertainment cable channel's *Biography* series in 1994-95.

Mae West on the Air: Rare Recordings 1934-1960 (Sandy Hook Records CSH-2098). Sandy Hook, Conn.: Radiola Records, 1987.

Mae West on the Chase and Sanborn Hour (CMR-1126). Sandy Hook, Conn.: Radiola Records, 1987.

Mae West: Sixteen Sultry Songs (RC 1315). New York: Rosetta Cassettes, 1987.

My Little Chickadee. February 1940. Universal Pictures. Produced by Lester Cowan. Directed by Edward Cline. Written by Mae West and W. C. Fields. Starring Mae West and W. C. Fields, with Joseph Calleia, Dick Foran, and Margaret Hamilton.

Myra Breckinridge. June 1970. Twentieth Century-Fox. Produced by Robert Fryer. Directed by Michael Sarne. Written by Michael Sarne and David Giler, from novel *Myra Breckinridge* by Gore Vidal. With Mae West, John Huston, Raquel Welch, Rex Reed, and Farrah Fawcett; also Tom Selleck, Calvin Lockhart, and John Carradine.

Night after Night. October 1932. Paramount Pictures. Produced by William LeBaron. Directed by Archie Mayo. Written by Vincent Lawrence, based on story "Single Night" by Louis Bromfield. Additional dialogue by Mae West. With George Raft, Constance Cummings, Wynne Gibson, Mae West, Alison Skipworth, and Roscoe Karns.

Red-Hot Riding Hood. Tex Avery cartoon with Mae West parody. 1943.

Sextette. March 1978. Crown International Pictures. Produced by Daniel Briggs and Robert Sullivan. Directed by Ken Hughes. Written by Herbert Baker, based on play *Sextette* by Mae West. Starring Mae West, with Timothy Dalton, Dom DeLuise, Tony Curtis, Ringo Starr, George Hamilton, Alice Cooper, Rona Barrett; also Keith Moon, Regis Philbin, Walter Pidgeon, George Raft, and Gil Stratton.

She Done Him Wrong. March 1933. Paramount Pictures. Produced by William LeBaron. Directed by Lowell Sherman. Written by John Bright and Harvey Thew, based on play *Diamond Lil* by Mae West. Starring Mae West, with Cary Grant, Gilbert Roland, Noah Beery, Rafaela Ottiano; with Owen Moore and Louise Beavers.

Who Killed Cock Robin? Walt Disney cartoon with Mae West parody. 1935.

Index

ABC (American Broadcasting
  Corporation), 148
Academy Awards, 82, 176 n.13
"Adam and Eve" sketch, xxi, 68-69; public
  reception of, 79-80, 81, 103, 104
Advertising Code, 47
Allen, Gracie, 89
Ameche, Don, 69, 79
Ames, Leon, 110
Anger, Kenneth, 25-26
Arbus, Diane, 12
Armstrong, Louis, 14, 209
Avery, Tex, 98, 179 n.35, 210

Babe Gordon (West), 16
Babuscio, Jack, 124
Baby Face, 45, 46, 50
"Baby, It's Cold Outside," 82
Balaban, Barney, 72
Ball, Lucille, 89
Bankhead, Tallulah, 124
Barthes, Roland, 91
Beavers, Louise, 14, 87, 120, 210
Beery, Noah, Sr., 210, fig. 33
Belle of the Nineties, xxi, 23, 57, 58, 209,
  figs. 8-11, 15, 18-19, 21, 28-32, 39, 46;
  censorship of, 51, 158 n.30, 168-69
  n.56; comedic "straight man" in, 86;
  male gaze in, 91; promotion for, 24,
  156 n.9; representation of African
  Americans in, 14, 15, 88;
  representation of Native Americans in,
  16; sexuality as means to higher class
  status in, 51-52; West as prostitute in,
  7, 28
Bergen, Edgar, 68-69, 79-80, 81
Bergman, Andrew, 75-76
Bible, the, 80
Billanti, Dean, 123

Biltmore Theater, 29
Bitter Tea of General Yen, The, 16, 159 n.33
block booking, 67-68, 173 n.30
Blonde Venus, 50
Blumer, Herbert, 47-48
Bogle, Donald, 14, 158 n.30
Booth, Mark, 191 n.13, 192 n.18
Bourdieu, Pierre, 43-44
Braun, Eric, 117
Breen, Joseph I., 26-27, 47; assessment of
  West's comedic style, 79-80, 90, 120;
  explicit responses to West, 64;
  negotiations to produce West's films,
  19-20, 102-3; role in censoring Klondike
  Annie, 60-62; role in PCA, 26
Brice, Fannie, 89
Briggs, Daniel, 122-23, 210
Bringing Up Baby, 118
Brolin, James, 130, 209
Brown, John Mack, 51
Butterworth, Charles, 20, 120, fig. 27

Calleia, Joseph, 86, 210
camp, xvii, xviii, xxii, 12, 107, 113, 114-
  16, 120-24, 186-87 n.42, 187 n.45, 192
  n.19
Carter, Angela, 188 n.53, 191 n.12
Carter, Lynne, 115
Catherine the Great, 21-22, 103, 107,
  160-61 n.52
Catherine Was Great, 21, 122
Cavanagh, Paul, 84, 209
CBS (Columbia Broadcasting System), 80,
  82-83, 105
Celluloid Closet, The (Russo), 118
censorship, xv, xx-xxi, 1, 78-83; of Belle of
  the Nineties, 51, 158 n.30, 168-69 n.56;
  of Diamond Lil, 29-40; as element in
  West's image, 24, 27, 81-82, 176 n.12;

representations of Native Americans in, 15; satire in, 103; West as showgirl in, 7

Myra Breckinridge, xxii, 210; as camp, 20, 136, 138; representations of African Americans in, 15; self-parody in, 99, 100, 125-26; screenplay for, 117, 183 n.16; transgressive sexual practices in, 113, 116-18

National Broadcasting Corporation (NBC), 81, 82
National Council of Catholic Women, 80
National Recovery Act, 56, 71
Neale, Steve, 101, 177 n.22, 178 n.27
Newton, Esther, 115, 121, 123, 124, 142-43, 186 n.37
New York State Board of Censors, 33, 49, 164 n.11
New York Sun, 61
New York Times, xiii, 136
Newsweek, 48, 81, fig. 6
Nicodemus, 14
Night after Night, 22, 23, 30, 106, 185 n.29, 210
Norr, Ray, 54, 150
Novak, Paul, 130, 185-86 n.31

Oboler, Arch, 79, 177 n.6
Odd Couple, 109
Otterson, John, 66

Parade (1929), xx, 3, 5, 7, 17, 18
Paramount Pictures Corporation, 23, 24, 78, 120, 138, 144, 174 n.35, 209, 210; economic difficulties, 65-66; efforts to sanitize West's image, 134; negotiations to produce *Diamond Lil*, 29-40; plots of West vehicles at, 7-8; publicity for West, 17-19, 23-24, figs. 15-16, 22-24, 26; West's contract with, 64-65, 66
parody, xv, xxi, 80, 101-2, 104, 109; of gender roles, 114, 129; of legendary female figures, 21, 79, 81-82, 103-4
Parsons, Louella O., 64
Payne Fund Studies, 47-48, 167-68 n.50
PCA. *See* Motion Picture Production Code Administration
Person to Person, 82-83
Personal Appearance. See Go West, Young Man

Philbin, Regis, 122, 210
Photoplay, 11, 142
Pickford, Mary, 104
Pidgeon, Walter, 122, 210
Pierce, Charles, xvi, xvii, 137, 139, 189 n.61, fig. 1
Pleasure Man, 3, 5, 17, 23, 116, 155 n.5
Possessed, 45
Pryor, Roger, 51, 209, fig. 46

Quigley, Martin, 41, 44, 69-70, 175 n.42

race: as element encoding West's image, 2-5, 12-17, 74-75, 87-88, 131, 157-58 n.27, 158 n.29; treatment and censorship of as "exotic" element in 1930s Hollywood films, 158 nn.30-32, 159 n.33
Raft, George, 23, 30, 122, 210
Rainey, Ma, 12, 13, 97
Ratoff, Gregory, 88, 119, 209
Red-Headed Woman, 45-46, 53
Red Hot Riding Hood, 98
Red Skelton Show, 83
Reed, Philip, 59, 209
Reed, Rex, 116, 189 n.61, 210
Riviere, Joan, 145
Robertson, Pamela, 138
Romay, Lina, 177 n.17, 209
Rooney, Mickey, 139, 190 n.7
Roosevelt, Franklin D., 47
Roseanne, xvi
Rosen, Marjorie, 22-23, 26, 126-27, 129, 134
Russell, Craig, 116
Russell, Jane, 122
Russo, Vito, 118, 185 n.29

Sabotage, 161 n.61
satire, 80, 100, 101; on gender roles, 110, 111; on marriage, 102-3
Satyricon, 111
Savoy, Bert, 18, 159 n.43, 160 n.44
Schallert, Edwin, 21
Scott, Hazel, 15, 158 n.31, 177 n.17, 209
Scott, Randolph, 118-19, 209, fig. 40
Screening the Sexes: Homosexuality in the Movies (Tyler), 116
self-parody, xxi-xxii, 100, 101, 105, 107-11, 113, 123
Sennwald, Andre, 10

Ramona Curry studied as an undergraduate at the University of Kansas and the University of Chicago, earned a master's degree in philosophy at the University of Tübingen (Germany), and in 1990 received a Ph.D. from Northwestern University in the Department of Radio, Television and Film. Between degrees, she traveled, watched movies, made short films, and researched the operations of cultural institutions firsthand by working for them. Since 1990, Curry has taught theory and history of film and other forms of popular culture at the University of Illinois at Urbana-Champaign. Her essays on female stars, feminist film and video productions, German cinema, and the historical impact of media institutions have appeared in numerous anthologies and U.S. and international journals.